After the New Testament: The Writings of the Apostolic Fathers
Part II

Professor Bart D. Ehrman

THE TEACHING COMPANY ®

PUBLISHED BY:

THE TEACHING COMPANY
4151 Lafayette Center Drive, Suite 100
Chantilly, Virginia 20151-1232
1-800-TEACH-12
Fax—703-378-3819
www.teach12.com

ISBN 1-59803-066-3

Bart D. Ehrman, Ph.D.

Professor and Chair of the Department of Religious Studies,
University of North Carolina at Chapel Hill

Bart Ehrman is the James A. Gray Professor and Chair of the Department of Religious Studies at the University of North Carolina at Chapel Hill. With degrees from Wheaton College (B.A.) and Princeton Theological Seminary (M.Div. and Ph.D., magna cum laude), he taught at Rutgers for four years before moving to UNC in 1988. During his tenure at UNC, he has garnered numerous awards and prizes, including the Students' Undergraduate Teaching Award (1993), the Ruth and Philip Hettleman Prize for Artistic and Scholarly Achievement (1994), the Bowman and Gordon Gray Award for Excellence in Teaching (1998), and the James A. Gray Chair in Biblical Studies (2003).

With a focus on early Christianity in its Greco-Roman environment and a special expertise in the textual criticism of the New Testament, Professor Ehrman has published dozens of book reviews and more than 20 scholarly articles for academic journals. He has authored or edited 16 books, including *The Monk and the Messiah: The Story of How the New Testament Came to be Changed* (San Francisco: HarperSanFrancisco, 2005); *Truth and Fiction in the Da Vinci Code* (New York: Oxford University Press, 2004); *Lost Christianities: The Battles for Scripture and the Faiths We Never Knew* (New York: Oxford University Press, 2003); *Jesus: Apocalyptic Prophet of the New Millennium* (Oxford University Press, 1999); *The New Testament: A Historical Introduction to the Early Christian Writings* (Oxford, 1997; 3rd ed., 2004); and *The Orthodox Corruption of Scripture* (Oxford, 1993). He is currently at work on a new commentary on several non-canonical Gospels for the *Hermeneia Commentary* series, published by Fortress Press.

Professor Ehrman is a popular lecturer, giving numerous talks each year for such groups as the Carolina Speakers Bureau, the UNC Program for the Humanities, the Biblical Archaeology Society, and select universities across the nation. He has served as the president of the Society of Biblical Literature, Southeast Region; book review editor of the *Journal of Biblical Literature*; editor of the Scholar's Press Monograph Series *The New Testament in the Greek Fathers*; and co-editor of the E. J. Brill series *New Testament Tools and*

Studies. Among his administrative responsibilities, he has served on the executive committee of the Southeast Council for the Study of Religion and has chaired the New Testament textual criticism section of the Society of Biblical Religion, as well as serving as Director of Graduate Studies and Chair of the Department of Religious Studies at UNC.

Table of Contents

After the New Testament:
The Writings of the Apostolic Fathers
Part II

Professor Biography i
Course Scope 1
Lecture Thirteen   Barnabas and the Opposition to the Jews............ 4
Lecture Fourteen   The Rise of Christian Anti-Semitism 20
Lecture Fifteen   2 Clement—An Early Sermon 38
Lecture Sixteen   The Use of Scripture in the Early Church........ 54
Lecture Seventeen   Papias—An Early Christian Interpreter 71
Lecture Eighteen   Oral Tradition in Early Christianity 86
Lecture Nineteen   The Shepherd of Hermas—An Apocalypse... 101
Lecture Twenty   Apocalypses in Early Christianity.................. 118
Lecture Twenty-One   The Letter to Diognetus—An Apology 135
Lecture Twenty-Two   Apologetics in Early Christianity................... 151
Lecture Twenty-Three The Apostolic Fathers as a Collection 166
Lecture Twenty-Four   The Apostolic Fathers and Proto-orthodoxy.. 183
Timeline 201
Glossary 203
Biographical Notes 207
Bibliography 216

After the New Testament:
The Writings of the Apostolic Fathers

Scope:

At the very foundation of the Christian religion stand the writings of the New Testament, a collection of 27 books that represent the earliest surviving literary productions of the burgeoning Church and that eventually came to be regarded as sacred Scripture. The writings produced by Christians *after* the New Testament are also important, however, as they can reveal to us how Christianity changed, developed, and grew after the first Christian century had passed.

The writings of the Apostolic Fathers are the most important books for understanding these developments in Christianity immediately after the New Testament period. The term *Apostolic Father* was coined by scholars who believed that the authors of these books were companions or followers of the apostles of Jesus. Scholars today do not accept this older view, because the books in the collection appear to have been written in a later generation. But most of them do date from the early to mid-2nd century, and as such, they are among the earliest Christian writings from outside the New Testament.

There are 10 (or 11) authors who are traditionally included in the collection of the Apostolic Fathers. Some of the works are by well-known figures of the early 2nd century (such as Ignatius of Antioch and Polycarp of Smyrna); others are anonymous. Together, they represent the early writings of *proto-orthodoxy*—that is, they represent the views that eventually came to influence and inform the shape of Christianity as it was to grow into a world religion that eventually converted the Roman Empire and became the major religious (and political, social, cultural, and economic) force of the Middle Ages.

In this course, we will examine the various writings of the Apostolic Fathers, both to see what each of the surviving books has to say and to see how these books can instruct us about the emerging Christian Church of the 2nd century.

In rough outline, the lectures of the course are set up in "pairs," in which the first lecture discusses the writing of one of the Apostolic Fathers and the next deals with the broader implications of the writing for understanding key issues in the early history of Christianity. We will begin with the letter of 1 Clement, written by the Christians of Rome to quell an uprising in the church of Corinth around A.D. 95; our examination of this letter will lead us, in the next lecture, to consider the development of a Church hierarchy in the early Christian communities.

Next, we will consider the Letters of Ignatius, one of the earliest Christian martyrs, whose writings urge adherence to the one bishop of each church and warn against false teachers. These letters will serve as a springboard to consider various kinds of "heresies" in early Christianity. Then, we will look at the letter written by Polycarp to the church in Philippi, which had experienced some turmoil when one of its elders was caught red-handed in some kind of shady dealings; this letter quotes numerous earlier Christian writings and, thus, will allow us, in the next lecture, to consider how Christians began to appreciate earlier writings as canonical Scripture.

Another writing of the Apostolic Fathers is an account of Polycarp's own martyrdom; this eyewitness report will lead us to consider how, why, when, and where Christians were persecuted for their faith in the early years of the religion. Also significant among these writings is a book called the Didache, which contains ethical instructions for Christians and indicates how the Christian rites of baptism, eucharist, prayer, and fasting were to be practiced; this work will lead us then to consider the emergence of distinctively Christian rituals in the Church.

Next, we will turn to the so-called Letter of Barnabas, which was written to show the superiority of Christianity to Judaism. This letter will allow us to explore the nature of early Jewish-Christian relations and the rise of Christian anti-Semitism. From there, we will move to a study of a book (mis-)named 2 Clement, which in fact, is the earliest surviving Christian sermon from outside the New Testament. Because 2 Clement uses an allegorical approach to interpreting Scripture, it will enable us to consider more fully, in the next lecture, the various methods of interpretation used by early Christians in understanding their sacred texts.

This matter of interpretation is equally important for the next author we examine, Papias, whose works have come down to us only in fragments. Papias tells us that he prefers oral traditions to written texts in trying to understand what happened during the life of Jesus.

This will bring us, in the next lecture, to a consideration of the importance of the oral transmission of early Christian tradition.

Next, we will turn to one of the earliest surviving apocalyptic writings of Christianity, The Shepherd of Hermas, which will, in turn, lead us to consider the importance of apocalyptic thought for the earliest followers of Jesus. As Christians moved away from an apocalyptic worldview, they began to have increased interactions with outsiders who were suspicious of their religion. The next writing we will consider is the anonymous Letter to Diognetus, which will serve as a springboard for considering the early *apologetic* movement, in which Christians defended themselves against charges of atheism and immorality and argued that their religion was, in fact, the only true one.

We will conclude our course by seeing how the Apostolic Fathers can instruct us concerning the development of Christianity in the early 2nd century, in the years between the foundation of the Church by Jesus and his disciples and the emergence of the Catholic Church of later times.

Lecture Thirteen
Barnabas and the Opposition to the Jews

Scope:

The next writing of the Apostolic Fathers we consider, the Letter of Barnabas, was allegedly written by the traveling companion of Paul, Barnabas, but in fact, was written in the early 2nd century. It is a long and intriguing letter that is chiefly concerned with one issue: how Christianity relates to its mother religion, Judaism. According to Barnabas, Christianity is superior to Judaism in every way, in that it is the religion that God had intended all along. Jews who do not realize this are condemned for their blindness and susceptibility to the teachings of an evil angel. More than that, the Jewish Scriptures, in fact, do not belong to the Jews; they belong to Christians.

These and other highly controversial teachings form the core of the Letter of Barnabas. In this lecture, we will consider how its anonymous author makes his case and ask whether and to what extent it is fair to consider this letter as an early instance of Christian anti-Semitism.

Outline

I. One of the most popular books outside of the New Testament in ancient times was the Letter of Barnabas.

   A. It was so popular in parts of the Church that some Christian writers (such as Clement of Alexandria) quoted it as Scripture.

   B. It is actually included as one of the books of the New Testament in our oldest surviving complete manuscript of the New Testament, Codex Sinaiticus.

   C. In part, its popularity stemmed from its reputed author: Barnabas, the companion of the apostle Paul (see Acts 13–14).

   D. The book itself is anonymous, however, and scholars today recognize that it was written decades after Barnabas's death.

   E. It is probably a good thing that the book never made it into the New Testament: This is one of the most virulently anti-Jewish books from the first two centuries of Christianity.

II. The overarching theme of the Letter of Barnabas is that Judaism is, and always has been, a false religion; that Jews have always misunderstood the Law of Moses God gave them; and that the Old Testament is, in fact, a Christian, not a Jewish, book.

A. After the introduction to the letter, the theme is stated in 2:4: God has no need of the Jewish sacrifices and has never wanted them.

    1. One key to understanding the letter is that Barnabas draws this lesson from the pages of the Jewish Scriptures themselves (specifically, the prophets, who were interested themselves in the revival of the Jewish religion, not its abolition)!

    2. In other words, Barnabas uses Jewish Scripture to undermine the Jewish religion.

B. This is a strikingly different approach to Scripture from that evidenced among other early Christian writers.

    1. Some early Christians, such as the Jewish-Christian Ebionites, had just the opposite view of Scripture: It was the only authoritative guide to faith and practice, to be adhered to closely by the followers of Jesus.

    2. Other early Christians, such as the apostle Paul, thought that the Scriptures had been fulfilled in Christ; its ritual laws were no longer a guide to how one was to live religiously.

    3. Still other early Christians, such as the 2nd-century teacher Marcion, thought that the Scriptures of the Jews were *only* for the Jews and were to have no bearing on the lives of Christians.

    4. Barnabas, in contrast to all these other positions, maintained that parts of the Scripture were literally to be accepted—those parts that condemned the Jews for their failure to worship God appropriately. But other parts— especially those that described how God wanted his people to live and worship—were to be taken figuratively.

    5. According to Barnabas, Jews had mistakenly taken God's Law given to Moses literally, when in fact, he intended the Law to be a figurative set of instructions about how to live.

C. For Barnabas, the Jewish people, who had always misunderstood God's purpose and intentions, were not really God's people, members of the covenant.

    1. In Barnabas's view, when God gave his covenant to his people on Mount Sinai, they immediately broke it, as symbolized in Moses' smashing of the tablets of the Ten Commandments (4:6b–8).

    2. For that reason, Jews never had been people of the covenant.

    3. God's covenant is reserved for those who actually do what he wants, in believing in his messiah, Jesus, and keeping the figurative meaning of the laws given to Moses.

III. Much of the Letter of Barnabas is devoted to showing how Jews misunderstood these laws, taking them literally when they were meant symbolically.

    A. This is seen in the law of circumcision, for example, which did not actually require Jews to cut the foreskins of their baby boys (as they were misled by an evil angel to believe) but was a symbolic statement of the need to believe in the cross of Jesus (ch. 9).

    B. This "misunderstanding" is also seen in the laws of kosher, which are not about what not to eat but how not to behave.

        1. Not eating pork means not behaving in the same manner as pigs, who are satisfied with their master (God) only when well fed (10:1–4).

        2. Not eating rabbit means not being sexually corrupt, like rabbits, who grow an additional orifice every year to increase their sexual appetite (10:6).

        3. Not eating the hyena means not being perverted, like hyenas, who alternate sex annually, one year being male and the next, female (10:7).

        4. Not eating the weasel means not engaging in illicit sexual activity, like weasels, who conceive their young through the mouth (10:8). And so on.

        5. On the other hand, the foods that are to be eaten are symbolic as well: Jews are to eat only animals that chew the cud and have split hooves. They are, in other words, to be those who meditate on God's word (chewing the cud) and who are both upright in this world and anticipate the world to come (split hooves).

C. The "misunderstanding" is further seen in other symbolic passages of Scripture, such as when the children of Israel won their battle with the Amalekites so long as Moses stood over them lifting his arms in the shape of a cross (ch. 12).

D. It is seen in the law of the Sabbath, which does not give Jews license not to work one day of the week, but refers to the future 1,000-year reign of Christ, the millennium (ch. 15).

IV. This is clearly a work that attacks the Jewish religion from a Christian perspective. But when was it written?

A. The text indicates that the Temple lay in ruins and that there is an expectation that it will soon be rebuilt (16:3–4).

B. This means that it must have been written after A.D.70, when the Jewish Temple was destroyed, and probably when the Temple was rebuilt by the Romans as a temple to Jupiter/Zeus around the year 130.

C. It may be that heightened Jewish-Christian tensions are what led to this vitriolic attack on all things Jewish.

D. To make sense of that context, we need to know more about the development of Christianity away from being a Jewish sect to becoming an anti-Jewish religion, which will be the subject of our next lecture.

Essential Reading:

Bart D. Ehrman, ed., "The Epistle of Barnabas," in *The Apostolic Fathers*, vol. 2, pp. 3–83.

Clayton Jefford, *Reading the Apostolic Fathers: An Introduction*, pp. 11–31.

Supplementary Reading:

Reidar Hvalvik, *The Struggle for Scripture and Covenant: The Purpose of the Epistle of Barnabas*.

James Carleton Paget, *The Epistle of Barnabas: Outlook and Background*.

Questions to Consider:

1. In your experience, how do Christians today deal with the fact that the Old Testament is still considered part of sacred Scripture, yet Christians do not think that they need to follow the laws that the Old Testament prescribes?

2. In your opinion, is it possible to be strongly opposed to all things Jewish, as is Barnabas, without being in danger of being anti-Semitic?

Lecture Thirteen—Transcript
Barnabas and the Opposition to the Jews

To this point in our course, we've considered several of the writings of the Apostolic Fathers: the Letter of First Clement, the Seven Epistles of Ignatius, Polycarp's Letter to the Philippians, and the Martyrdom of Polycarp. One of the most popular books outside of the New Testament in ancient times was the Letter of Barnabas, another one of the Apostolic Fathers. The Letter of Barnabas was so popular in parts of the church that some Christian writers actually quoted it as scripture, for example, the 2nd-century church father writing out of Alexandria, Egypt, Clement, who considered Barnabas to be one of the New Testament texts. It's actually included as one of the books of the New Testament in our oldest surviving complete manuscript of the New Testament, the Codex Sinaiticus.

As you may know, we don't have the original copies of any of the books of the New Testament. We only have later manuscripts. These later manuscripts that we have are usually not complete New Testaments. They often contain just a portion of the New Testament—just the Gospels, for example, or just the letters of Paul. The first time we get a complete copy of the New Testament is in the 4th century—probably around the year 350—in this manuscript that's called Codex Sinaiticus. It's called that because it was discovered on Mount Sinai.

Codex Sinaiticus though, in addition to including all 27 books of the New Testament, also includes the Epistle of Barnabas and another book we'll be looking at later in this course, The Shepherd of Hermas, as canonical scripture. This shows that down into the 4th century some people considered Barnabas to be part of the New Testament. In part, its popularity was due to its reputed author, Barnabas, who was understood to be the companion of the apostle Paul. We meet Barnabas in the pages of the New Testament, especially in the book of Acts, The Acts of the Apostles, where Barnabas plays a very important role in the spread of early Christianity.

The way the story goes is that the apostle Paul, before he was the apostle, was the persecutor, Saul of Tarsus, who was a persecutor of the Christian church. Saul had a vision of Christ on the road to Damascus as he was going to Damascus to persecute the Christians there. This vision of Christ converted him to become a believer in Christ. Paul then made a journey to Jerusalem in order to meet the disciples of Jesus, who were now the apostles of Jesus, the heads of the church in Jerusalem. But they refuse to meet him because they know of him as a persecutor, and they don't believe that he's become a believer.

It's Barnabas who intercedes on his behalf, who takes Paul and introduces him to the apostles and thereby sets him up as one of the favored persons to the Jerusalem church, who then is sent out with Barnabas to the city of Antioch, where they together start up the church in the important city of Antioch. So Barnabas is a companion of Paul. He's one of the starters of the church in Antioch, and then he goes with Paul on his missionary journeys, for example, in Acts, chapters 13-14.

Barnabas, the historical Barnabas, was a very important figure in the history of early Christianity. The Epistle of Barnabas is allegedly written by Barnabas, but it's worth noting that the book itself does not claim to be written by Barnabas, and, in fact, the name "Barnabas" does not occur in this book. There are good reasons for thinking, as we'll see at the end of this lecture, that the Epistle of Barnabas was actually written around the year 130 or 135, which would have been something like 60 or 70 years after the real Barnabas had died. So this book was attributed to Barnabas, which is partly the reason for its popularity, but in fact it wasn't really written by Barnabas. It's been falsely attributed. It's an anonymous book written decades after Barnabas's death.

It's probably a good thing that the Epistle of Barnabas never made it into the New Testament when the New Testament was finally canonized, for this is one of the most virulently anti-Jewish books from the first two centuries of Christianity. The overarching theme of the Letter of Barnabas is that Judaism is, and always has been, a false religion, that Jews have always misunderstood the Law of Moses that God gave them and that the Old Testament is in fact a Christian, not a Jewish, book. This is not the kind of book that is useful for Jewish-Christian dialogue, either in the modern world or the ancient world, because in fact this book is virulently anti-Jewish.

The book begins with the anonymous author greeting his readers: "Greetings sons and daughters in the name of the Lord who loved us in peace. So great and abundant are the righteous acts of God towards you that I am exceedingly overjoyed beyond measure by your blessed and glorious spirits." And then he launches into his discourse. The author states the theme of his book early on in the epistle. We call this an epistle by the way—or a letter—even though in fact it doesn't have the characteristics of an ancient letter. Normally an ancient letter would name the recipients of the letter at the beginning and would name the sender of the letter at the beginning. This letter doesn't do either. So we simply call it a letter by way of convenience. It's probably more like a tractate that's being written for a group of Christian readers.

The author states his theme in what is now chapter 2: "Since then the days are evil and the one who is at work holds sway, we should commit ourselves to seeking out the righteous acts of the Lord." And this is the key point, "For through all the prophets He has shown us that He has no need of sacrifices, whole burnt offerings or regular offerings," for, as he says in one place, "What is the multitude of your offerings to me? says the Lord." And he goes on to give a quotation from the Old Testament Book of Isaiah.

A little bit of background is necessary for us to understand what this theme is all about. Jews from time immemorial had maintained that their religion was based on the revelation God had given to their forefathers. In particular, God had chosen the Father of the Jews, Abraham, to be in a special relationship with him and his people were to inherit the land of Israel. The people of Israel, though, became enslaved to the nation of Egypt, and 400 years later, God raised up a prophet, Moses, to save them from their slavery in Egypt. God made a covenant with Moses, an agreement with Moses, that he would be the protector and defender of the Jewish people. In exchange, the people were to follow the law that God had given Moses on Mount Sinai – the Law of Moses – sometimes called the Torah.

Jewish people understood that they had a covenant with God, that he would be their God, he would protect and defend them, and they would keep his law. This law included a wide range of sacrifices that were to be made to God on a regular basis whenever people violated the law. So when the law would come to be broken, whether a person would become ritually impure by, for example, touching a dead body or a woman who menstruates—there are a wide range of ways that a person becomes ritually impure—a sacrifice would be necessary. If a person sinned against God, a sacrifice would be necessary. The sacrificial system was absolutely part of the Torah of Moses, the Law of Moses, a good bit of which describes how these sacrifices are to be performed.

Later on in the history of ancient Israel, prophets arose who condemned the people of God for straying from the will of God—such as Isaiah and Jeremiah and Amos and Josiah and Joel. These prophets' writings are found in what is now the Hebrew Bible—the Old Testament. Many of these prophets attacked the people of Israel for thinking that if they simply followed the ritual prescriptions of Torah they would be right with God and ignoring the fact that they had to also follow the laws that governed how they were to relate to one another. "You shall not murder. You shall not commit adultery. You shall not bear false witness. You shall not covet your neighbor's wife," et cetera.

People had substituted the sacrificial system for the laws that govern the relationships with one another. According to the prophets, this just was not right and was not pleasing to God. And so the prophets attacked the people of Israel for not maintaining a lifestyle that was acceptable to God.

Barnabas takes over the prophetic critique of the Jewish covenantal theology in order to turn it against Judaism itself. The Jewish prophets of course never ceased being Jewish. They were completely Jewish, and they understood themselves to be Jewish and understood themselves to be people of the covenant and were trying to reform Judaism. Barnabas uses the prophetic writings in order to reject Judaism—a key difference, obviously.

One of the most important aspects of the book of Barnabas is that Barnabas draws his lesson that the sacrifices are of no use to God from the pages of the Jewish scriptures themselves, in other words, specifically from the prophets who were interested in reviving the Jewish religion, not in abolishing it. In other words, Barnabas uses Jewish scripture in order to undermine the Jewish religion, which is a bit of an irony. This is a strikingly different approach to scripture from that evidenced among other early Christian writers.

Some early Christians, such as the Jewish Christian Ebionites whom we've met before—Christians who believed that the law was to be followed—these Jewish Christian Ebionites had just the opposite view of scripture. For them, it was the only authoritative guide to faith and practice. Scripture was to be adhered to closely by the followers of Jesus for the Ebionites. Other early Christian authors, such as the apostle Paul, thought that the scripture had been fulfilled by Christ. Christ hadn't abolished the scripture; he had fulfilled the scripture. Paul, nevertheless, thought that the ritual laws of the scripture applied to Jews and not to Gentiles. And so Paul was against the idea of Gentile believers in Christ following the Jewish law when it came to things like circumcision and kosher observance and Sabbath observance. But he didn't throw out the law itself or condemn Judaism as Judaism.

There were other Christian authors, such as the 2nd-century teacher that we've met before, Marcion, who thought that the scriptures of the Jews were only for the Jews, that they were to have no bearing at all on the lives of Christians. The Jewish scriptures are unrelated to anything Christian for Marcion. Barnabas stands in contrast to all of these other positions. Barnabas maintained that parts of the scripture were literally to be accepted. Parts of the Hebrew Bible—what Christians called the Old Testament—were to be literally accepted, those parts that condemned the Jews for their failure to worship God appropriately. Those parts—the condemnations of Jews—were accepted literally. But other parts of scripture were not to be taken literally. Other parts that described how God wanted his people to live and worship were to be taken figuratively. And this was God's intention all along—that his laws were to be taken figuratively, not literally.

According to Barnabas, Jews had always mistaken God's purpose. They had mistakenly taken God's law, given to Moses in a literal sense, when in fact God intended the law to be a figurative set of instructions about how to live. I'll give you illustrations of this in a moment. The key point at this stage is that for Barnabas the Jewish people who had always misunderstood God's purpose and intentions were not really God's people, members of the covenant. In other words, he absolutely denied the Jewish understanding that Jews were the people of God because the Jews have always misunderstood their own law.

According to Barnabas, when God originally gave his covenant to his people on Mount Sinai, when God gave the law to Moses on Mount Sinai, they immediately broke the law. The passage that he bases this on is found in the book of Exodus, chapters 31-32. Let me read you a passage from Barnabas to show you how he gets to this idea. Barnabas says in chapter 4, "Watch yourselves now and do not become like some people by piling up your sins, saying that the covenant is both theirs and ours"—in other words, saying that both the Jews and Christians belonged to the people of God—"for it is ours. But they"—the Jews—"permanently lost it in this way when Moses had just received it." So as soon as Moses got the law, they lost it. As soon as they made the covenant, it was gone. For the scripture says, "Moses was on the mountain fasting for 40 days and 40 nights and he received the covenant from the Lord, stone tablets written with the finger of the Lord's own hand. But when the people turned back to idols, they lost it. For the Lord says this…" So God is talking to Moses on Mount Sinai. You may remember this passage. God says to Moses, "Moses, Moses, go down quickly because your people whom you've led from the land of Egypt have broken the law." They've made these golden calves because they don't know where Moses has gone. They start worshiping the old gods they used to have.

Moses understood and he cast the two tablets from his hand. So he's got the two tablets of the Decalog, the Ten Commandments; he sees the people committing idolatry and he throws them down—in the book of Exodus—and he smashes the two books of the covenant. And according to Barnabas, therefore, their covenant was smashed, that the covenant of his beloved one, Jesus, might be sealed in our hearts in the hope brought by faith in him. Jews broke the covenant as soon as they got the covenant, as shown clearly by the fact that Moses smashed the two tables of the law. Jews never had been the people of God. They mistakenly thought they were the people of God, not realizing that the covenant had been shattered.

God's covenant instead is reserved for those who are actually doing what he wants them to do in believing in his Messiah Jesus and keeping the figurative meaning of the law that God gave to Moses. Barnabas goes on to give a figurative interpretation of the laws given to Moses to show what they're really all about. For example, in the Law of Moses, we're told that the people of Israel are to circumcise their baby boys on the eighth day. This is a sign of the covenant. According to Barnabas, however, God did not literally mean that Israelites were supposed to cut the foreskin off the penises of their baby boys. God is not interested in the mutilation of human flesh. What is the law of circumcision really about?

Well, Barnabas points out that the Father of the Jews, Abraham, was the one who was first given the commandment to circumcise. And at one point in the book of Genesis, Abraham circumcised 318 of his servants prior to their going off to battle to show that they were among God's people, so they would be fighting the enemy as God's people. And Barnabas is intrigued by this passage. Why is it that Abraham circumcises 318 people? Why does the Father of the Jews do this? What's his connection with the 318 and what's that connection with circumcision?

According to Barnabas, it's a symbolic passage, not a literal passage. It's symbolic because of the number involved. The number is 318. Now, in ancient languages, they typically used the letters of the alphabet for their numbers. We don't do this today. We use Roman letters for our alphabet, but we use Arabic numerals for our numbers. In ancient languages, they used the letters of the alphabet for their numbers. So that, for example, in Greek, the language Barnabas is writing in, alpha, the first letter of the Greek alphabet is 1, beta is 2, gamma is 3, and so forth and so on.

When you write out the number 318, it is spelled *tau iota eta*. Tau is like our letter "T." It's in the shape of a cross. *Iota eta* are the first two letters of the name "Jesus." Abraham circumcised 318 servants. What does this signify? It signifies the cross of Jesus—*Tau iota eta*. So this is not a literal statement about something that happened; it's a prediction of how the new covenant will actually come into being. It will come into being through Jesus dying on the cross. Barnabas assures his readers that no one has ever learned a better lesson from him. I'm sure he's right about that.

The figurative laws of the Jews can be seen in a number of other ways. For example, Jews were well known in the ancient world for keeping kosher food laws. There were certain foods that Jews were not allowed to eat. Well, what is that all about? According to Barnabas, these kosher food laws were not meant to be taken literally; they were meant to be taken figuratively. For example, Jews, as is well known, were not allowed to eat pork. Why can't you eat pig? Pig is a perfectly fine food. That's not meant to be taken literally. It's not meant to say that you're not to eat pork. It's a figurative statement meaning you're not to live like pigs. How do pigs live? Well, pigs grunt and make a lot of noise when they're hungry, but when they're fed, they're silent. "Don't be like that" says Barnabas. Don't be somebody that makes a lot of noise to God, who prays to God when you're hungry—in other words, when you're in need—and then when you're satisfied, you don't pray any longer. Don't be like a pig. Instead, pray to God at all times. That's what it means not to eat the pig.

He goes on and gives a number of very peculiar interpretations of some of the animals that were forbidden as food for the ancient Jews. For example, in verse 6 of chapter 10, he says, "The Commandment—do not eat the hair—for what reason? You must not, he says, be someone who corrupts children or be like such people"—in other words, corrupts them sexually. "For," he says, "the rabbit adds an orifice every year. It has as many holes as years it has lived." So rabbits, why do rabbits propagate so much? Because every year they grow a new orifice, and so they're able to have sex a lot and have a lot of babies, and you're not to be like that, he says. And so don't be sexually perverse.

"Nor shall you eat the hyena," he says. One of the commandments in Torah is don't eat the hyena. Why not? Well, "You must not," he said, "be an adulterer or a pervert, nor be like such people." For what reason? How does he get that symbolic meaning? Well, because, as everyone knows, the hyena changes its nature every year. At one time it's male; the next time it's female. So in alternate years, the hyena is male or female. Well, that's perverted, and so you're not supposed to be perverted. I guess it means you're not to cross-dress or something like the hyena.

And he also fully hated the weasel. What's wrong with eating the weasel? Well, he tells you, it's a figurative law. It's not meant to be taken literally. "You must not be like those who are reputed to perform a lawless deed in their mouth because of their uncleanness, nor cling to unclean women who perform the lawless deed in their mouth, for this animal conceives with its mouth." Why not eat the weasel? Well, because the weasel conceives through the mouth, and so it's a figurative meaning. You're not to have oral sex. And so Barnabas goes on and gives a lengthy interpretation of the food laws found in the scriptures.

He ends up this discussion, this very peculiar discussion, which is based, by the way, on an ancient bestiary, an ancient understanding of the animals. In the ancient world, they used to have these books that would describe each animal and its unique customs and peculiar features of them. A lot of this was just legendary material that he of course is taking over. He ends up his discussion by pointing out that in the Law of Moses people were allowed to eat animals that both chewed the cud and had split hooves. So an animal had to both chew the cud and have split hooves, like the cow, for example.

Well, what does that mean, he says? Well, it isn't to be taken literally. Animals that chew the cud, that means you're to associate with people who meditate on God's word. That's what chewing the cud means. It means somebody who actually meditates on God's word. And someone with a split hoof, who is that? That's somebody who is both upright in the present world and who anticipates the world to come. So they're split between this world and the coming world. And so you're to associate with people like that. That's the meaning of Moses' Law.

There are other passages that he deals with—quite interesting—that he takes in a symbolic way. I'll give you one other example. He finds Jesus represented figuratively throughout the Hebrew Bible, and passages that originally in the Hebrew bible of course had nothing to do with Jesus. For example, there's a passage in Exodus, chapter 17, of the war of the children of Israel against the Amalakites. He gives a figurative interpretation of this passage which is very interesting. In the passage, in Exodus, chapter 17, Moses sends Joshua, his underling, out to fight the Amalakites, and Moses stands upon a hill overlooking the battle. And he holds up his arms and as long as his arms are held up, the Israelites win the battle. But as soon as his arms get tired and he puts them down, then they lose the battle. And so he has two of his companions, Aaron and Hur, stand next to him and hold his arms up. So he stands like this with his arms crossed out for the duration of the battle, and the Israelites win.

Well, Barnabas points out that when his arms are outstretched, he is standing in the form of a cross. In other words, it's the cross of Jesus that brings victory over the enemies. This is referring to Jesus. It's not referring to a war against the Amalakites. Barnabas's figurative interpretation applies to the law of the Sabbath. Jews understand that God created the world in six days, and then he rested on the seventh day. Moreover, people are to emulate his example by working six days of the week and then resting on the Sabbath—not working on the Sabbath.

This, according to Barnabas, is a law that was not in fact meant to give Jews license not to work one day of the week. In fact, it refers to the future thousand-year reign of Christ, the millennium. God worked six days and on the seventh day he rested. Barnabas points out that in scripture we're told that with God a day is as a thousand years and a thousand years is as one day. Well, that means that God created the world for 6,000 years and on the seventh day—another thousand-year period—he rested. In other words, for Barnabas, God's involvement with the world from the beginning of creation to the end of this age would be 6,000 years, and then there would be a thousand-year millennium.

This is the first time in Christian history that anybody indicated that the world would last for 6,000 years, which was a very important teaching some years ago when we turned to the year 2000. You may recall that people thought the year 2000 would be the end of the world. Why did they think that? Well, in part because of this idea that the world would last 6,000 years. It's a little bit complicated, but there was a 17th-century scholar named James Usher who calculated when the world was created. The world was created around the year 4000 B.C. Well, if it was created in the year 4000, and it lasts 6,000 years, then the year 2000 should be it. Right? So the world should end then, and we should enter into the millennium.

So Jesus is coming back in the year 2000, and many fundamentalists actually believed this. The problem was they got their dating wrong. Because what Usher actually said was that the world was created in the year 4004 B.C. In fact, it was created on October 23, 4004 B.C. Why 4004? Because Usher knew that the person who came up with our calendar miscalculated things with the turning of the era and Usher knew that Jesus was probably born in the year 4 B.C. So it's off four years. So 4004 B.C., on October 23, this means if the world was to last 6,000 years, it should have ended on October 23, 1997. So all the hoopla about the year 2000 was completely off base because it misunderstood our calendar. Well, the world didn't end in 1997 or in the year 2000. The world just keeps on ticking. But, in any event, Barnabas was the one who, in fact, was responsible to some extent for all the hype. He's the first one who came up with this understanding of things.

In any event, the Epistle of Barnabas is clearly a work that attacks the Jewish religion from a Christian perspective. When was the book written though? Can we put it in a historical context? At one place in the book of Barnabas we're told, in chapter 16, that the temple of the Jews lies in ruins, but there's an expectation that it will soon be rebuilt. This book then was clearly written after the destruction of Jerusalem and the destruction of the temple, and we know when that was from a variety of sources, including Roman sources. Romans were the ones who destroyed the temple. The temple was destroyed in the year 70 A.D.

So this book was clearly written after 70 A.D., and it seems to be presupposing that the temple is going to be rebuilt. The temple was destroyed because there was a Jewish uprising against the Romans, and the Romans attacked and destroyed Jerusalem and destroyed the temple. And it's been destroyed till this day.

About 60 years later, there was some expectation that the temple would be rebuilt. There was another Jewish uprising against the Romans, with an expectation that possibly if they drove the Romans out of the Promised Land the temple would be rebuilt. This expectation evidently was at its height around the year 130. The revolt actually happened in the year 135, and the Jews lost again, and they got kicked out of the Promised Land. This means that probably Barnabas was written sometime after 70 and some time near 135. Scholars typically put this letter sometime around the year 130—about 60 or 70 years probably after Barnabas himself had died. It may be that the heightened Jewish-Christian tensions around the year 130 are what led to this vitriolic attack on all things Jewish in the Epistle of Barnabas.

Well, to make sense of that context of Jewish-Christian tensions that were on the rise, we need to know more about the development of Christianity, away from being a Jewish sect, which it originally was, to becoming an anti-Jewish religion. How did Christianity move from being a Jewish sect to an anti-Jewish religion? That will be the subject of our next lecture.

Lecture Fourteen
The Rise of Christian Anti-Semitism

Scope:

The anti-Jewish stance of the Letter of Barnabas leads us to consider more broadly one of the key questions surrounding early Christianity. It is widely acknowledged by scholars today that Christianity began with the preaching of Jesus, who was himself thoroughly and ineluctably Jewish; yet within a century, many of his followers were avidly opposed to all things Jewish. How could this be? How is it that Christianity was so quickly transformed from a sect within Judaism to an anti-Jewish religion?

This is the question we will address in this lecture, as we trace the roots of anti-Jewish attitudes among some of Jesus' early followers, some of them well known, such as the apostle Paul and the writer of Matthew, and some of them less known but equally important, such as the 2nd-century bishop of Sardis, Melito.

Outline

I. The Letter of Barnabas raises a set of important questions about the relationships between Christians and Jews in antiquity.

    A. As we saw in the previous lecture, Barnabas is opposed to the Jewish religion.

        1. He maintains that Jews broke the covenant God had made with them as soon as it was given and that it was never restored.

        2. As a result, they were misled by an evil angel into thinking that their laws were to be taken literally instead of figuratively.

        3. For this reason, they have never worshiped God in a way appropriate to him.

        4. It is the Christians, the followers of Jesus, who correctly understand the Law of Moses and do what it requires. Jews are not, therefore, the true people of God.

    B. One might wonder why Barnabas is so obsessed with showing that Christians, rather than Jews, are the true people of God.

1. Ultimately, the answer has to do with Christianity's own historical root because the Christian religion started out as a sect of Jews.
2. Jesus himself was a Jew, as were his 12 disciples.
3. After his death, these Jewish followers formed a distinctive sect within Judaism and still considered themselves to be Jews.

C. Thus, one of the most salient questions for historians of antiquity is: How is it that a Jewish sect became an avidly anti-Jewish religion, all within a century?

II. To answer the question, we need to return to the beginnings of Christianity in the life and ministry of Jesus.

A. There is an enormous range of scholarly opinion today about how to understand the life of Jesus and how to know what he actually said and did.

B. The one thing virtually all scholars are agreed on, however, is that however Jesus is to be understood, he must be understood as a 1st-century Jew living in Palestine.
1. Jesus was born Jewish and raised Jewish. He followed Jewish customs, kept the Jewish Law, became a Jewish teacher, and acquired Jewish followers, whom he taught his own vision of what it meant to be an observant Jew, one who truly kept the Law God had given the Jewish people through Moses.
2. Throughout his lifetime, Jesus preached his message to Jews, and at the end of his life, he was executed by the Romans for claiming to be the Jewish king.
3. From beginning to end, Jesus was thoroughly and ineluctably Jewish.

C. So, too, were his earliest followers, who continued to keep his instructions about the Law and continued, according to our earliest records, to worship in the Jewish Temple in Jerusalem.

III. Even decades after his death, many of Jesus' followers continued to insist that in following Jesus, they had found the secret to keeping the Jewish Law and observing the Jewish religion in the way that the Jewish God wanted them to.

    A. This can be seen, for example, in one of our later Gospels, Matthew, written about 50 years after Jesus' death.

    B. Above all, Matthew is concerned to show that Jesus is the Jewish messiah sent from the Jewish God to the Jewish people in fulfillment of the Jewish Scriptures.

    C. Throughout Matthew's Gospel, Jesus continually emphasizes the need to observe the Jewish Law (for example, 5:17–20).

    D. It would be a mistake to think that Matthew didn't really mean this. The followers of Jesus, for Matthew, were to be good Jews.

IV. Other influential early Christians, however, had other ideas, especially the apostle Paul.

    A. Paul himself started out as a religious Jew, who was, in fact, opposed to Christians who claimed that Jesus was the messiah.

    B. For Paul, originally, Jesus could *not* be the messiah of God, because rather than being God's chosen one, he obviously stood under God's curse. He was, after all, crucified!

    C. But in one of the greatest turnarounds in history, Paul experienced a conversion, in which he came to see that Jesus really was the Son of God and that his death was not God's condemnation of Jesus but God's way of making his righteous one pay for the sins of others.

    D. Paul, then, became an outspoken proponent of faith in Jesus. But this had implications for his understanding of his former Judaism.

        1. Because faith in Jesus was the way to have a right standing before God, the Law of Moses was of no value in making one right before God.

        2. The salvation of Jesus was for all people, Jew and Gentile. And keeping the Law could not assist in bringing salvation.

3. The Jewish religion, therefore, had been transcended, and salvation now came to those who had faith in Christ.

E. Paul had opponents who thought otherwise, for example, enemies in the region of Galatia who maintained that following Christ required one to follow the Law as well.

1. Paul castigated such views as dangerous and anti-Christian.

2. But were his opponents people who held to a view more like Matthew's?

V. In the struggles that ensued within Christian circles, Paul's views eventually won out.

A. By the end of the 1st century, most converts to the new religion were pagans, not Jews.

B. In part, this was because the Christian message about Jesus never did make sense to most Jews, who saw Jesus not as the promised, powerful messiah but as a weak, crucified criminal.

C. But even within most Gentile circles of Christianity, there continued to be an emphasis on the need to retain the Old Testament as Scripture, even if keeping its laws could not in itself bring salvation.

1. In part, this was because of the staying power of the tradition that Jesus and his followers were all faithful Jews.

2. But there was another reason for Christians to hold on to their Jewish roots: Without them, Christianity could appear to be a novelty, an innovation; in the ancient world, "new" philosophies and religions were always seen as suspect and not credible.

3. Possibly to gain credibility in the world at large, or even to prevent their own persecution, Christians claimed that they were the true heirs of the ancient religion of Judaism.

4. But what was one to do about the fact that Jews were still around and were more naturally thought to be the heirs of their own religion?

5. Christians were almost forced by the logic of their own position to go on the attack against non-Christian Jews, to show that they were actually apostates from the

Jewish religion and that it was Christianity, not Judaism, that was the legitimate heir to the ancient traditions of Israel.

VI. That is the context within which the Letter of Barnabas and other 2nd-century Christian anti-Jewish literature was written.

A. Some 2nd-century writers, such as Justin Martyr, were quite unforgiving toward Jews, saying, for example, that the mark of circumcision was given by God to mark Jews for persecution.

B. Others, such as Melito of Sardis, were even more vitriolic, claiming that because Jesus was divine and because the Jewish people were responsible for his death, the Jews had killed their own God.

C. Eventually, of course, this led to a history of anti-Semitism, of hatred and violence against the Jews, ironically, by a Christian religion that itself started out as a sect within Judaism.

Essential Reading:

Bart D. Ehrman, ed., *After the New Testament: A Reader in Early Christianity*, pp. 95–130.

Rosemary Ruether, *Faith and Fratricide: The Theological Roots of Anti-Semitism*.

Supplementary Reading:

John Gager, *The Origins of Anti-Semitism*.

Marcel Simon, *Verus Israel: A Study of the Relations between Christians and Jews in the Roman Empire (135–425)*.

Questions to Consider:

1. In your opinion, is it possible to believe that Jesus is the fulfillment of Judaism *without*, at least indirectly, casting aspersions on the Jewish religion as it has come down through the centuries?

2. In your experience, how much of modern anti-Semitism can be traced to Christian influences? Does it seem ironic that a religion that urges love of all people should have a history of such hatred

toward Jews, especially given that the religion started off as Jewish?

Lecture Fourteen—Transcript
The Rise of Christian Anti-Semitism

The Letter of Barnabas raises a set of important questions about the relationships between Christians and Jews in antiquity. As we saw in the previous lecture, Barnabas is opposed to the Jewish religion. He maintains that Jews broke the covenant that God had made with them as soon as it was given and that it was never restored. As a result, Jews were misled by an evil angel into thinking that their laws were to be taken literally instead of figuratively. Jews, therefore, have never worshiped God in a way that's appropriate to him, according to Barnabas. For him, it's the Christians, the followers of Jesus, who correctly understand the Law of Moses and do what it requires. Jews, therefore, for Barnabas, are not the true people of God.

One might wonder why Barnabas is so obsessed with showing that Christians, rather than Jews, are people of the covenant, people who belong to the God of Israel. Ultimately, the answer has to do with Christianity's own historical roots. For the Christian religion started out as a sect of Jews. Jesus himself was a Jew, as were his twelve disciples. After his death, these Jewish followers of Jesus formed a distinctive sect within Judaism. They met in synagogues. They followed Jewish customs. They still considered themselves to be Jews.

And so one of the most salient questions for historians of antiquity is, How is it that a Jewish sect became an avidly anti-Jewish religion all within a century? To answer the question, we need to return to the beginnings of Christianity in the life and ministry of Jesus himself. As you probably know, there's an enormous range of scholarly opinion today about how to understand the life of Jesus, to know what he actually said and did. Scholars who have devoted their entire lives to the project of understanding the historical Jesus have come up with radically different solutions.

This is an interesting phenomenon in itself. Why is it that otherwise intelligent people, who are highly trained, are able to look at the same sources and come up with such radically different conclusions? These are people, by the way, who are quite learned in order to be a scholar of the historical Jesus. To be a serious scholar of the historical Jesus, one has to be able, of course, to read both Greek and Hebrew, but also one should be able to read Aramaic because that was the language that Jesus spoke. Greek was the language the gospels were written in. Hebrew was the language of the Old Testament.

Moreover, it's good to be able to read Latin because many of the traditions are preserved in Latin, and Coptic, because Coptic is a language that some of the ancient gospels are written in. And you can probably throw in a couple more ancient languages, not to mention French and German, because you have to read what other European scholars have said about Jesus. So these people who were investigating the historical Jesus are very highly trained, and many of them are very, very smart, and they come up with radically different interpretations, some claiming that Jesus is best understood as a Jewish rabbi, some that he's best understood as a Palestinian holy man, some that he's best seen as a Jewish cynic philosopher, and some claiming that Jesus was a Jewish apocalyptic prophet.

The reason for all of these differences, by the way, has to do with the nature of our sources. Our source material for understanding who Jesus really was is not adequate for historians who want to make a complete reconstruction. And these sources can be read in a variety of ways and interpreted in a variety of ways, so the people who devote themselves to the task come up with a variety of interpretations.

The one thing that virtually all scholars are agree on, however, is that however Jesus is to be understood ultimately, he must be understood as a 1st-century Jew living in Palestine. Jesus was born Jewish, and he was raised Jewish. He followed Jewish customs. He kept the Jewish law. He became a Jewish teacher. He acquired Jewish followers, whom he taught his own vision of what it meant to be an observant Jew, one who truly kept the law of God that God had given to the Jewish people through Moses.

We find this throughout the earliest sources we have for the historical Jesus, that Jesus is thoroughly Jewish. Let me give you one kind of key example, a key moment in the life of Jesus for those engaged in this kind of historical research: Jesus at one point in his ministry is asked by a Jewish scribe—in other words, an expert in the Jewish law—what is the summary of the law? What is the most important commandment of the law? And Jesus replies, "The most important commandment of all is that you shall love the Lord your

God with all your heart, soul, and strength," a quotation from Deuteronomy, chapter 6. But then he goes on to say, "And the second commandment is, you shall love your neighbor as yourself," a quotation from Leviticus, chapter 19. "Love God above all else. Love your neighbor as yourself. On these two commandments hang all the law and the prophets," says Jesus.

It's a mistake to think that Jesus himself came up with the idea that you should love your neighbor as yourself. This is a quotation from the Torah, from the Law of Moses. Jesus understood himself as an interpreter of the Law of Moses, as a teacher who understood the essence of the Law of Moses, and tried to convey this essence to his followers who then were expected to follow the Law of Moses.

Throughout his lifetime, Jesus preached his message to Jews. And at the end of his life, he was executed by the Romans for claiming to be the Jewish King. And by the way, when you read accounts of the historical Jesus by scholars, one of the pressure points that you want to pay particular attention to is the relationship that is portrayed between Jesus' life and his death. Because if you can't make coherent sense of his execution for claiming to be King of the Jews on the basis of what the reconstruction of his life is, then the reconstruction is probably wrong. In other words, the most secure thing we know about Jesus—the one thing that everybody agrees on—is that Jesus was crucified by Pontius Pilate.

If you reconstruct his life in such a way that you can't really explain why Pontius Pilate wanted to crucify him, then you've got a problem. And some of these explanations that scholars have given don't explain very well why Jesus got crucified for being king of the Jews. If you say that Jesus was a Jewish rabbi who was really only concerned, principally concerned, about loving one another, why did Pilate kill him? Was it against the Roman law to love one another? Oh, you want people to love one another—to the cross! Well, no, that doesn't exactly make sense. Was it because Jesus said "Love your enemies," and Romans didn't want to be loved? They wanted to be hated? "Oh, you can't love us. We'll kill you if you love us." That doesn't make sense. So any reconstruction of who Jesus really was has to make sense of his death—just as a side note—because he was executed for being called King of the Jews.

For this lecture, what's important is that from beginning to end Jesus was thoroughly Jewish. So too were his earliest followers who continued to keep his instructions about the law and continued, according to our earliest records, to worship in the Jewish temple in Jerusalem. Even decades after Jesus' death, many of his followers continued to insist that in following Jesus they had found the secret to keeping the Jewish law and observing the Jewish religion in the way the Jewish God wanted them to. Decades after his death, there were Christians who were saying that you have to be a follower of Jesus, the Jew, by being Jewish.

This can be seen, for example, in one of our later gospels, the Gospel of Matthew. Now Matthew was written about 50 years after Jesus' death. Nonetheless, it seems to embody many of Jesus' own concerns with regard to the Jewish law. Matthew is, above all, concerned to show that Jesus is the Jewish Messiah sent from the Jewish God to the Jewish people in fulfillment of the Jewish scriptures. In other words, this gospel goes out of its way to emphasize Jesus' Jewishness.

What's striking is that in this gospel, unlike some of the other gospels we have, Jesus continually emphasizes the need to observe the Jewish law. As he says in an important passage in chapter 5, at the beginning of the Sermon on the Mount in Matthew's gospel, Jesus says to his disciples, "Don't think that I've come to abolish the law. I've come not to abolish the law, but to fulfill the law. Truly I tell you, every letter of the law, every stroke of a letter of the law, will not pass away until all has been fulfilled." He goes on to say that his followers have to keep the law even better than the scribes and the Pharisees if they want to enter the kingdom of heaven. Well the scribes and Pharisees were very good at keeping the law. This is what they committed themselves to doing. Jesus' followers have to keep it even better than the scribes and the Pharisees.

It would be a mistake to think that Matthew didn't really mean this. One common interpretation of Matthew is that what Jesus did—this is the interpretation people sometimes give—is that in Matthew, Jesus tries to show that the law can't be kept, and, therefore, if you can't keep the law, you need Jesus. In fact, Matthew gives no indication that that's what he's thinking. When Matthew intensifies the law and says you have to keep the law better than the scribes and the Pharisees, he seems to be assuming that it's possible. He never says you can't do it.

For example, the famous antithesis in Matthew, where Jesus states one of the laws and then gives his interpretation of it, which is a radical interpretation of it because it radicalizes the command of the law, this antithesis begins with such comments as, "The law says you shall not murder, but I say to you, you shouldn't be angry at another. The law says you shall not commit adultery. I say to you, you should not lust after another. The law says to fulfill your vows when you swear an oath. I say, don't swear an oath at all." Well, these are intensifications of the law because it's obviously much harder not to get angry than it is not to murder. But Matthew seems to think that people can do this. And, of course, it is possible not to vent your wrath on somebody. And it's possible not to murder somebody. It's also possible not to vent your wrath on somebody. And so it's possible not only to keep your vows but it's also possible not to vow at all. I mean it is humanly possible to do this, and Matthew assumes that Jesus' followers are going to act in this way, which means Matthew's Jesus is very Jewish and is insisting not that his people overthrow the law. He doesn't tell them, "The law is wrong so go ahead and commit murder. Go ahead and commit adultery." No, he radicalizes the law and says you have to keep this radical version of the law if you expect to enter the kingdom of heaven. That's Matthew's view of things 50 years after Jesus.

Other influential early Christians, however, had other ideas, especially the apostle Paul. It's a remarkable phenomenon that both Paul and Matthew made it into the same canon of scripture. Both Matthew and Paul are in the New Testament. But it would be an interesting situation to see Matthew and Paul having a conversation about what they really thought following Jesus meant because Paul is quite adamant that following Jesus, for non-Jews at least, does not mean following the Jewish law. Paul insists that non-Jews not keep the law, in fact.

He doesn't mean that non-Jews should go out and commit adultery and murder people, but he does mean that non-Jews should not practice parts of the law that make Jews Jewish. Gentiles should not go out and get circumcised. Gentiles should not keep kosher. Gentiles should not have to observe the Sabbath because these are things that make Jews Jewish, and Christ's salvation comes not just to Jews but to all people, according to Paul. So Paul's followers were not told that they had to keep the Jewish law.

Paul's relationship to Jesus is a very interesting one, and understanding this will help us unpack a little bit Paul's understanding of the role of the Jewish law. Paul, as I indicated in a previous lecture, started out not as a disciple of Jesus. He didn't know the earthly Jesus. He wasn't a follower of the earthly Jesus. Paul grew up outside of Palestine. He was a Greek-speaking Jew from outside of Palestine, not an Aramaic-speaking Jew like Jesus' followers. When Paul first heard of Christianity, he was incensed by it, and he became one the chief persecutors of the Christian church. Neither Paul nor the book of Acts actually tells us why Paul persecuted the Christian church, so we have to reconstruct and kind of read between the lines of our sources to try and figure it out.

What a number of scholars think is that Paul persecuted the Christians originally precisely because they were proclaiming that Jesus was the Messiah. Well, what was the problem with that? The problem with that is that Paul, like every other Jew we know about from the first century prior to Christianity, did not think that the Messiah was somebody who would be crucified. Who was the Messiah going to be for ancient Jews? Well, we know what ancient Jews thought about the Messiah because we have some writings from ancient Jews. My guess is most ancient Jews weren't expecting a Messiah any more than most modern Jews are expecting a Messiah. But there were Jews who were expecting a Messiah, and we know about what these Messianic expectations were like because of surviving Jewish writings. There were a variety of expectations of the Messiah among 1st-century Jews. Some Jews thought the Messiah—probably most Jews who thought about it—thought that the Messiah would be a future political leader who would be a military man. He would be a warrior who drove out God's enemies from the Promised Land and set up a kingdom in Israel—a sovereign state in Israel—and would rule in Jerusalem over Israel as a sovereign state much as David, his ancestor, had done. He'd be a descendent of David who, like David, was a warrior and a king—the Messiah.

There were other Jews who thought that the Messiah, in fact, would be a heavenly figure. He'd be a cosmic figure who came from heaven in judgment on the evil forces in the world who would overthrow the forces of evil and set up God's kingdom on earth. Those were two of the most prominent expectations of who the

Messiah would be. In both cases, the Messiah is going to be somebody who is powerful and grand. Power and grandeur were the marks of the Messiah.

Prior to Christianity, we know of no Jew who thought that the Messiah was one who was going to suffer and die. Well, why do Christians think that the Messiah is somebody who is supposed to suffer and die? Because Christians think that Jesus is the Messiah, and they know that Jesus suffered and died. Therefore, the Messiah must suffer and die. Christians point to passages in the Hebrew Bible that talk about a righteous person of God who suffers and dies, and they say this refers to the Messiah.

The debate between Christians and Jews in the ancient world was over whether these passages actually were talking about the Messiah or not, because these passages, such as Isaiah 53 and Psalm 22 that talk about somebody suffering and dying, in fact don't ever use the term "Messiah." And Jews never interpreted these passages messianically because the Messiah wasn't going to be somebody who suffered and died. He was going to be somebody who was exalted, who was powerful, who was mighty.

If Jesus is the Messiah, then he must be powerful and mighty. He must be the king in Israel. He must be the one who drove out the Romans. Right? Well, wrong. Jesus, in fact, didn't drive the Romans out of the Promised Land. He never raised an army. And, in fact, he was arrested by the Romans and subjected to the most horrible, humiliating, painful death the Romans had devised. He was crucified as a common criminal.

Most Jews thought that this claim that Jesus is the Messiah was crazy, because Jesus obviously isn't the Messiah. He's a low-life criminal who got on the bad side of the law and got crucified. Why did Paul persecute the Christians? Probably because Paul thought that their claim that Jesus was the Messiah was absolutely ludicrous and blasphemous against God.

But then in one of the great turnarounds in history, Paul experienced a conversion in which he came to see that Jesus really was the Son of God. Paul claims that he had a vision of Jesus after his death and this convinced him that Jesus was in fact alive. Jesus was alive. Well, how could Jesus be alive if he had been crucified? Paul starts thinking backwards from his experience, and he starts reasoning backwards leading to the distinctive theology that Paul develops as a Christian theologian.

The way the backward thinking works is this: Jesus is alive. How could he be alive? God must have raised him from the dead. How else could he be alive? Well, if God raised him from the dead, then he must be somebody who's entirely special before God. If he's special before God, why did he die such a humiliating death? Well, God must have wanted him to. Why would God want him to die such a humiliating death? Well, it must not have been for anything that he had done wrong. It must have been that he died for the sake of others. Because if he's under God's special favor, well, then, clearly God wouldn't want him to die for anything wrong he'd done because he hadn't done anything wrong if he's under God's special favor. He must have died for others. That means that Jesus' death is for the sake of others and it's according to God's plan that Jesus died.

Well, then, that must mean that a person is put into a right standing before God because Jesus died for his sins. A right standing before God therefore—see how this backwards reasoning is working—a right standing before God then comes through Jesus' death. Well, what about the law that God gave Moses? Isn't that important for a person standing before God? Well, no, because evidently the law can't make you right with God because, if it did, God wouldn't have had Jesus die. So the law is not something that can put you in a right relationship with God, which means that whether you're a Jew who follows the law or a Gentile who doesn't even know the law, the only way to be right with God is through the death of Christ. Therefore, Gentiles don't have to keep the law in order to be right with God because being right with God has nothing to do with keeping the Law of Moses.

This led then to Paul's theology as a Christian in which he maintained that Jesus was the way to have a right standing before God and the Law of Moses was of no value for somebody standing before God. The salvation of Jesus comes to all people, Jew and Gentile, and the law assists in no way in bringing about salvation. For Paul therefore, the Jewish religion in a sense had been transcended in that now it's those who had faith in Christ who'd be right with the God of Israel. But Paul didn't see that the Jewish religion had been transcended; he saw it that the Jewish religion had been fulfilled. This is what God had planned all along. So Paul remains Jewish, and he sees Jesus as the fulfillment of the expectation of the Jews. But the irony is the fulfillment of the Jewish law indicates that the law is not necessary for salvation.

Paul had opponents who thought otherwise. If he knew Matthew, Matthew might well have been one of his opponents, but Matthew lived after Paul's day. At least it's possible that Matthew would have been an opponent of Paul. Matthew does insist that the followers of Jesus are to keep the law better than the scribes and Pharisees and Paul insists that salvation comes apart from the law.

There were opponents of Paul during his lifetime that he knew about who in fact took opposing views. For example, after Paul established the churches in the region of Galatia, which is in the central part of Asia Minor—central part of modern-day Turkey—some other Christian missionaries showed up, and these other Christian missionaries insisted that the Christians in Galatia were to be circumcised if they were to be true followers of God. God says in the Old Testament that circumcision is given as a sign of the covenant, and it's to be for all people who are to be people of the covenant, and so even followers of Jesus need to be circumcised. Paul writes his letter to the Galatians to oppose this view, which he sees as extremely dangerous. It's not just that if a person gets circumcised, they've done something that they really don't need to do, it's just an act of super arrogation for Paul. It's not that. If you get circumcised, it shows that you don't believe the death of Christ is sufficient for salvation, which means you don't understand the gospel, which means you probably do not have a right standing with God. This is a very important issue for Paul. If people think that by keeping the law they have a better standing before God, they've absolutely missed the boat.

In the struggles that ensued between Paul's view and other views— Paul's view and what I've called the Judaizing view of others that think you have to keep the Jewish law—as you well know, Paul's views are the ones that eventually won out. By the end of the 1st century, most converts to the new religion of Jesus were actually not Jews; they were former pagans that Paul and others had converted. In part, Gentiles, or pagans, converted more frequently than Jews because the Christian message about Jesus never did make sense to most Jews who saw Jesus not as the promised, powerful Messiah, but as a weak, crucified criminal. And, of course, the Christian message continues not to make sense to most Jews.

But even within Gentile circles of Christianity, there continued to be an emphasis on the need to retain the Old Testament of scripture, even if keeping its laws could not in itself bring salvation. Why did Christians keep the Old Testament if the laws didn't bring salvation? Well, in part they kept the Old Testament because it was the Bible of Jesus and his followers, and they knew that this started out as a Jewish sect, and it had always been their scripture. And so Christians kept to the scripture. But there was another reason for Christians to hold on to their Jewish roots.

Without their Jewish roots, Christians could appear to be a novelty on the religious scene. Christianity could be seen as an innovation. But—this is the key point—in the ancient world, new philosophies and religions were always seen as suspect and not credible. If something is new in the ancient world, it can't be right. This is quite different from the way we think of things today where it's always the new and better that we go for. I bought a computer two weeks ago, and it's out of date. We want the new stuff. We don't care about the old. And new religions spring up all the time. My daughter just moved to California. I hear all about new religious movements. Just open up the Yellow Pages in Los Angeles sometime and look up "Churches." The new is better in our world. In the ancient world, the old is better because, if it's not old, it obviously can't be true because everybody before us got it wrong. And so the old was respected; the new was suspected. Christianity had to claim to be old in order to be respected.

But Christianity wasn't old. It just started with Jesus who was just around some years ago. Christians claim though that their religion was old because their religion was true Judaism. The Jewish religion is in fact Christianity. The Old Testament—the Hebrew Bible—is a Christian book, not a Jewish book. Possibly in order to gain credibility in the world at large or even to prevent their own persecution by Romans who were opposed to new religions, Christians claimed that they were the true heirs of the ancient religion of Israel.

Well, if Christians made the claim that they were the true heirs of the true religion of Israel, what were they supposed to do about the fact that there were still Jews around who were more naturally thought to be the heirs of the religion of Israel since they were, after all, Jews? I mean, Christians claimed to be the fulfillment of the expectations of the Hebrew Bible, that Jesus is the fulfillment of the law, but Christians didn't keep the law. Did this really make sense? Jews said, "We're the heirs of the Old Testament law because, yes, we actually keep the law." And so this is a point of tension between Christians and Jews.

Christians were more or less forced by the logic of their own position to go on the attack against non-Christian Jews to show that non-Christian Jews actually were apostates from the Jewish religion and that it was Christianity, not Judaism, that was the legitimate heir to the ancient traditions of Israel. That's the context in which the Letter of Barnabas and other 2nd-century Christians' anti-Jewish literature was written. We have a range of anti-Jewish literature written from the 2nd century.

For example, there's a 2nd-century author known as Justin Martyr—Martyr is not his last name; martyr is what happened to him—but he's known to history as Justin Martyr. He was a Christian philosopher who was quite unforgiving toward Jews. Justin, in one of his writings that still survives, says—he's talking about circumcision—"Circumcision can't have any bearing on salvation." He says, "Look, Abraham was made right with God before he was circumcised, as were the saints before Abraham." Moreover, he points out, "If circumcision shows you're right with God, what about women? Women aren't circumcised. Does that mean half the population can't be right with God? What's circumcision for then?" He says, "Circumcision is to cut off the Jewish people," making a pun on the term "cut off," to show them as distinctive, yes. They're the ones who are distinctive so everybody knows who is to be persecuted: the Jews. So it's a physical sign of who is to undergo persecution.

There were other 2nd-century authors who were even more vitriolic—for example, an author named Melito—Melito, who was the bishop of the city of Sardis, who claimed that—as became popular in the 2nd century—Jesus himself was divine; Jesus in some sense was God. Melito claimed that the Jewish people were responsible for Jesus' death, and Melito drew the conclusion that since Jews had killed Jesus and since Jesus is God, the Jews had killed their own God.

Well, that's a serious charge. This is the first instance in history that we know of in which the charge of deicide—the murder of God—was leveled against the Jews.

Eventually, of course, this led to a very ugly history of anti-Semitism, of hatred and violence against Jews that carried on down through the Middle Ages, based on the theological claims of people like Barnabas and Justin and Melito, hatred and violence against Jews, ironically, by a Christian religion that itself started out as a sect within Judaism.

Lecture Fifteen
2 Clement—An Early Sermon

Scope:

One of the lesser-known works of the Apostolic Fathers is a book traditionally called the letter of 2 Clement. The title is a misnomer: The book was not written by Clement, the bishop of Rome, and it is not even a letter. It is, instead, an anonymous sermon. As such, it is the first surviving sermon to come down to us from early Christianity (outside of the New Testament).

The topic of the sermon has to do with the joy of salvation that has been graciously granted to Christians through the merciful act of God in Christ. It prompts Christians to be thankful for what they have received as believers and urges them to exhibit appropriate ethical behavior in response. The sermon is based on an interpretation of certain key texts of the "Old" Testament. In this lecture, we will consider the main themes of this sermon and the nature of its exposition of scriptural passages in order to make its points.

Outline

I. Probably the least known and the most under-studied book of the Apostolic Fathers is the so-called letter of 2 Clement.

    A. The title of the book is a misnomer.

        1. It was not written by the author of 1 Clement or by Clement of Rome in the late 1st century.

        2. And it is not even a letter; it appears, instead, to be a sermon delivered by some anonymous preacher, then written down for broader circulation.

    B. It was discovered in the 17th century, in the same manuscript that contains 1 Clement, which was published in 1633.

    C. It is a very difficult document to date, because there are no references to datable events in the text and we don't know who wrote it. Based on its theological perspective, scholars have tended to date it to the mid-2nd century, possibly in the 140s—some 50 years after 1 Clement was written by a different author.

D. Despite its relative unpopularity, it is an interesting book and worth some sustained reflection.

II. Even a quick read through the book shows that it is probably best understood as a sermon that was originally delivered orally.

  A. This can be seen in the author's comments in 19:1.

  B. Its genre is significant: This is the first Christian sermon from outside the New Testament to survive from Christian antiquity.

  1. There are several sermons found in the New Testament, for example, in the book of Acts (chs. 2, 3, 15, for instance).

  2. And some scholars think that the book of Hebrews originated as a sermon.

  3. But, as we will see, 2 Clement is significant because it gives clues as to how the Christians' worship services, in which the sermon was given, were conducted.

  C. It appears that the audience of the sermon was comprised of Christians who had been converted from paganism (cf. 1:6).

III. The sermon involves an exposition of Scripture and exhortation to appropriate behavior.

  A. The theme of the sermon is stated at the outset (1:1–2).

  B. The author elaborates his theme through an exposition of a passage of Scripture, using a figurative mode of interpretation (2:1–3).

  1. It is clear that the "Old" Testament is taken as an authoritative text.

  2. However, it is not the historical, literal meaning of the text that matters, but its figurative application to the congregation in the present.

  3. In the next lecture, we will deal with this mode of scriptural interpretation at length, as it is both interesting and widespread in early Judaism and Christianity.

  C. It is striking, though, that not only the Old Testament but the teachings of Jesus are treated as "Scripture" (2:4).

  1. It looks as if 2 Clement is well on the way to accepting a *bipartite canon* of "Old" Testament and "New" Testament, both equally authoritative.

2. The quotations of Jesus, though, may not all come from books: Some may have come to the author through the oral tradition.

3. Some of these quotations are familiar to students of the New Testament (for example, 4:1–2; cf. Matthew 7:21; 9:10–11; cf. Matthew 12:50).

4. Others, however, do not have a precise parallel in any other known account of Jesus' words (cf. 4:5).

D. Some of the unusual sayings of Jesus that form the basis for the book's exposition appear to derive from Gospels that did not make it into the New Testament.

1. The saying of 5:2–4, for example, appears to be from the lost Gospel of Peter.

2. And the saying of 12:1–2 appears to come from the Coptic Gospel of Thomas.

IV. All of the authorities quoted—Old Testament Scriptures and sayings of Jesus—are used for the purposes of exhortation.

A. This can be seen even in the sayings of Jesus that derive from non-canonical sources (for example, 12:3–6).

B. And it appears to be the point of the entire sermon (cf. 17:1, 3).

V. Thus, it becomes clear from 2 Clement how the worship service of this community was constructed.

A. There was a reading from Old Testament Scripture (Isaiah 54:1).

B. This was the basis for reflection and exposition, as the text was explained.

C. This exposition was then the basis of moral exhortation.

D. It is possible, as well, that hymns were sung during the services, as seen from other evidence from the 2nd century.

VI. In sum, 2 Clement is a significant book, in part because it can reveal to us what worship services were like in the mid-2nd century; as it turns out, they were probably not all that different from Christian worship services in our own time.

Essential Reading:

Bart D. Ehrman, ed., "Second Letter of Clement," in *The Apostolic Fathers*, vol. 1, pp. 154–199.

Clayton Jefford, *Reading the Apostolic Fathers: An Introduction*, pp.117–133.

Supplementary Reading:

Karl Donfried, *The Setting of Second Clement in Early Christianity.*

Alistair Stewart-Sykes, *From Prophecy to Preaching: A Search for the Origins of the Christian Homily.*

Questions to Consider:

1. If you have ever had any experiences in worship services today, how were they like and unlike those attested to by 2 Clement?

2. Given the range of authorities cited by 2 Clement, what do you suppose we can say about the formation of the canon of Scripture for Christians in the 2nd century: Was the collection of books into a set canon completed yet?

Lecture Fifteen—Transcript
2 Clement—An Early Sermon

Probably the least known and most understudied book of the Apostolic Fathers is the so-called Second Letter of Clement. The title of the book is a misnomer. This book was not written by the author of First Clement, or by Clement of Rome in the late 1st century. And it is not even a letter. It appears, instead, to be a sermon delivered by some anonymous preacher and then written down for broader circulation.

The document that contains this letter—the text within which it is found—was discovered in the 17th century in the same manuscript that contains First Clement, which was published then in 1633. It's very difficult to know when this book of Second Clement—which I'll continue to call it Second Clement even though it's misnamed; since I don't know what else to call it, we'll call it Second Clement—it's difficult to know when Second Clement was written.

This is true of many documents from the ancient world. It's very hard to date ancient documents unless the documents give you some reference to an external event of some kind. In that case, you can date a document. But just taking the gospels of the New Testament, for example, the gospels of the New Testament obviously happened sometime after the death of Jesus. So if you can date the death of Jesus, you know a time after which they were written.

But there are very few other external references in the gospels that allow you to determine what they were written before. Some people think that in the Gospel of Mark there are illusions to the coming Jewish War—the Jewish War took place between 66 and 70 A.D.—so that it sounds like war is in the works or at least Mark knows that war is brewing because of some of the things that he says later on in his gospel which make people think that probably Mark was written around the year 70.

The Gospel of Luke, on the other hand, had several sayings of Jesus that seem to presuppose that Jerusalem has already been destroyed and been trampled over by the Gentiles, by Romans. And he describes the siege of the city and its destruction. That would presuppose that Luke was written after the destruction of Jerusalem in the year 70. Moreover, there are reasons for thinking that whoever wrote the Gospel of Luke had used the Gospel of Mark for one of his sources, which means it has to be after Mark, so that people end up making guesstimates that Mark was probably written around the year 70. Luke was probably written 10 or 15 years later, around 80 or 85, but they're just guesstimates because there aren't any explicit references to external events that allow people to date these documents.

We noted in the Letter of Barnabas that there are a couple of external events that are mentioned, because in Barnabas the temple is already in ruins. So it's clearly after 70, but it's clear that there's been no rebuilding of the temple yet. And so it must be before the year 135. Why 135? Because in the year 135, all hopes of building the temple were dashed when the Emperor Hadrian had a temple built to Zeus on the site of the Jewish temple. Well that dashed all hopes of the Jewish temple being rebuilt, and so Barnabas must be written before that happened, and so it has to be written between 70 and 135.

When we're dealing with a text like Second Clement, there are no external references to datable events in the text. So we don't know who wrote the book and we don't know when it was written. Based on its basic theological perspectives, scholars have tended to give it a rough date sometime in the middle of the 2nd century. In other words, the theology that it embraces appears to be similar to the theology of other books written about the middle of the 2nd century. And so usually it's dated possibly in the 140s, some 50 years or so after First Clement and, as I've indicated, by a different author.

Despite its relative unpopularity—this isn't the book that's read most widely among the Apostolic Fathers—Second Clement is an interesting book and worth some sustained reflection. Even a quick read through the book shows that probably the book is best understood as a sermon that was originally delivered orally rather than a book that was written to be read. So this appears to be a written version of a sermon that somebody actually gave in an oral setting originally.

You get a sense of this near the end of the book in chapter 19 where the author says, "So then, brothers and sisters, now that we have heard this word from the God of truth, I am reading you a request to pay attention to what has been written so that you may save yourselves and the one who is your reader." This is somebody who's reading something out loud to a congregation. And he's saying,

"Now that you've heard God's word"—in other words, now that you've heard a scripture reading—"I'm giving you this exhortation." His exhortation, interestingly enough, is that they ought to pay attention, which of course is highly appropriate in a church setting. So this appears to have been some kind of sermon that was delivered that was later then written down.

Its genre is significant because if it's right that this is a sermon and if it's right that it dates sometime in the middle of the 2nd century, say, in the 140s, this would be the first Christian sermon to survive from outside the New Testament. This would be the first Christian sermon that we have from outside the New Testament. Now I say from outside the New Testament because there are several passages in the New Testament that scholars have identified as possibly originating as sermons that got implemented in the text of the New Testament itself. For example, there are several passages, a large number of passages, in the book of Acts in which there are speeches given by one of the characters, and some scholars think these speeches actually embody sermons that had been given by Christian preachers that the author of Acts had incorporated into his text.

Remember, the book of Acts is about the spread of Christianity throughout the Roman world after the death of Jesus. So it details several narratives in which apostles are preaching to crowds in order to convert them, and there are other passages where the apostles will talk to a gathering of Christians. And so there are a variety of speeches given in the book of Acts. In fact, a large portion of the book of Acts is taken up by speeches.

Let me give you one of the earlier ones. This is a speech that the apostle Peter gives in Acts, chapter 3. The situation in Acts, chapter 3, is that Peter has just healed a man who was lame, and Jewish people have gathered around and seen this and they're marveling at it. And so Peter takes this as an opportunity to tell them that Jesus is the Messiah and they need to repent of their sins so that they can be saved. And so he uses this as an evangelistic opportunity. Verse 12 of chapter 3: "When Peter saw this," the people that gathered around, "he addressed the people, 'You Israelites, why do you wonder at this?'" that I've healed this person, or, 'Why do you stare at us as though by our own power or piety we made this man walk? The God of Abraham, the God of Isaac, the God of Jacob and the God of our ancestors has glorified his servant Jesus whom you handed over and rejected in the presence of Pilate, though he had decided to release him. But you rejected the holy and righteous one and asked to have a murderer'—Barabbas—'given to you. And you killed the author of life whom God raised from the dead. To this we are witnesses and by faith in His name, His name itself has made this man strong, whom you see and know.'" So he goes on to say that Jesus is the one who's healed this person through me, "this Jesus whom you rejected."

And he goes on to say, "So you need to repent." And he gives them reason for this by citing the scriptures. "For Moses said that the Lord will raise up for you from your own people a prophet like me," like Moses. "You must listen to whatever he tells you." And so he goes on to talk about this prophet that Moses had predicted and that Jesus is the fulfillment of. According to this passage in Acts, chapter 3, then, Jesus is the prophet that Moses predicted in the Hebrew Bible. He goes on then and tells these people they need to repent and believe in Jesus, and there's a massive conversion based on his preaching.

Now, this sermon in Acts 3 is not really the same as the sermon we're going to find in Second Clement, because in Acts 3 this is an evangelistic sermon to outsiders in order to convince them to believe, whereas Second Clement is a sermon to insiders—people who already believe—exhorting them to proper understanding of their faith. At the same time, the passage in Acts 3 is similar to the passage in Second Clement because it's based on an exposition of scripture that is probably ultimately designed for Christian readers, by which I mean, in the book of Acts it's an evangelistic sermon trying to convert people. But when the author of Acts sticks it in Acts 3, he's meaning this for his Christian readers to read. And so to that extent, it's a sermon that's being read by Christian readers, so that in some sense it's like the sermon preserved outside the New Testament, Second Clement.

There are scholars who think that some other books of the New Testament contain sermons. For example, there's a wide scholarly view that the book of Hebrews in the New Testament is best understood as originating as a sermon rather than as a letter. In any event, as we'll see, Second Clement—which is outside the New Testament, one of our Apostolic Fathers—is significant because it gives clues. As a sermon, it gives clues about how the worship services of the Christians in which the sermon was given were conducted.

It appears first off—the first point to make—that the audience of the sermon of Second Clement was comprised of Christians who had been converted from paganism. In other words, the congregation is not made up of converted Jews; it's made up of converted pagans. We get this sense from the very beginning of the sermon: "What praise then shall we give God or what can we pay in exchange for what we have received?" The whole sermon is filled with gratitude to God for the salvation that he's provided. "We were maimed in our understanding. We were worshiping stones and pieces of wood and gold and silver and copper, all of them made by humans. And our entire life was nothing other than death." And so this author admits that before they converted to faith in Christ, they were worshiping idols. So this shows that the congregation, including the author, is made up of converted pagans, people who previously were polytheists who now have become followers of the God of Israel through his son Jesus.

That makes it interesting, how the sermon progresses, because, in fact, the sermon involves an exposition of the Jewish scripture and an exhortation to appropriate behavior based on the scripture, so that even though the converts are not people who grew up in Judaism who had the Jewish scripture originally as their scripture, this author presupposes the authority of the Jewish Bible and he assumes that these former pagans are going to accept the authority of the Jewish Bible as part of their faith.

The theme of the sermon is stated at the outset—chapter 1, verses 1 and 2. This is how it begins. You'll see it doesn't start like a letter. It doesn't start with the author introducing himself and addressing himself to his recipients. It starts off right off the bat sounding like a sermon: "Brothers," he says "we must think about Jesus Christ as we think about God, as about the judge of the living and the dead, and we must not give little thought to our salvation. For when we think little about Him, we also hope to receive but little." So we should think great things about our salvation because our salvation in fact is great.

This is an interesting phrase that he begins with: "We should think of Jesus as we think of God." This is being written in a period in which Christians are increasingly thinking of Jesus as himself divine, as we've seen in a previous lecture. That movement toward understanding Jesus himself as in some sense God is already seen here in the sermon: "You should think of Jesus as God." And so the theme of the sermon is going to be that the salvation that God has provided is an amazing act on his part and we should in fact be completely grateful for this glorious salvation that God has provided.

The author elaborates his theme through an exposition of a particular passage of scripture which appears to be simply the passage of scripture that was read for that day, so that what we need to imagine is that there's a worship service with a congregation in some unknown place, some unknown Greek-speaking place, somewhere in the Roman Empire, where there are pagans who have converted to believe in the God of Israel and Jesus as his son who are gathered together for a worship service, and there's been a reading of the scripture and now there's a sermon based on that scripture.

The scripture that was read was Isaiah, chapter 54, verse 1. And the author quotes a passage from Isaiah 54, which apparently the whole passage had just been read; then he quotes a passage and interprets it. So he goes through this passage, giving an interpretation as he goes. And so it starts this in chapter 2, verse 1, where he quotes the passage, Isaiah 54: "Be jubilant, you who are infertile and who do not bear children. Let your voice burst forth and cry out, you who experience no pains of labor. For the one who has been deserted has more children than the one who has a husband." That's the scripture quotation.

What does this mean, "You who are infertile should be jubilant; your voice should burst out and cry out, you who have experienced no pains of labor?" So a woman who hasn't born a child should rejoice. "For the one who has been deserted," in other words, who doesn't have a husband, "has more children than the one who has a husband." What's that referring to? When you read this passage in Isaiah itself—Isaiah, chapter 54—it's clear that this is a reference not to an actual woman who's given birth or not given birth. It's actually a symbolic reference to the city of Jerusalem.

This is a passage that was written during the Babylonian exile. Now if you know your history of ancient Israel well enough, you'll remember that in the 6th century B.C., the nation of Israel was overthrown by the Babylonians in a military conquest. Israel was overthrown, Jerusalem was destroyed, the temple was burned, and Jerusalem was depopulated. They took the people of Israel out of Jerusalem, and they led them into exile back to Babylon.

Jerusalem, in this passage, is being portrayed then as a woman who has no children because there are no inhabitants there. And the prophet is saying, "Rejoice, for the one who has been deserted"—Jerusalem—"has more children than the one who has a husband." In other words, Jerusalem is going to acquire a huge number of inhabitants. So he's saying that the exiles are going to return to Jerusalem. That's what the passage meant originally in the book of Isaiah.

And so it's interesting that this author interprets it in a completely different way. He doesn't interpret it at all the way Isaiah interprets it. He says, "Now when it says 'Be jubilant, you who are infertile and who did not bear children,' it's referring to us. For our church was infertile before children were given to it." It's referring to Christians because the church had no children before people converted to become Christian. "And when the text says, 'Cry out you who experience no pains of labor,' it means this: we should raise our prayers up to God sincerely and not grow weary like women in labor." So just as a woman in labor grows weary and cries out, well, that's how Christians would act or to cry out to God. "And when it says 'for the one who has been deserted has more children than the one who has a husband,' it's because our people appear to be deserted by God"—the pagans appear to be deserted by God—"but now that we believe we have become more numerous than those who appear to have God." The pagans are more numerous than the Jews in the body of Christ in the church.

What we have here then is a sermon that's based on an exposition of scripture. We will be looking at this approach to scripture in our next lecture. In this lecture, I want to continue by talking about some of the interesting other features of Second Clement, one of which is that not only the Old Testament, Isaiah 54, but also the teachings of Jesus are considered by this author to be scripture. Remember, as we've seen, the words of Jesus begin to take on scriptural authority for Christians in the beginning of the 2nd century. Well, we have that here in chapter 2, verse 4, he says, "Also another scripture says 'I did not come to call the upright, but the sinners,'" a reference to the passage of what Jesus himself said, for example, in Mark, chapter 2, verse 17, and Matthew, chapter 9, verse 13. So Jesus' teachings are accepted as scripture. That's interesting because it shows that there's a movement by this author toward a bipartite canna—a canon of scripture—with two parts in it, an Old Testament and a New Testament: the writings of the prophets and the words of Jesus.

Some of the quotations of Jesus may not have come from books. It may not be that he's quoting Matthew. It may be that he simply heard the traditions about Jesus. Some of the quotations that are found of the words of Jesus are familiar to those who read the New Testament. For example, in chapter 4, he says, "For this reason we should not merely call him Lord, for this will not save us, simply calling him Lord, for he says not everyone who says to me, 'Lord, Lord,' will be saved, but only the ones who practice righteousness." That seems to be a quotation from Matthew, chapter 7, verse 21. And so these are some of the quotations of Jesus that sound familiar to students of the New Testament.

There are other passages though that don't sound familiar to people who know the New Testament because they're not found in the New Testament. I'll give you an example, chapter 4, verse 5, an interesting passage, where it says, "For this reason, when you do these things, the Lord has said" and then he quotes the Lord Jesus, "Even if you were nestled close to my breast but did not do what I have commanded, I would cast you away and say to you 'leave me. I do not know where you are from, you who are lawless.'" Well, that's an interesting quotation from Jesus, but we don't have it anywhere else. It's not in any of the gospels that we have, and so it's not clear where he got it. He may have another gospel that we don't have in which this would be a quotation from Jesus. In fact, it appears to me he probably does have another gospel we don't have.

Some of the unusual sayings of Jesus that formed the basis for this book's exposition then appeared to come from gospels that didn't make it into the New Testament, and we have a couple of instances in which we're pretty sure—in fact, we know—that the quotations about Jesus come from gospels that are not found in the New Testament. I'll give you one of the most intriguing passages in Second Clement where the author is giving an exposition of a saying of Jesus. The first part of this exposition—the first part of the quotation—is something found in the New Testament. "For the Lord said, 'You will be like sheep in the midst of wolves.'" Now that's a reference to when Jesus is sending out his disciples two by two in order to tell the people that the kingdom of God is coming. He sends them out two by two, and he says, "You'll be like sheep in the midst of wolves." So it's not going to be any easy time for you.

But in this quotation from the words of Jesus, we have a continuation of the passage that's not found in the New Testament that's rather interesting. "Peter replied to Jesus, 'What if the wolves rip apart the sheep?'" What if we get torn to shreds? Jesus said to Peter, "After they are dead, the sheep should fear the wolves no longer." I guess that's true. If they're dead, they don't have to fear the wolves any longer. "So to you, do not fear those who kill you and then can do nothing more to you. But fear the one who, after you die, has the power to cast your body and soul into the hell of fire." So you have this very interesting passage where Peter is concerned that they're going to be ripped to shreds, and Jesus says don't worry about that because when you die, you don't have to fear those who can do that, but fear God, who after your death can punish you. That's probably a good Christian lesson.

So where did he get the saying from though? because only the first part of the saying, "You'll be like sheep among wolves," occurs in the New Testament. He must have gotten this from another gospel. Well, what other gospel did he get it from? We are fortunate in recent times to have discovered the answer to this question.

Occasionally, archeologists in Egypt turn up portions of manuscripts, fragments of manuscripts, that contain gospel materials. In the second half of the 20th century in an archeological dig, there was discovered several fragments of a gospel that contained sayings of Jesus. And one of these passages has this saying in it, slightly different. In this fragment that's been discovered, "The Lord said, 'You'll be like sheep in the midst of wolves,' and I replied to him, 'What if the wolves rip apart the sheep?' and Jesus said to me..." Then it continues on. It gives the rest of it.

What does this show? This shows that this fragment was originally from the Gospel of Peter because Second Clement quotes this as being a conversation between Peter and Jesus, and this fragment, which is just a fragment of a manuscript, records it as a conversation between the Lord and me, which shows this must have come from the Gospel of Peter, which is really interesting for a lot of reasons, one of which is that, as I've indicated earlier, we've discovered a

Gospel of Peter, but it's only a fragmentary copy of the Gospel of Peter and it doesn't contain this saying.

The larger chunk of the Gospel of Peter that was discovered—I say we discovered it; I wasn't born yet, but a century before I was born, it was discovered in the middle of the 19th century by French archeologists digging in Egypt who had uncovered the tomb of a monk and had found a book buried with him. This book that was buried with him was a book that contained several writings, including a gospel by Peter, which recounts the events surrounding Jesus' trial, his death, and his resurrection.

Scholars wondered when this Gospel of Peter—and we know that's a gospel of Peter because Peter writes in the first person in this gospel, so we know that that's a gospel that was by Peter. But people wondered, did the Gospel of Peter that was found in the 19th century in this tomb of the monk, did it originally consist just of a passion narrative or was it an entire gospel? Was it just about Jesus' trial, death, and resurrection, or was it an entire gospel with his ministry ahead of time? What scholars tend to think now is that this fragment discovered more recently was part of the same gospel, and it shows that this Gospel of Peter was originally an entire gospel with the ministry of Jesus preceding his Passion. And it appears that this author, Second Clement, in the 140s, had access to this gospel, and so he's quoting it. He's quoting the lost portion of the Gospel of Peter.

I'll give you a second example of this author quoting something that's only recently turned up. In chapter 12, the author says, "For this reason, we should await the kingdom of God with love and righteousness every hour, since we do not know the day when God will appear. For when the Lord himself was asked by someone when his kingdom would come, he said the following…," and now there's going to come a quotation of Jesus that we don't have in any of our New Testament Gospels. "The Lord said, 'When the two are one and the outside is like the inside and the male with the female is neither male nor female, then the kingdom will come." What? That's a very strange saying, when the two are one, the outside is like the inside, the male is like the female, so there's neither male nor female, then the Kingdom will come.

Well, we now know where this quotation came from. In the 1940s they discovered a collection of manuscripts near Nag Hammadi, Egypt, as I've mentioned earlier. Among these manuscripts was a gospel that is called the Coptic Gospel of Thomas which contains 114 sayings of Jesus. This is one of the sayings that's found in the Coptic Gospel of Thomas, so that Second Clement is actually quoting this Coptic Gospel of Thomas. This is a striking fact because both the Gospel of Peter and the Gospel of Thomas were ultimately eliminated from consideration for the New Testament canon because they were considered heretical.

This author, who is completely proto-orthodox, considers them to contain sayings of Jesus. And he elaborates on these sayings of Jesus and gives an exposition of these sayings of Jesus. In my next lecture, hopefully, I'll tell you how he in fact interprets this saying about the outside and the inside and the male and the female.

In any event, all of the authorities that the author Second Clement quotes—the Old Testament and the sayings of Jesus—are used by him in order to exhort his congregation to certain actions, even this quotation from a non-canonical source. It appears, in fact, that the entire point of his sermon is to exhort people, as he says, for example, at the end of his sermon. He says, "Well, on the basis of all this, we should repent from our whole heart lest any of us perish and not only should we appear to believe and pay attention now while we're being admonished by the presbyters." So he's referring to people who are in the church service: "Just don't pay attention now, we're being exhorted, "but also when we return home, we should remember the commandments of the Lord and not be dragged away by worldly desire." So don't just be a Sunday-morning Christian; you should be a Christian throughout the week. So the entire point of the sermon is an exhortation for Christian behavior.

In any event, it appears clear from Second Clement how the worship service of this community was actually constructed, and I'll conclude with this: The way they had their worship service evidently, reading between the lines of this book, is that they would have a reading from the Old Testament scripture, in this case, Isaiah, chapter 54. So this was one of the congregations that thought the Old Testament was still valid for Christians.

This Old Testament scripture was the basis for reflection and exposition as the text was explained for its relevance for the community. This exposition then was the basis for moral exhortation to the community. It's possible that hymns were also sung during the services, as we know from other evidence from the 2nd century.

In sum, Second Clement is a significant book, in part because it can reveal to us what worship services were like in the mid-2nd century. As it turns out, in many respects the worship services then were probably not all that different from Christian worship services in our own time.

Lecture Sixteen
The Use of Scripture in the Early Church

Scope:

The fact that Scripture is so central to the exposition of 2 Clement allows us to consider further the question of how Scripture functioned for the early Christian communities. Much of that sermon is based on a creative reading of a particular passage in the Old Testament, Isaiah 54:1, a passage that at first glance seems to have nothing to do with the situation addressed by 2 Clement. But by using an allegorical mode of interpretation, the preacher is able to make the words of the text applicable to his congregation's own situation.

In this lecture, we will see that this was not an unusual approach to Scripture among early Christians. Rather than taking a literal approach to the text, they often read the text figuratively. In this, they were following accepted interpretive practices of Judaism. Eventually, however, the practice of allegorical reading among Christians came under fire, as Christian leaders began to realize that if a text can be taken to mean something other than it literally says, it could be used to support "false" teachings as well as true ones.

Outline

I. In our last lecture, we saw how Scripture played an important role in the worship services presupposed by 2 Clement.

   A. The Old Testament was not interpreted literally, however, but figuratively, to show its relevance in the here and now for the congregation of Christians.

   B. We might call this a *presentist* mode of interpretation, one in which the text is taken out of its own historical context and made to apply to a present situation—even if that present situation is quite different from the one to which the text was originally addressed.

   C. Thus, the exposition of Isaiah 54:1 in 2 Clement applies not to Israel in the Babylonian exile but to Christians in the Roman world.

D. This kind of presentist interpretation of Scripture has always been popular among Christians and is still found widely today, as seen, for example, in the scriptural expositions of "prophecy experts" who claim that the predictions of Scripture are coming true in the here and now (e.g., Edgar Whisenant on Matthew 24).

    1. Edgar Whisenant published a book (*88 Reasons Why the Rapture is in 1988)* prophesying the "rapture" or Second Coming of Christ would occur in 1988.

    2. One of the reasons many found this a convincing idea was Whisenant's interpretation of the parable of the fig tree, found in Matthew 24.

    3. Whisenant pointed out that in Scripture the fig tree symbolizes Israel. He interpreted the parabolic image of the fig tree sprouting leaves as the foundation of the state of Israel in 1948. To this he added his interpretation of the parable's words "This generation shall not pass till all these things be done" to mean that the rapture would happen in 40 years, or one Biblical generation, from the founding of Israel in 1948.

II. There is a long history of this mode of interpretation among both Jewish and Christian interpreters.

    A. Around the time of the beginning of Christianity, this approach to interpretation was prevalent among the Jewish community that produced the Dead Sea Scrolls.

        1. Scholars believe the Dead Sea Scrolls, discovered in 1947, were written by Essenes, apocalyptic Jewish Christians, who believed the end of the world was imminent; God would soon intervene to overthrow the forces of evil (i.e. the Romans), and they, the Essenes, would be given the kingdom of Israel.

        2. There are a variety of kinds of writings found among the scrolls discovered beginning in 1947: Scripture texts, rules for the community's life together, books of psalms, and most important for our purposes here, examples of scriptural interpretation.

        3. Among the latter are commentaries on Scripture, such as the famous Commentary on Habakkuk, which applies a mode of interpretation called *pesher*—in effect, a simple presentist form of interpreting the text.

B. We find similar modes of interpretation among the early Christians.

    1. Something similar happens in Matthew's interpretation of the life of Jesus (for example, Matthew 2:15).

    2. Another presentist interpretation appears in 2 Clement in response to the Gnostic idea of a fragmented material world separated from the divine world. The Gnostics worked toward unifying the two worlds into a future world in which spirit and body would be one and male would not be distinguished from female. The author of 2 Clement interprets the symbolic Gnostic words "two become one" to mean "when we speak truth to one another—when we agree." The Gnostic "outside like inside" is interpreted in 2 Clement to mean that the soul should be visible through good works. The Gnostic "male and female are neither male nor female" is interpreted to mean that males and females will be equals in society.

    3. An even more obvious example occurs in the apostle Paul's interpretation of the book of Genesis, in which he allegorizes the partners of Abraham, Sarah, and Hagar (Gal. 2:21–31).

C. We can see similar approaches to interpretation in writings of other church fathers. Recall the interpretations of the laws of circumcision and *kashrut* in Barnabas, for example.

III. Eventually, this mode of interpretation ran into problems in proto-orthodox Christian circles.

A. One problem is that if a text doesn't mean what it literally says, but means something else instead, it is difficult to control the meaning of the text, allowing interpreters to make the text mean anything they want it to mean.

B. This became a problem because certain "heretical" groups could appeal to Scripture in support of their views, even when those views were not literally taught in Scripture.

    1. For example, Gnostics believed that there were 30 gods in the divine realm; Gnostic interpreters claimed that the fact that Jesus was baptized when he was 30 supported this view.

   2. Further, Gnostics held that the 12th deity of the final group of 12 "fell" from the divine realm, leading to the creation of this world; this was "seen" in the fact that Jesus' 12th disciple, Judas Iscariot, was the one who betrayed him.

   3. The dove that descended upon Jesus was interpreted to mean that at that point, a divine being came into the man Jesus to empower him for his ministry before leaving him prior to his death; this was based on the fact that the letters in the Greek word for "dove" have the same numerical value as alpha and omega, the number of God.

C. Proto-orthodox Christians opposed these interpretations by claiming they had no ties to the literal meaning of the text.

   1. The father Irenaeus, in particular, asserted that Gnostic interpreters were like someone who took a beautiful mosaic of a king and rearranged the stones into the shape of a mongrel, claiming that that image was what the artist intended all along.

   2. But in some ways, the proto-orthodox interpretations of texts were no less bizarre and unrelated to the literal meaning than those of the Gnostics.

   3. The difference—at least according to the proto-orthodox Christians—was that they derived their doctrines from the clear meaning of Scripture (meaning a literal interpretation) and their figurative interpretations were valid only insofar as they did not contradict these literal meanings.

   4. It is for that reason that the literal meaning of Scripture has often been given the greatest priority in interpreting the text.

IV. It is important to realize that texts don't provide their own interpretations.

A. Interpreters are the ones who instill meaning in texts.

B. And interpreters all have different ways of looking at and understanding the world.

C. These different perspectives affect how texts are read.

D. That was just as true in antiquity as it is today, as can be seen, for example, in the interpretations of Scripture advanced by the book of 2 Clement.

Essential Reading:

Karlfried Froehlich, *Biblical Interpretation in the Early Church*.

Robert Grant and David Tracy, *A Short History of the Interpretation of the Bible*.

Supplementary Reading:

Peter R. Akroyd, ed. *Cambridge History of the Bible*, vol. 1.

R. P. C. Hanson, *Allegory and Event*.

Questions to Consider:

1. Do you think that texts have "common sense" interpretations? If so, why do so many otherwise intelligent people disagree about how to interpret texts, such as those of the New Testament? Is it just that some people are smarter than others?

2. In your opinion, should the texts of Scripture be interpreted in just the same way as all other texts are interpreted (such as novels, short stories, and newspaper articles), or should there be "special" rules? If there are special rules, who gets to decide the rules, and how would you know if they are right?

Lecture Sixteen—Transcript
The Use of Scripture in the Early Church

In our last lecture, we saw how scripture played an important role in the worship services presupposed by the book of Second Clement. The Old Testament was not interpreted literally, however, but in a figurative way to show its relevance in the here and now for the congregation of Christians. We might call this approach to scripture a "presentist" mode of interpretation, as it is one in which the text is taken out of its own historical context and made to apply to a present situation even if that present situation is quite different from the one to which the text was originally addressed—a "presentist" interpretation. And so is the exposition of Isaiah, chapter 54, verse 1, in Second Clement. Isaiah 54 originally was using the image of the barren woman as a reference to Jerusalem, which had lost its children, its inhabitants, to the Babylonian exile. And Isaiah is telling the people of Israel that they should rejoice because in fact this woman who is barren will have more children than the one who has a husband. In other words, Jerusalem will become repopulated. That was the original meaning of Isaiah 54.

Second Clement, however, took the text to refer not to Israel in the Babylonian exile but to Christians in the Roman world. He interpreted it in light of his own congregation and their situation. This kind of "presentist" interpretation of scripture has always been popular among Christians, and it is still found widely today, as seen, for example, in the scriptural expositions of people who call themselves "prophecy experts" who claim that the predictions of scripture are coming through in the here and now.

This is a very common phenomenon in modern Christianity. You need only go to any Christian bookstore and look on the shelves and you'll see shelf after shelf of prophecy books that talk about how the prophecies of old are coming to be fulfilled in our own day. There have been a number of occasions in my life when I've been made acutely aware of this approach to the Bible, perhaps none more interesting than when I arrived at my teaching position at Chapel Hill in 1988. I had been teaching at Rutgers in New Jersey and moved to North Carolina in August of that year and had never been in the South prior to my move, and I was confronted with a situation, namely, that there was a book that was floating around many

Christian congregations in the South that was causing a bit of a disturbance.

This book was quite popular, not just in the South, but far more in the South than in New Jersey. It was a book by a fundamentalist person named Edgar Whisenant, and the book was called *88 Reasons Why the Rapture Will Occur in 1988.* Some of you may remember the book. As I said, there are eight million copies in print. It was causing quite a splash. When I arrived in Chapel Hill, I started getting phone calls from newspapers and journals wanting to know my opinion about whether the rapture was going to occur. The rapture, as you know, is the teaching of evangelical Christians that Jesus will return from heaven and the people who have died who are Christians will rise up to meet Jesus in the air. And then people who are on earth who are believers in Jesus will also be taken up into the air. And so the only people who will be left on earth will be the unbelievers, And then there will be a seven-year period of absolute chaos on earth—the tribulation—in which the antichrist will arise, and at the end of the seven years Christ will come back in judgment and overthrow the antichrist and set up his kingdom on earth.

This is a teaching found among many fundamentalist groups, including the group that Edgar Whisenant belonged to. And he had solid reasons for thinking; in fact, he had 88 reasons for thinking that this was going to occur in 1988. In fact, he was a little bit more specific than that. He insisted that this was going to happen during the Jewish festival of Rosh Hashanah in 1988, which happened near the end of October.

So what are his reasons? Well, I can't give you all 88, but let me give you one of the reasons to show you a presentist interpretation of scripture. This was one of the 88 reasons and one that many people found to be fairly convincing. Jesus, in the Gospel of Matthew, chapter 25, tells a parable about the coming of the end. He says, "When these things have been fulfilled, you know that the end is near. Learn the parable from the fig tree. When the fig tree puts forth its leaves, you know that summer is near. So, too, when all these things take place, you know that the end is near. Truly I tell you this generation will not pass away before all these things take place."

Well, how is one to interpret this parable? Edgar Whisenant points out that in scripture the fig tree is commonly used as a symbol for the nation of Israel. When the fig tree puts forth its leaves, what would that mean? Well, the fig tree has lain dormant through the winter. It puts forth its leaves in the spring. That's a sign of the fig tree coming back to life. When does Israel come back to life? 1948, when Israel reestablishes itself as a sovereign state. "Truly I tell you, this generation will not pass away before all these things take place." How long is a generation in the Bible? 40 years. 1948 plus 40—bingo!—1988. That's one of his 88 reasons. I won't give you the others.

Now, some people were upset with this, even evangelical Christians, who queried Whisenant and said, "Look, Jesus himself says that no one knows the day or the hour when the Son of Man will return." Whisenant's reply was, "I don't know the day or the hour. I just know which week." And so it goes. This approach toward interpreting Biblical prophecy of course didn't die out in 1988.

By the way, when it didn't happen in 1988, Whisenant wrote another book in which he pointed out that he had forgotten that when the calendar was devised they didn't include the year 0. They went from 1 B.C. to A.D. 1, so he was a year off; so it's actually going to happen in 1989. Well, it didn't happen in 1989. So he wrote another book, and so it goes.

This mode of interpretation is still alive and well among us. One of the amazing publishing phenomena of the beginning of the 21st century is the "Left Behind" series—this series of books in which two authors give, in novelistic form, what will happen after the rapture here on earth. In other words, it is the book of Revelation that these novels are based on. The book of Revelation isn't about past time—it's not about what was going on in the author's day. The book of Revelation is about us and our day.

Of course, every generation from the time of Jesus onward has thought that the prophecies applied to its own day. As I tell my students, everyone who has predicted the end of the world and set a date—everyone in the history of Christianity, from day one until now—everyone has had one thing in common: Every single one of them has been absolutely wrong. That should give one pause when thinking that one knows what's going to happen in the near future. Well, in any event, there is a long history of presentist modes of interpretation among both Jewish and Christian interpreters. This is not found simply in Second Clement and in modern times. In fact, there's a long and noble history of this approach to scripture.

Around the time of the beginning of Christianity, this approach, this interpretive approach, was prevalent among the Jewish community that produced the Dead Sea Scrolls. I mentioned in an earlier lecture that the Dead Sea Scrolls were discovered by pure serendipity. A shepherd boy was searching for a lost sheep and threw a stone into a cave and heard it plunk against a jar. He didn't know it was a jar until he went back the next day with a buddy. They climbed up and went into the cave, and there were jars in there, and these jars were filled with scrolls. This was in 1947.

When this boy and his friend told their family members about this—these were Bedouin—they went and they discovered that cave and started to search around and found other caves. And eventually, scholars found out that this discovery had been made, and then scholars went out and started searching for these caves in this area. This is an area in what is now Israel to the west of the Dead Sea, a wilderness area, where there are a lot of caves. So they looked in every cave and little hole around the entire area to find what they could find. They uncovered 11 different caves over the years—mainly in the 1950s—11 different caves that had manuscripts in them.

And scholars became convinced that these manuscripts were produced by a group of Jews known as the Essenes because there was a settlement that was discovered nearby these caves that has been excavated. It appears that this community, which is called Qumran, Qumran was a natural community of Essene Jewish Christians. These Essenes were people who believed that the end of the age was near. They were sort of 1st-century B.C. counterparts to Edgar Whisenant in some respects. They thought that the end was coming right away and they had a sense it was going to happen within their own generation. They were apocalyptic Jews, holding to the perspectives of apocalypticism, that the end of the age was imminent and that God would soon intervene in the course of history to overthrow the forces of evil and bring in His good kingdom.

These Essenes had moved out into the wilderness at some point in their history. Evidently, the community had as an early leader, a figure whom the community called the "teacher of righteousness," who was talked about in some of the Dead Sea Scrolls. This teacher of righteousness was apparently a very charismatic interpreter of scripture who had been offended and opposed by a priest in Jerusalem. Both the teacher of righteousness and the "wicked priest," as he was called, are left unnamed in the Dead Sea Scrolls. And so there are a lot of theories about who these people actually were.

This wicked priest opposed the teacher of righteousness and drove him out of Jerusalem. And so that was part of the establishment of this community—a kind of monastic-like community—off in the wilderness. These Essenes were in the wilderness trying to maintain their purity according to their interpretation of scripture so that they would be pure when the end arrived. They thought that God was soon going to intervene and there would be a major war against the Romans. Their nickname for the Romans was the "kittim." The kittim were going to attack Israel, and God would intervene, and after a 40-year war, would overthrow the kittim. And then they, the children of light, who were on God's side after all, would be given the kingdom of Israel after this major war. So that was the expectation of this Essene community that produced the Dead Sea Scrolls.

There were a number of different kinds of writings among the Dead Sea Scrolls. In one set of writings they actually had copies of the books of scripture. So there is a complete copy of the Book of Isaiah, for example, and in fact there are fragments at least of every book of the Hebrew Bible, except for the Book of Esther, found among the Dead Sea Scrolls, which is significant because the next earliest copy of the Hebrew Bible that we have dates from the year 1000 A.D., so these scrolls were made before Christ, and so the 1st century before Christ or so. So these are at least a thousand years older than our next earliest copy of the Hebrew Bible; so you can check to see whether the scribes in the intervening centuries copied the text accurately or not. So they're very useful for that. And the answer is sometimes they did and sometimes they didn't.

In any event, there are copies of scripture found among the Dead Sea Scrolls and there are rules for the community's life together which are very interesting because you can see how these Jewish monks lived their lives together. There are books of psalms, and, most important for our purposes here, there are examples of scriptural interpretation, books that give commentaries on texts of scripture.

I'll give you some examples from one of the most famous of these, which is a commentary on the Old Testament prophet Habakkuk. We're told, in the commentary on Habakkuk discovered in the Dead Sea Scrolls, that God told Habakkuk to write down that which would happen to the final generation—what would happen at the end of time—but God did not make known to Habakkuk when time would come to an end. So Habakkuk talked about things happening at the end of time but didn't know actually what he was talking about because he didn't know when the end was going to come. The author of this commentary knows when it's going to come though—it's going to come in our lifetime. So Habakkuk is referring to our day. This is a presentist mode of interpretation.

Scholars sometimes call this form of interpretation a "pesher" interpretation. Pesher interpretation is from the Hebrew word which means interpretation. What happens in this Habakkuk commentary is the author will quote a passage from scripture and then give its pesher—give its interpretation—which is always a presentist interpretation. For example, I'll read you a few passages from the Habakkuk commentary discovered at Qumran: "For behold, I rouse the Chaldeans,"—that's the Babylonians—"that bitter and hasty nation." So Habakkuk was written when the Babylonians were about to attack Israel. Interpreted, this author says—the pesher for this is—"This concerns the kittim," in other words, the Romans, "who are quick and valiant in war." So when Habakkuk was talking about the Babylonians, he wasn't really talking about the Babylonians; he's talking about the Romans—our enemies today.

A second example: "Oh, traitors,"—this is from Habakkuk, chapter 1, verse 13—"Oh, traitors, why do you stare and stay silent when the wicked swallows up one more righteous than he?" Then the pesher—the interpretation: "This concerns the house of Absalom," which was a prominent group of Jews in Jerusalem in his day, in the author's day, "and the members of its council who were silent at the time of the chastisement of the teacher of righteousness"—this is referring to when the teacher of righteousness was confronted by the wicked priest—"and gave him no help against the liar," which is the wicked priest, "who flouted the law in the midst of their whole congregation." So Habakkuk's referring in fact to our own day. And it goes on and it gives other such things, other presentist commentaries, on this Book of Habakkuk. So presentist modes of interpretation were already established within Jewish circles as we now know from the discovery of the Dead Sea Scrolls.

We find similar modes of interpretation among the early Christians as well. Not just Jews but also Christians in the early times were interpreting scripture in a presentist way. We find this, for example, in the Gospel of Matthew. In the Gospel of Matthew, in the birth narrative when Jesus is born, we are told that all sorts of things happened to fulfill the scriptures. For example, Jesus is born in Bethlehem. Why? because Micah, chapter 5, verse 2 says that from Bethlehem will come forth a savior. Now Matthew isn't actually looking forward to the time of Jesus. He's referring to something in his own day, but they take Micah as referring to the birth of Jesus.

Or an even clearer example is in Matthew, chapter 2, verse 15. If you remember in Matthew, King Herod is out to kill the newborn child Jesus, and so Joseph takes Mary and Jesus and they flee to Egypt. Well, why do they do that? Why Egypt? I mean, why not somewhere else? It's because of the scripture. Matthew, chapter 2, verse 15, tells us that this is to fulfill what was spoken by the prophet that "Out of Egypt have I called my son." So Jesus, the Son of God, is to come forth out of Egypt. Originally, when Hosea is talking about "Out of Egypt have I called my son," he's referring to the exodus of the children of Israel out of Egypt. But Matthew takes it in a presentist mode to refer not to what happened in ancient Israel but what happened in fact to Jesus the Messiah. And so it's a presentist mode of interpretation.

We also get a presentist mode of interpretation, as I've indicated, in Second Clement, not just of Isaiah, chapter 54, but also this very interesting passage that I quoted in the previous lecture, this passage about when the kingdom will come, quoted from the Gospel of Thomas. When the Lord himself was asked by someone when his kingdom would come, he said, "When the two are one and the outside like the inside and the male and female is neither male nor female, then the kingdom will come."

Originally, when this is penned, at least in the Gospel of Thomas, this appears to refer to the Gnostic idea that this world is fragmented and the world needs to move toward unity. Gnostics were very much into kind of a fragmented understanding of this world. They came to understand that this world is actually separated from the divine realm, that this is a material world where the divine realm is spiritual, that human beings represent divine sparks that are trapped within material bodies. And the goal of the Gnostic religion is to provide the necessary knowledge, the gnosis, for the divine spark to escape its entrapment.

And so the idea is that the Gnostic religion then works toward unifying that which has been fragmented. Even Jesus is fragmented in the Gnostic understanding because, for Gnostics, there's a difference between Jesus the man and Christ the god. According to Gnostics, Jesus was a man; he was a human being. But a divine being, the Christ, came into Jesus at his baptism, allowing Jesus to teach the secret teachings of the divine realm to his followers so that then they could have the necessary gnosis to escape their entrapment.

Jesus was not himself an entrapped spark. Jesus Christ was two beings—Jesus the human being and Christ the divine being—who provided the necessary knowledge for salvation. So there's that kind of split in the understanding of the Gnostic religion and this saying is about how the split is going to be unified. The kingdom will come when the two are made one. Now you're two: you are spirit—you've got a trapped spirit—and you are body. But you will be one. You'll be just spirit. The outside will be like the inside. Right now, the outside is not at all like the inside because the outside is material and the inside is spiritual. And the male and female will be neither male nor female because in the kingdom that's coming there will be no distinctions between sexes. There will be unity rather than fragmentation. So that's what the saying probably meant in its original form.

Second Clement though takes it to mean something quite different. He says, "The two are one when we speak truth to one another so that we agree with one another." That's what it means when the two become one. So you and I agree; two become one. "The outside like the inside means that your body is visible; so too your soul should be visible in your good works." Well that's an interesting interpretation, but it's not what the saying originally meant. And the words, "the male and the female are neither male nor female," mean this, that a brother who sees a sister should think nothing about her being female, and she should think nothing about his being male. So you shouldn't make kind of distinctions like that in your community but you should treat one another equally. That's an interesting interpretation, but it's not the interpretation that at least you get in the Gospel of Thomas.

Let me give you one other example of an early Christian use of a presentist mode of interpretation. The apostle Paul, our earliest Christian author, in chapter 4 of the book of Galatians, gives a very interesting allegorical reading of an event that happened in the Old Testament. In the Old Testament, Abraham, the father of the Jews, is promised by God that he will have many offspring. Well, Abraham grows up and he's an old man and his wife is an old lady, and there's no offspring. And so Abraham decides that what God must mean is that he's not going to have offspring from his wife Sarah but he has to bring up offspring from someone else. So Sarah hands over her maid, Hagar, her slave Hagar, and Abraham has sex with Hagar and they have a child, Ishmael. But then God says, "No, that's not what I meant," and so it turns out, in fact, "I meant Sarah was going to get pregnant." And so then Abraham has sex with Sarah, and even though she's a very, very old woman she conceives and bears a son, Israel. And so this is the beginning of the nation of Israel then. And so you get Israel and Ishmael.

That's an interesting story in the Old Testament. Israel then is the Father of the Jews and Ishmael is the one who is cast out because he's not the one who's the heir of the promise. Paul interprets this allegorically, where he says that Sarah and Hagar actually don't refer just to the women, Sarah and Hagar. Hagar was the slave woman. She refers to Jerusalem in the present, which is a city in slavery because its people are still enslaved to the law. In other words, it refers to Jews. Sarah is the free woman. This represents the people who are freed from the law, the people of the promise. That represents the Christians who are not in slavery to the law but who are free from the law. And so it's the Christians who are heirs of the promise of Abraham, not the Jews. Well, a very interesting interpretation, but again it's a presentist mode of interpretation, which, of course, would not be convincing to anybody except for someone who already agreed with the premises of the interpretation.

We can see similar approaches to interpretation in the writings of other church fathers. Remember the interpretation of the laws of kosher in Barnabas where not eating a pig means not living like a pig; not eating a hyena means not being like a hyena; and not eating a weasel means not being like a weasel. These are presentist modes of interpretation.

Eventually, this mode of interpretation came to be considered to be somewhat problematic in proto-orthodox Christian circles. The reason it became seen as problematic is that this kind of presentist interpretation that gives a figurative meaning to the text is very difficult to control. How can you control interpretation if the text means something other than what it says? If the text doesn't mean what it says, how can you control how people interpret the text?

Christians had a particular problem with this when it came to Gnostics who were interpreting scripture. As I think you know, the Gnostics had a variety of understandings of their religion. But in various forms of Gnosticism, there were figurative modes of interpretation that led them to their understanding of their religion. In some Gnostic understandings of things, there's not just one God because God can't have created this world because this world is obviously a cesspool of misery and suffering. The good God couldn't have created that. Well, then, how did we get this world? Well, there were a number of gods in the divine realm. In some Gnostic systems, there were 30 gods, and one of these gods accidentally fell from the divine realm, and the fall from the divine realm led to a natural disaster that eventuated in the creation of this world. So this world is a cosmic disaster. Thirty gods? Yes. Well, some Gnostics pointed to the fact that Jesus was baptized when he was 30 years old and they concluded that he was baptized when he was 30 years old because there were 30 gods in the divine realm.

Orthodox people said, "That's not what the text says." The Gnostics replied, "Yes, but that's what the text means." Or this idea that Jesus has the Christ come into him when he's baptized so that the Christ enters Jesus to give him the gnosis that he needs for salvation. In the Gospels we're told that a dove descends upon Jesus; in Mark's gospel it says the dove entered into Jesus. The Gnostics made a big deal of this. There was one Gnostic group that pointed out that the word "dove" in Greek—you take the Greek letters and you add up the numerical equivalents; remember each Greek letter has a numerical equivalent—you add up the Greek numbers in the word "dove," and it adds up to 801, which is interesting because that's also the number you get when you add up the letters alpha and omega, because omega is 800 and alpha is one. This means that the alpha and the omega descended upon Jesus. In other words, God descended upon Jesus. That's why Jesus and Christ are separate beings, because the Christ is the dove, the alpha and omega, which entered into Jesus. In the book of Revelation, for example, Christ says, "I am the alpha and the omega."

Well proto-orthodox Christians opposed these Gnostic interpretations by claiming that they had no ties to the literal meaning of the text. One church father, named Irenaeus, makes the point that the Gnostic interpreters can be likened to somebody who takes a beautiful mosaic—a stonework portrayal—of a king and takes the colored stones out and rearranges them so that now instead of having this beautiful portrait of a king you've got the portrait of a mongrel dog. The Gnostics have rearranged the colored stones from being a king to being a mongrel dog and claiming that's what the author meant to mean in the first place. So they've taken scripture and rearranged its meaning all over the place and ended up with something that's so bizarre that it's unrelated to the original meaning.

I should point out that in some way proto-orthodox interpretations of the text were no less bizarre or unrelated to the literal meaning than some of the Gnostic interpretations, just thinking again of Barnabas. Eventually though, it came to be the case that some proto-orthodox—and then eventually this became the dominant view— maintained that they derived their doctrines from the clear meaning of scripture with a literal interpretation and that figurative interpretations were valid only insofar as they did not contradict the literal meanings.

Proto-orthodox Christians came to champion the idea that the literal meaning has to be primary, that you have to read the text for what it literally says and base your doctrines on that, not on some figurative interpretation of the text. That point of view, of course, eventually won the day.

To sum up the matter, it's important for us to realize that in fact texts do not provide their own interpretations. Texts are not self-interpreting. They require interpreters. Interpreters are the ones who instill meanings in texts. And interpreters all have different ways of looking at and understanding the world. And these different perspectives affect the way that interpreters read their texts. Texts don't mean something by themselves. They have to be read and interpreted, and your perspectives affect your interpretation of these texts. You can't help that. There's not a way around that.

There's not an objective science that can make you interpret a text and make it say what it really means because texts don't really mean anything. Texts mean what readers say they mean. There's no way around that. And that was true just as much in antiquity as it is today, as can be seen, for example, in the interpretations of scripture by the book of Second Clement.

Lecture Seventeen
Papias—An Early Christian Interpreter

Scope:

The questions of interpretation dealt with in the previous lecture make a natural segue into the fragmentary writings of another Apostolic Father, Papias. Unfortunately, we do not have Papias's writings preserved for us completely but only in small snippets as they were quoted for us in later authors. However, what we know about Papias is significant: He wrote one of the earliest detailed commentaries on the sayings of Jesus, called An Exposition of the Sayings of the Lord.

The quotations from this work that we still have are very interesting, because they contain a number of legendary details both about what Jesus taught—for example, about the coming millennial age—and about his followers—for example, about the fate of Judas Iscariot.

Outline

I. One of the most interesting but least known Apostolic Fathers was Papias, an enigmatic figure of the early 2nd century.

    A. Unfortunately, the writings of Papias have come down to us only in snippets.

        1. With the other Apostolic Fathers, we actually have manuscripts of their writings, completely preserved.

        2. The writings of Papias, on the other hand, were not preserved. We know of them only insofar as small portions of them were quoted by later church fathers.

    B. At one time, however, Papias's works were recognized as significant. He was the first known author to collect the sayings of Jesus and provide an extended interpretation of them.

        1. His lost work was in five volumes and was called An Exposition of the Sayings of the Lord.

        2. Given its length, Papias obviously collected a lot of material not found in the Gospels of the New Testament.

        3. We are fortunate that he tells us what his sources of information were: Principally they were the companions

of the apostles themselves, whom Papias had met and interviewed for information about what Jesus' apostles had said about him (fragment 3.3).

C. The traditions we have about Papias indicate that he was a companion of Polycarp's and, along with Polycarp, had actually been a disciple of John, the son of Zebedee.
   1. Later traditions indicate that he was John's secretary (fragment 15); however, this appears to be a legend.
   2. What we can say about him is that he appears to have been a generation removed from the companions of Jesus' disciples; he seems to have been active around A.D. 110–130.
   3. The connections these later legends make from Papias and Polycarp to John appear to be part of the attempt by later orthodox writers to trace the line of apostolic succession from the days of Jesus down to their own time.

II. In large measure because of his quirky views, Papias came to be regarded as suspicious by later authors.

A. In particular, it was his literal interpretation of the future millennium that led to his falling out of favor with the later representatives of orthodoxy.

B. From the earliest of times, Christians had maintained an apocalyptic worldview, starting with Jesus himself, who proclaimed the coming of a future kingdom of God to Earth.
   1. The kingdom of God for Jesus was not "heaven" in the world above: It appears to have been a real kingdom, here on Earth, that would be ruled over by earthly rulers (the 12 disciples) and headed by the future messiah.
   2. This kingdom was expected to replace the wicked kingdoms of Earth.
   3. In making this proclamation, Jesus was standing in a long line of prophets who predicted that God would eventually reassert his control over this world.
   4. Expectations of what this would be like go all the way back to the Hebrew prophets of the Old Testament, such as Isaiah (cf. Isa. 11:1–9).
   5. Jesus, though, had a more apocalyptic vision of what this future kingdom would be like: He anticipated that it

would involve not just a good kingdom on Earth but the overthrow of the forces of evil with the arrival of the Son of Man (cf. Mark 8:38–9:1; Mark 13:24–31).

C. Jesus' preaching of the future kingdom was taken up by his followers, as can be seen from the writings of the apostle Paul.

    1. Paul expected that it would be Jesus himself who would return from heaven in judgment on the Earth.

    2. And Paul anticipated that he himself would be alive to see this cataclysmic event take place (1 Thessalonians 4:14–18; 1 Corinthians 15:51–53).

D. Papias, two generations later, continued to subscribe to this kind of apocalyptic vision, literally anticipating a future paradise here on Earth (fragment 1:2).

E. Later church fathers found this view, which they called *chiliasm*, to be far too literalistic and naïve.

    1. Instead, there developed the idea that the kingdom of God was not to be taken literally as an event that would take place on Earth.

    2. The kingdom of God increasingly was taken as a metaphor for God's rule over his people, both here on Earth and in heaven after death.

    3. It is probably because of his literalistic interpretations that Papias was castigated by later writers, such as Eusebius, the father of Church history, who called Papias "a man of exceedingly small intelligence" (*Church History* 3.39).

III. It is interesting to observe that the apocalyptic vision of Jesus and his earlier followers came to be transformed in later generations.

A. In part, this transformation resulted from the "failure" of the end to appear.

B. We can see the beginnings of that transformation already among some of Paul's congregations, for example, the Christians in the church of Corinth.

C. Paul's avid opposition to their views came to be embodied in the New Testament, but ironically, his perspective ended up not carrying the day.

D. Today, the vast majority of Christians think of the kingdom of God as the experience of God's rule in the here and now and in the afterlife, rather than as a literal kingdom here on Earth.

IV. In sum, Papias was faithful to the earliest Christian tradition about the coming of the end, and it was because he failed to adjust that vision with the passage of time that he ended up being regarded as a naïve and unsophisticated thinker, even though he was one of the first to collect the sayings of Jesus and interpret them according to the teachings of Jesus' own followers.

Essential Reading:

Bart D. Ehrman, ed., "Fragments of Papias," in *The Apostolic Fathers*, vol. 2, pp. 86–119.

William R. Schoedel, "Papias," in the *Anchor Bible Dictionary*, D. N. Freedman, ed., vol. 5, pp. 140–142.

Supplementary Reading:

William R. Schoedel, "Papias," in the series *Aufstieg und Niedergang der Roemischen Welt*, pp. 235–270.

William R. Schoedel, "Fragments of Papias," in *The Apostolic Fathers: A New Translation*, Robert M. Grant, ed., vol. 5.

Questions to Consider:

1. There continue to be people today, of course, who still expect the end of this world to happen soon. How are such people widely viewed, and why are they viewed in this way?

2. In your opinion, could Jesus and Paul really have expected the end of the age to come within their own generation? Were they wrong?

Lecture Seventeen—Transcript
Papias—An Early Christian Interpreter

One of the most interesting, but least known, of the Apostolic Fathers, was the enigmatic figure of the 2nd century, the early 2nd century, Papias. Unfortunately, the writings of Papias have come down to us only in snippets. With the other Apostolic Fathers, we actually have manuscripts of their writings completely preserved, manuscripts that have been transmitted down through the Middle Ages, or else manuscripts that have been discovered in modern times.

The writings of Papias, on the other hand, were not preserved in manuscript form. We know of them only insofar as small portions of his writings were quoted by later church fathers such as the father of church history, Eusebius, in the 4th century. At one time, however, Papias's works were recognized as significant. He was the first known author to collect the sayings of Jesus and provide an extended interpretation of them.

His last work was in five volumes and was called An Exposition of the Sayings of the Lord. It's not clear whether this book, An Exposition of the Sayings of the Lord, actually was dealing only with the sayings of Jesus or whether it was an extended commentary on everything involving Jesus' life. In any event, whether it dealt just with the sayings or with a fuller narrative, it is quite clear that there was a narrative about Jesus' life found in Papias's own exposition in the comments that he made at least on the sayings of Jesus.

Given its length—it was five volumes long—Papias obviously had collected a lot of material that is not found in the gospels of the New Testament. We are fortunate that Papias tells us what his sources of information were. As it turns out, principally, they were the companions of the apostles themselves whom Papias had met and interviewed for information about what Jesus' disciples had said about him.

We learn this from one of the fragments that have been preserved of Papias's writings as it's quoted in the church fathers. This particular fragment is from Eusebius from his church history where Papias is quoted as saying, "I also will not hesitate to draw up for you," his reader, "along with these expositions an orderly account of all the things I carefully learned and have carefully recalled from the elders.

For I have certified their truth," he says. And he goes on to say, "Whenever someone arrived who had been a companion of one of the elders," in other words, when anyone who had been a companion of one of the early apostles arrived in town, "I would carefully inquire after their words to find out what Andrew or Peter had said or what Philip or what Thomas had said, or James or John or Matthew, or any of the other disciples of the Lord." So he has interrogated and questioned—interviewed—these companions of the disciples, "and I would seek to find out what things Ariston and the elder John, who are disciples of the Lord, were saying."

Eusebius makes a point when Eusebius, who is writing this in a volume of his church history, is talking about Papias. He makes the point that Papias appears to differentiate between two groups of people who provided authorization for his message. On the one hand, there are the disciples of Jesus himself whose companions he's talked to on occasion. He doesn't indicate he's ever talked to any of the disciples, but he's talked to their companions, so he's probably living after the disciples have died. But the companions are still around.

But the second group is a group that he calls the "elders," such as the elder John and this person named Ariston. They're also disciples to the extent that they're followers of Jesus. But these appear not to have been Jesus' own earthly twelve disciples. So they may be important figures from the 2nd century. He concludes this quotation with the following words: "For I did not suppose that what came out of books would benefit me as much as that which came from a living and abiding voice."

In other words, Papias preferred talking to people who were connected with the apostles of Jesus to reading things in books; so that he would much prefer talking to a companion of Matthew than reading the Gospel of Matthew. He thought that the living voice was more valuable. We'll see the significance of that in the next lecture when I talk about the importance of oral tradition for early Christianity more broadly and with respect to Papias himself.

The traditions we have about Papias indicate that he himself was a companion of Polycarp—Polycarp, the bishop of Smyrna—whom we've met on numerous occasions, and along with Polycarp, Papias had been actually a disciple of John, the son of Zebedee. This is a later tradition that is very hard to verify. In fact, if you listened

©2005 The Teaching Company Limited Partnership

carefully to that quotation, there's reason to think that Papias was not actually a disciple of John the son of Zebedee because he refers to his interviewing companions of John to find out what John had said. That suggests that he himself wasn't one of the companions of John.

Later traditions though indicate that not only was he a disciple of John, he actually was John's secretary to whom John dictated his gospel. And so we find, for example, in the later tradition, when the last of the apostles, John—who was called the son of Thunder—had become a very old man, fearful heresies had sprouted up. And so he dictated the gospel to his own disciple, the respectable Papias of Hierapolis, so as to complete the work of those before him who had proclaimed the word to the nations throughout the world.

What that's indicating is that the three other gospel writers had produced their works— Matthew, Mark and Luke—that John as a very old man produced his gospel and he dictated it then to Papias. This is a later tradition again that does not appear to be authentic. What we can say about Papias is that he appears to have been, based on his own words, a generation removed from the companions of Jesus' disciples. This would make him active sometime around the years A.D. 110 to 130—is the best guesstimate.

The connections that the later legends make between Papias and Polycarp, and then Papias and Polycarp and John, appear to be part of the attempt by later Orthodox writers to trace the line of apostolic succession from the days of Jesus down to their own time. And so the way it worked is, you have the writings of Papias and you want to know if these are worth anything or not. "Oh yes, they're worth a lot." "Why?" "Well, because he was a companion of Polycarp and Polycarp was a bishop of the church of Smyrna. Not only that, but Polycarp and Papias were disciples of John, and John was a disciple of Jesus, and Jesus came from God, and so this writing is perfectly acceptable." So these legends about his relationship, especially his relationship with John, were probably propagated in order to provide a secure understanding of his authority to write the five-volume book that he did.

It was in large measure because of his quirky views that Papias came to be regarded as suspicious by later authors. I'm not saying that I myself find them quirky in comparison with other writings from the early church, but it is clear that there were church fathers, especially in proto-orthodox circles, who came to think that Papias represented a quirky perspective in one respect in particular.

In particular, it was Papias's literal interpretation of the future millennium that led to his falling out of favor with the later representatives of orthodoxy. And so I need to give some background to make sense of what Papias's understanding of the future millennium was in order to put all of this in context.

If you'll recall from our earlier lectures, from the earliest of times Christians had maintained an apocalyptic worldview starting with Jesus himself, who is probably best understood to have been an apocalyptic prophet who proclaimed that there was coming a future kingdom of God to earth. The kingdom of God that Jesus predicted as coming soon was not heaven in the world above. In other words, Jesus does not appear to have had the view that we'll talk about later in this lecture that's common among Christians today, that a person dies and his soul goes to heaven, and then he's in the kingdom of God. That isn't what the kingdom of God was for Jesus. The kingdom of God for Jesus appears to have been a real kingdom, a kingdom here on earth which would be ruled over by earthly rulers—the twelve disciples, in fact, as it turns out—and it would be headed by the future Messiah.

Jesus was living at a time in which the kingdoms of earth were ruled, in the opinion of many Jews, by evil rulers who were empowered by evil cosmic forces; demonic forces have set up the major kingdoms of earth as we find, for example, in the book of Revelation in the New Testament. Many Jews, including Jesus, seemed to think that God was going to overthrow these evil kingdoms and set up his own kingdom, but it would be a kingdom here on earth where God would rule through his appointed Messiah and his Messiah would rule through his underlings, in Jesus' case, the twelve apostles, who were going to be the twelve rulers of the future kingdom.

For example, Jesus says in the Gospel of Mark, our earliest gospel—this is the earliest recorded saying of Jesus, in Mark, chapter 1, verse 15—where Jesus says, "The time has been fulfilled. The kingdom of God is at hand. Repent and believe the good news." This is an apocalyptic image. This age has an allotted amount of time that has been given to it and the time has been fulfilled. So, in other words, the time is almost up. "The kingdom of God is at hand," meaning it's very near. People are to repent and prepare for its coming. This kingdom, as I've indicated, would be a real kingdom ruled by real rulers. In particular, Jesus indicates at one time in a saying that must be authentic, I think, that his own twelve disciples would be the rulers of the kingdom. At one point, Jesus is talking to his disciples in the Gospel of Luke—and it's also found in the Gospel of Matthew—where Jesus says, "Truly I tell you, you twelve will be sitting on twelve thrones ruling the tribes of Israel." His understanding was that there would be a future Son of Man, a future cosmic deliverer, who would be over the kingdom of God, and the twelve disciples would be twelve rulers over the kingdom.

There is a very good reason for thinking that this is something that Jesus actually said. We know there are a lot of sayings in our gospels, not just Matthew, Mark, Luke, and John, but in the Gospel of Peter and the Gospel of Thomas and all of our other gospels. There are a lot of sayings that Christians made up and put on Jesus' lips. That sometimes happens even in the canonical gospels. But this is not a saying that a Christian would have made up and put on his lips, which means it must be a saying that Jesus actually said.

Why is it that nobody would have made up this saying? Because Jesus is talking to his twelve disciples, and he tells them they will be the twelve ruling in the kingdom. But one of the twelve was Judas Iscariot, and later Christians knew that Judas Iscariot had turned Jesus in. So no Christian thought that Judas Iscariot would be one of the twelve rulers, but the saying indicates that all twelve will be rulers, so Jesus must have actually said this during his lifetime. Jesus actually anticipated his twelve disciples would be twelve rulers over the kingdom when it arrived.

This kingdom was expected to replace the wicked kingdoms of earth. Now in making this proclamation of the coming kingdom, Jesus was in fact standing in a long line of prophets who predicted that God would eventually reassert his control over this world. This world obviously is not completely under God's control. If this world was under God's control, why is it that thousands of people die every day of starvation and other poverty-related causes? Why is it that we have tsunamis where millions of people are left homeless and uncounted people are killed? How do you explain that if God's in charge? Well, according to the prophets, even if God doesn't appear to be in charge now, he's going to become in charge and he's going to reassert control over this world, and when he does, it's going to be a paradise-like existence.

Expectations of what it would be like when God reasserted control of this world go all the way back to the Hebrew prophets of the Old Testament—the Jewish Bible. Take, for example, the prophet Isaiah, who was prophesying in the 8th century B.C., so 750 years before Jesus or so. Isaiah has this very famous passage, parts of which will sound familiar to you. It begins in chapter 11: "A shoot shall come forth from the stump of Jesse and a branch shall grow out of his roots"—Jesse was the father of King David—and this is saying that there's going to be a shoot from the family tree. This is a reference to a future son of David, who will be like David, will be a Messianic figure. "The spirit of the Lord shall rest on him, the spirit of wisdom and understanding, the spirit of counsel and might, the spirit of knowledge and the fear of the Lord. His delight shall be in the fear of the Lord." So it goes on to say that this future son of David will be like David, will be a person of wisdom and understanding and counsel and might.

It goes on to describe what life will be like once this son of David arrives and begins his rule—verse 6: "The wolf shall live with the lamb; the leopard shall lie down with the kid; the calf and the lion and the fatling together; and a little child shall lead them. The cow and the bear shall graze. Their young shall lie down together. And the lion shall eat straw like the ox. The nursing child shall play over the hole of the asp and the weaned child shall put its hand on the adder's den. They will not hurt or destroy on all my holy mountain, for the earth will be full of the knowledge of the Lord as the waters cover the sea." This is a beautiful passage, describing the utopian-like existence that will come about in the future age when a son of David once again reascends the throne and becomes the King of Israel.

Jesus, though, had a somewhat more apocalyptic vision of what it would be like when the future kingdom arrived. As he anticipated that this future kingdom would not simply be a utopian existence on earth, he actually anticipated that with the coming of the kingdom there would be an overthrow of the forces of evil when a figure whom he called the Son of Man arrived from heaven in judgment on the earth. Jesus had a different view from many of the prophets of the Old Testament in that he thought that the reason people were suffering now was not because God was punishing them but because there were powers of evil in the world—cosmic forces—that were causing the disasters that were striking the earth.

When the kingdom comes, according to Jesus, these cosmic forces that have so thoroughly infiltrated this world will be destroyed. God will remake the heavens and the earth for a place of habitation for his followers. For example, Mark, chapter 8, verse 38 through chapter 9, verse 1, Jesus says, "Whoever is ashamed of me and of my words in this adulterous and sinful generation, of that person the Son of Man will be ashamed when he comes on the clouds of heaven in the presence of the holy angels. Truly I tell you, some of you standing here will not taste death before they see that the kingdom of God has come in power." Jesus anticipates there will be some coming figure that he calls the Son of Man.

In this passage, it's not at all clear that he's talking about himself as the Son of Man, in fact, quite the contrary. If you didn't think Jesus was the Son of Man, you would never think so on the basis of this passage, which is one reason for thinking this is something that Jesus actually said. Because if a Christian wanted to make up a saying of Jesus and put it on his lips, he wouldn't leave it ambiguous as to whether Jesus thought he was the Son of Man, because Christians thought Jesus was the Son of Man. This is ambiguous. I mean, it doesn't look like Jesus is talking about himself here, and so it's probably something that Jesus said. Jesus expected the Son of Man to arrive in judgment, and he expected it would happen before all of his disciples died.

Or as he says later on in Mark, in the famous passage of chapter 13 where Jesus narrates what it will be like when the end comes, "In those days, after all that suffering, the sun will be darkened and the moon will not give its light. And the stars will be falling from heaven and the powers in the heavens will be shaken. Then they will see the Son of Man coming in clouds with great power and glory. Then he will send out the angels and gather his elect from the four winds, from the ends of the earth to the ends of heaven. The coming of the end will be a cataclysmic event of cosmic proportions in which this cosmos is destroyed and remade and the kingdom of God then will arrive."

Jesus' preaching of the future kingdom was taken up by his followers, as can be seen by the writings of the apostle Paul. Paul, too, expected the end to come within his own generation. Paul's expectation had shifted somewhat from that of Jesus. Jesus had anticipated that a figure called the Son of Man was going to arrive on the clouds of heaven. Paul thought that Jesus, who had been raised from the dead and exalted to heaven, was himself the Son of Man who was going to come on the clouds of heaven.

And so Paul talks about Jesus returning in judgment on the earth, and Paul anticipates that when this happens, when Jesus returns, he himself will still be alive. One of the key passages is I Thessalonians, chapter 4, verse 13 and following. Paul says, "We do not want you to be uninformed, brothers and sisters, about the people who have died so that you may not grieve as others who have no hope."

A little background—Paul is writing this letter to his congregation in Thessalonica. He had evidently started this church by convincing former pagans to worship the God of Israel and Jesus his son, and he taught them that Jesus is soon to return in judgment on the earth, and when he does, the kingdom will come. In the interim, between the time Paul left the community and the time that he is now writing this letter, some members of the community had died. Paul has been informed that some of the members of the congregation are upset by the fact that these people have died because they think that these people have lost out on the benefits of the coming kingdom.

And so Paul has to write to explain to them that, in fact, they haven't lost out on the benefits of the coming kingdom. And so he says that, "You should not be informed about those who have died so that you may not grieve," verse 14, "for since we believe that Jesus died and rose again, even so through Jesus, God will bring with him those who have died. For this we declare to you by a word of the Lord"— this is the key passage—"that we who are alive who are left until the coming of the Lord," so Paul's including himself, "we who are alive who are left until the coming of the Lord will by no means precede those who have died. For the Lord himself with a cry of command and the archangels call and the sound of God's trumpet will descend from heaven and the dead in Christ will rise first. Then, we who are alive who are left will be caught up in the clouds together with them to meet the Lord in the air and so we will be with the Lord forever. Therefore, encourage one another with these words."

This is the passage that evangelical Christians have used to talk about the rapture—when Jesus returns and people rise up to meet him in the air. The term rapture, as you've noted, does not actually occur in this passage. This understanding of the end times presupposes that there are three stories to our universe—that the universe is built on three stories—that we have the place where we live now and down below us is the realm of the dead and up above us is the place of God. Jesus was here with us, living, He died; he went to the place of the dead. But he arose, and then he ascended to the place of God, and he's going to come back down from the place of God, down to the place of the living. And the people who are dead, who are down below, are going to rise up. And those who are living on this plane are also going to rise up and live with Christ in the air—the place of God. And so it's built on this kind of three-story universe. That, of course, is not the view of the universe that people have today, even though people continue to ascribe to a literal understanding of this passage, some people, and some people subscribe to a literal understanding of this passage in I Thessalonians.

A similar passage can be found in Paul's Letter to the Corinthians, I Corinthians, chapter 15. "What I'm saying, brothers and sisters, is this: Flesh and blood cannot inherit the kingdom of God, nor does the perishable inherit the imperishable." In other words, the kingdom can't come to us while we're still just mortals—flesh and blood. "Listen, I'll tell you a mystery. We will not all die, but we will all be changed in a moment, in the twinkling of an eye at the last trumpet. For the trumpet will sound and the dead will be raised imperishable and we will be changed." Again, he's including himself. "For this perishable body must put on imperishability and this mortal body must put on immortality." So bodies are going to be transformed. At the last trumpet, people are going to be changed then—bodily changed—into immortal bodies so that they can inherit the kingdom. The kingdom of God is a future kingdom that will be lived in bodily by people whose bodies have been transformed at the coming of Jesus. This is the understanding of Paul, again, an apocalyptic sense of what happens at the end time.

Papias, writing two generations later, continued to subscribe to some kind of apocalyptic vision—literally anticipating a future paradise here on earth. His description of what it's going to be like here on earth is very interesting and intriguing. He claims that he got this information from people who were familiar with John, the disciple of the Lord, who remembered how the Lord used to teach about the coming times by saying, "The days are coming when vines will come forth, each with 10,000 bows, and on a single bow will be 10,000 branches, and indeed on a single branch will be 10,000 shoots, and on every shoot there will be 10,000 clusters, and in every cluster there will be 10,000 grapes, and every grape when pressed will yield 25 measures of wine."

Well, this is a terrific harvest you've got going here in the utopian kingdom that's coming. "And when one of the saints grabs hold of one of the clusters, another cluster will cry out, 'I'm better, take me. Bless the Lord through me.' So too a grain of wheat will produce 10,000 heads and every head will have 10,000 grains. And every grain will yield 10 pounds of pure, exceptionally fine flours." Every grain of wheat will yield 10 pounds of flour. "So, too, with the remaining fruits and seeds and vegetation, they will produce in similar proportions, and all the animals who eat this food drawn from the earth will come to be at peace and harmony with one another, yielding in complete submission to humans." That's the utopian existence that Papias imagines is happening when the kingdom of God arrives on earth.

Later church fathers found this view, which they called a chiliasm—chiliasm, from the Latin word meaning a thousand—to be far too literalistic and naïve. Instead, there developed the idea that the kingdom of God was not to be taken literally as an event that would take place on earth according to later church fathers. The kingdom of God came increasingly to be seen as a metaphor for God's rule over his people both here on earth and in heaven after death.

It was probably because of his literalistic interpretations that Papias was castigated by later church writers such as the father of church history, Eusebius, who in one passage called him, "A man of exceedingly small intelligence." Eusebius wasn't very fond of this chiliastic understanding of the end of time. And that's probably why Papias's writings were not preserved.

It's interesting to observe that the apocalyptic vision of Jesus and his earlier followers then came to be transformed in later generations. No doubt this earlier vision of the apocalypse got transformed because it didn't come. It didn't happen, and so people had to transform its meaning. Eventually, the understanding that the kingdom of God is a kingdom here came to be that the kingdom of God is a kingdom there, in heaven. The kingdom of God came to be equated with heaven.

The New Testament does not teach the doctrines of heaven and hell that most people have today—that when you die, your soul goes to heaven or your soul goes to hell. Most of the authors of the New Testament thought that the kingdom of Heaven would be a place here, and it would be a bodily existence here in this world, not in the world of God up in heaven. Paul himself had that point of view and Paul advocated this view quite strenuously, as had Jesus before him and Paul's followers after him.

Today, the vast majority of Christian people may think of the kingdom of God maybe as the experience of God's kingdom—his rule in the here and now and in the afterlife— rather than a literal kingdom here on earth. But these are later views that you might call deapocalypticized views. When the apocalypse doesn't happen, you modify the meaning of the words so that now "kingdom of God" actually refers to the "kingdom of Heaven," which refers to heaven, the place where you go when you die.

To sum up, Papias was faithful to the earliest Christian tradition about the coming of the end. And it was because he failed to adjust that vision with the passage of time that he ended up being regarded as naïve and as an unsophisticated thinker, even though he was one of the first to collect the sayings of Jesus and to interpret them according to the teaching of Jesus' own followers.

Lecture Eighteen
Oral Tradition in Early Christianity

Scope:

One of the most striking features of Papias's writings is that he claims to prefer learning about Jesus from companions of his disciples rather than from the books that had been written about him (that is, the Gospels). For Papias, it was better to have a living, breathing authority for a tradition about Jesus than a book, principally because the living authority could be questioned.

In this lecture, we will consider this issue of oral tradition versus written text. Included in our discussion will be the problem of the oral circulation of traditions—because stories tend to be changed and even made up in the process of retelling. To what extent did that happen with the traditions about Jesus, given that they were in oral circulation among Christian communities for decades before they were written down in the Gospels?

Outline

I. One of the interesting things we learned about Papias in the preceding lecture was that he showed a distinct preference for oral over written traditions about Jesus (fragment 3: 3–4).

   A. This preference stands at odds with modern sensitivities.

   1. People today tend to distrust oral traditions as "hearsay" and prefer to have written documentation for events of the past.

   2. But in antiquity, oral sources were widely regarded as being superior to written, because they could be questioned and probed for additional clarification.

   3. This preference for oral over written communication had a strong philosophical basis, from the time of Plato up to the Gnostics.

   B. Eventually within Christianity, the written word came to play a more important role than spoken tradition—at least among "official" representatives of "orthodox" theology.

   1. This was precisely because the written word, in theory, was established and secure.

2. Moreover, the "ancient" written records could be trusted to set forth the more ancient views, of Jesus and his apostles, unchanged with the passing of time.

C. Even so, in the earliest periods of Christianity, oral tradition played a vital role in the religion.

   1. This can be seen in some of the comments made by the apostle Paul in the years before there were any written accounts of Jesus' words and deeds (cf. 1 Cor. 11:22–24; 1 Cor. 15:3–5).

   2. It can also be seen in the claims of one of the Gospel writers, Luke (Luke 1:1–4).

D. Modern scholars are convinced that the fact that the traditions about Jesus circulated orally for so long before being written down played an important role in how they came to be changed over time.

   1. It is important to remember that the Gospels of the New Testament were written 35–65 years after Jesus had died.

   2. The authors of these Gospels relied on traditions they had *heard* about Jesus in producing their accounts.

   3. Naturally, traditions passed along orally change in transmission (cf. the children's game "telephone").

   4. In oral cultures, it was not thought that traditions should remain the same with each retelling; quite the contrary, traditions were to be modified according to the audience and the circumstances of the retelling.

   5. The concern for verbatim accuracy only came into being with the advent of written culture; this was not a dominant concern before accuracy could be verified.

II. Traditions about Jesus continued to circulate orally and, in that process, came to be changed, even after the Gospels were written, as can be seen in the traditions found in Papias's book, An Exposition of the Sayings of the Lord.

A. There is, for example, a striking tradition about the death of Judas.

   1. The New Testament accounts of Judas's death show evidence of modification over time; there are similarities but irreconcilable differences between the two accounts we have (Matthew 27 and Acts 1).

2. Papias's account is different still and even more gory (fragment 4).

3. Later authors tried to reconcile all of these by conflating the versions together (fragment 4:1).

B. In addition, there is an oral tradition in Papias about the writers of the Gospels of Matthew and Mark (fragment 3:15), although there is some question about whether he is referring to *our* Gospels of Matthew and Mark.

III. Oral traditions about Jesus also came to be embodied in yet later written accounts.

A. This can be seen, for example, in the stories of Jesus' youth in the so-called Infancy Gospel of Thomas.

B. It can also be seen in the stories of Jesus' Passion in the Gospel of Peter.

IV. In short, as the fragments of Papias show, oral tradition played an enormously important role in early Christianity, both before and after the accounts of Jesus' life were written down by the anonymous authors of our New Testament Gospels.

Essential Reading:

Bart D. Ehrman, *The New Testament: A Historical Introduction to the Early Christian Writings*, chapter 3.

———, ed., *The New Testament and Other Early Christian Writings*, pp. 116–142.

Supplementary Reading:

W. J. Ong, *Orality and Literacy.*

William R. Schoedel, "Papias," in the *Anchor Bible Dictionary*, D. N. Freedman, ed., vol. 5, pp. 140–142.

Questions to Consider:

1. What do you see as the benefits and difficulties of using oral traditions to reconstruct the events of the fairly recent past, for example, the events of the Second World War?

2. Have you ever experienced an instance in which something you did or experienced came to be changed as it was told by someone else later?

Lecture Eighteen—Transcript
Oral Tradition in Early Christianity

One of the interesting things we learned about Papias in the preceding lecture was that he showed a distinct preference for oral over written tradition about Jesus. Let me reread for you the fragment of Papias's writings as preserved in the church father Eusebius where Papias points out that he used to interview the companions of the elders, meaning the companions of the original apostles—companions of Andrew, Peter, Philip, Thomas, James, John or Matthew—to see what these disciples had said about Jesus. He also interviewed as well the companions of the second-generation Christians, such as the elder John and Ariston.

Why did he interview these people instead of simply reading the books that were widely becoming available to early Christians? It's because, he says, "I did not suppose that what came out of books would benefit me as much as that which came from a living and abiding voice." This preference for oral rather than written communication stands somewhat at odds with modern sensitivities. People today tend to distrust oral traditions as hearsay and to prefer to have written documentation for events of the past. You just don't want to hear some rumor that somebody's spreading around. You want to see it written down in black and white.

But in antiquity, oral sources were widely considered to be superior to written sources since oral sources could be questioned and probed for additional clarification. The problem with the writing is that in most cases you don't have the author there to ask about any difficulties you have; whereas, if you were talking to an authority, you can communicate with him and thereby elicit further information and clarification.

This preference for oral over written communication had a strong philosophical basis from at least in the time of Plato up to the Gnostics. Plato himself had an understanding that oral communication was superior to written communication, especially when it came to philosophical discourse. Plato thought that the written word was too wooden and not sufficiently elastic to contain the truth. Truth had to be worked out dialogically as a person would talk to another person, and the back and forth—the point and the counterpoint—out of that back and forth would emerge the truth. So Plato evidently did not put down his full philosophy in writing in any of the dialogues of Plato that survived, but he communicated the deeper truth to his students orally.

In a religious vein, something similar could be said about the early Christian Gnostics and their understanding of true revelation. Gnostics did think that written texts could contain truth. But, as you know, Gnostics believed in secret knowledge that could lead to salvation. People needed to learn the secrets of the world we live in and especially of our own existence in order to escape this evil material world. People needed the secret gnosis necessary for salvation. This gnosis could be embodied in the written text, but the written text is like the human body. It's a prison within which the truth is kept. The human body is a prison for the spirit, and the written word is a prison for the actual truth, the actual meaning of a text.

It's interesting that in one of our Gnostic gospels, the Gospel of Thomas—we're told at the very beginning—the author says, "These are the secret teachings which the living Jesus spoke and Didymus Judas Thomas wrote them down. Anyone who finds the meaning of these words will not taste death." Well, the words are written down, so they're not saying the writing is of no use. But reading the written words is not what brings eternal life. It's having the proper interpretation of those words which gets passed on orally. It's the oral communication that provides the secret gnosis necessary for salvation. Otherwise, the divine being Christ would not have come down to inhabit the man Jesus to deliver his secret teachings. He could have simply sent a book from heaven if that would solve the problem. No, it's oral communication that contains the words of salvation.

So at an early stage, and even on into later periods, there were people who preferred oral to written communication. That has a philosophical background at least as far back as Plato, and it is manifest in Papias. Eventually though, within Christianity, it was the written word that came to play a more important role than spoken tradition, at least among the official representatives of Orthodox theology. And the reason isn't too hard to find. The reason that the Orthodox Christians ended up preferring the written word, rather than the oral word, was precisely because the written word in theory was established and secure. Once something's written, it's written. You might be able to change it by erasing it and writing something else, but, by and large, something that's in print is written and it stays the same. It stays written; it stays the way it was without getting changed so some heretic can't come along and change it except by actually manually scraping off the page and writing something else, which did happen but didn't happen nearly as much as happened at the oral level when you can take any saying that somebody gives to you and say it differently. It's much harder to change written texts.

Moreover, the ancient written records that the Orthodox Christians had available to them could be trusted, they said, to set forth the more ancient views of Jesus and his apostles—unchanged with the passing of time. And so if you have an ancient book, this ancient book records ancient views, and it stays the same. It's the same ancient view as it was when it was written a hundred years ago.

Even with this ultimate preference, this eventful preference for written over oral communication in the earliest periods of Christianity, oral tradition played a vital role in the Christian religion. We can see this already in some of the comments that were made by the apostle Paul in the years before there were any written accounts of Jesus' words and deeds. So let me just read a couple passages from Paul, which indicate that Paul himself is dependent on oral tradition for some very important information. Paul is writing his Letter to the Corinthians in order to solve some of the problems in the community. One of the problems the Corinthians had was that they were misusing the Lord's Supper. And so Paul writes to them the proper way to celebrate the Lord's Supper, and he bases his interpretation of this ritual on words that have been handed down to him orally about how Jesus celebrated the Last Supper.

I Corinthians 11, verse 23 and following: "For I received from the Lord what I also handed on to you." So he received this orally, maybe through a prophecy, and he hands it on to these others, this Corinthian congregation, "that the Lord Jesus on the night when he was betrayed took a loaf of bread and when he had given thanks, he broke it and said, 'This is my body that is for you. Do this in remembrance of me.'" This is an oral tradition that came to Paul orally that he passed along orally, and it's the basis for his discussion then of how the Corinthians ought to celebrate the Last Supper—the Lord's Supper.

A second example, from I Corinthians, chapter 15: Paul wants to remind his readers of the basic gospel message that he proclaimed to them in the beginning. He says, "For I handed on to you as of first importance what I in turn had received, that Christ Jesus died, according to the scriptures, and that he was buried and that he was raised on the third day, according to the scriptures, and he appeared to Cephas and the Twelve." The two fundamental components of Paul's proclamation of his gospel, that Christ died in accordance with the scriptures—in other words, fulfilling prophecy of scripture— and that he was raised in accordance with the scriptures, these two fundamental beliefs of Christians were passed on orally to Paul, and he passed them on orally then to his Corinthian congregations.

Not just Paul, but other early writers indicate the importance of oral tradition. The Gospel of Luke, for example, is forthright in explaining to its readers where the author acquired his information about Jesus. The author points out that he had had many predecessors who had written down accounts of Jesus based on eyewitnesses and servants of the word, he says. In other words, people had written accounts based on what eyewitness reports had said as these have been passed on orally. And he goes on to say that he also has gathered information and he's going to then provide an accurate account of what Jesus said and did during his ministry. This is based largely on oral traditions.

Modern scholars are convinced that the fact that the traditions about Jesus circulated orally for so long, before being written down, played an important role in how these traditions came to be changed over time. This will be an important thesis of this lecture, that over time, when you're dealing with oral tradition, the traditions get changed.

It's important for us to remember that the gospels of the New Testament were written between 35 and 65 years after Jesus had died. Jesus' death is usually put to sometime around the year 30 A.D. It may have been 29; it may have been 33; it may have been 30, sometime right around there. The Gospel of Mark was probably our first gospel written. It was written sometime around 65 or 70, which would be 35 years or maybe 40 years after Jesus' death. The Gospel of John was probably our last gospel of the New Testament to be written, written maybe around 90 or 95 A.D., which would be 60 to 65 years after Jesus' death. So there's a 35- to 65-year gap between Jesus' death and these, our earliest accounts of his life—35 to65 years.

Many of the stories found in these gospels have come to the authors of the gospels through oral tradition. In other words, people have been passing on traditions about Jesus orally for decades before they come to be written down in our gospels. Now some people don't see this as a problem. I've met a number of elderly people who say, "I remember perfectly well what happened 60 years ago." I've never found that argument to be particularly persuasive, I have to say, partly because of personal experience.

I've had perfectly vivid recollections of something that's happened to me in the past that it turns out later that I've completely mis-remembered. I don't know if you've had this experience, but it's not because I have a bad memory. In fact, I have a very good memory, but there are things—one just occurred to me this morning, in fact. For years, I remembered from my high school days, I was on the high school debate team, and we had won the state championship in debate in Kansas when I was a senior in high school. We were off to the National Debate Tournament, and I remember driving to the National Debate Tournament and I remember perfectly well having parking problems in downtown Pittsburgh, Pennsylvania, and for years after that telling people that my first time in Pittsburgh was at the National Debate Tournament.

About two years ago, a friend of mine who was on my debate team with me and I were having a discussion about going to the National Debate Tournament, and he mentioned that it was the first time he'd ever been in Wake Forest, North Carolina. I said, "Wake Forest, North Carolina? It was in Pittsburgh." He said, "No, it wasn't Pittsburgh; it was in Wake Forest." "You're kidding? No, it wasn't, it was in Pittsburgh." He said, "No, it was in Wake Forest." And it turns out he was absolutely right. I'd remembered this for years incorrectly. And with nobody to correct me, I just assumed that I remembered it properly. I think this happens all the time. And even people who are convinced, "Oh no, I remember exactly what so and so said 20 years ago. I remember the exact words. I remember what I was wearing." They might remember it, or they might not remember it. But the reality is you really don't know and things get changed in your head. They not only get changed in your head, they get changed when stories get told. The stories about Jesus were being told for 30, 40, 50 years around the Roman Empire. These stories surely got changed in the process of transmission. How could they not change? Everybody who tells a story tells it somewhat differently from someone else who tells the same story.

This is especially true in old oral cultures. Some people have the idea that in oral societies, since everything is oral instead of written, there's special care-taking to make sure that things don't get changed in oral transmission. That's a common view, and it's absolutely wrong. Cultural anthropologists have shown, on the contrary, that in oral societies there is not a concern for verbatim, accurate reproduction of traditions. Oral cultures understand that when you're telling a story, you tell it for the occasion, for the audience you're talking to, for the particular situation that you're in. And the same story gets told differently on different occasions, depending who your audience is and why you're telling it and what the point is.

The early Christians lived in an oral society, and these stories got changed in the process of transmission. The life of Jesus was lived in 1st century Palestine. Jesus himself spoke Aramaic. By the time the gospels get written, these stories have been in circulation, not just in Palestine, they've moved outside of Palestine, and they've been translated from Aramaic into a different language, Greek, and they've circulated in Greek throughout the entire Mediterranean.

Some people have suggested that the stories couldn't be changed because the apostles were around to make sure that there would only be active traditions preserved. That's a crazy idea from my point of view. How could the apostles possibly be everywhere that somebody is telling a story about Jesus? There are hundreds of people being converted in major urban areas throughout the entire Mediterranean, and you've only got twelve apostles. They can't be guaranteeing the accuracy of everybody's story that's being told.

So, stories are being told about Jesus, and they're getting changed. And, I should say, this isn't just kind of the liberal view from the professor from Chapel Hill. This, in fact, has evidence behind it. The evidence we have that stories were getting changed in the process of transmission is the fact that we have different versions of the same story in our written sources.

People don't notice the differences in the gospel accounts of the same story because of the way people read the gospels. When people read the gospels, typically what they do is, they do what you do when you read a book. If you're going to read Matthew, you read through Matthew. And then you're going to read the next book—that's Mark. You read through Mark, and it sounds a lot like Matthew. And you read through Luke and that sounds a lot like Matthew and Mark. So they sound a lot alike. And you don't notice that there are discrepancies between them because of the way you've read them. And I'm not saying you shouldn't read them that way—that's, of course, the natural way to read a book. But if you want to notice that there are discrepancies in the way the stories are told, you don't read them from top to bottom—in other words, vertically. You read them side to side. You read them horizontally. In other words, you take a story found in Matthew, the same story found in Mark, and the same story found in Luke, and you read the three stories against each other, and you compare that. And when you do it that way, you almost always find discrepancies. Sometimes these discrepancies are so enormous that they cannot be reconciled.

I spent a good deal of my time in my New Testament class at Chapel Hill trying to convince my students that there are all these discrepancies in the gospels. And the point of it is not what my students think, that I just want to show the Bible is full of contradictions, you know, as if that's the thesis of the class. The Bible is full of contradictions, and I'm going to spend the semester proving it to you. That's not the point at all. The point is these are different books, and you can't assume that when Mark says something, he means what Matthew means, because he's told the story differently. And if you don't see that there are any discrepancies, you won't read the gospels that way. You'll read Matthew as if it's saying the same thing Mark is saying, which is saying the same thing Luke is saying, same thing that John is saying, and so you read all the gospels as if it's one big muddied mess, and they're all saying the same thing—they're not saying all the same thing. And the way you know they're not saying all the same thing is because you have these different traditions.

These different traditions that you find when you read the gospels horizontally applies when you actually read other traditions outside of the New Testament about the same materials. I'll give you an example. This has to do with Papias, you'll be glad to know. There are traditions about Jesus that continued to circulate orally after the writing of the gospels. And in the process, as they continued to be told even after the gospel writers wrote them down, these stories came to be changed. This can be seen from some traditions found in Papias' book, An Exposition of the Sayings of the Lord.

A striking example is the account that Papias gives of the death of Judas. Now this is an interesting instance because of what happens within the New Testament itself. Everybody assumes or thinks that Judas went out and hanged himself after betraying Jesus. As it turns out, three of our gospels don't say anything about what happened to Judas after his death. The death of Judas is recorded in only one of our gospels. It's found in the Gospel of Matthew, but it occurs in one other book as well, namely, the book of Acts, which was written by the same author who wrote the Gospel of Luke. And so you've got an account by Matthew, and you have an account by Luke. And as it turns out, it's very hard to reconcile these two accounts. And as we'll see, Papias's account is different also.

People don't notice that Matthew and Acts disagree on this account unless they're told to read these accounts right next to each other. The way it works in Matthew is—and you can look this up for yourself—it's in Matthew chapter 27, verse 3 and following; just read it for yourself and you'll see what happens—Judas has been paid thirty pieces of silver to betray Jesus. Well, when he sees that Jesus is bound for death—when they voted for his death—he repents of what he's done, and he brings the thirty pieces of silver—Judas brings the thirty pieces of silver—back to the chief priest and the elders. And he says, "I've sinned by betraying innocent blood." And they say, "Well what's that to us?" So he throws down the coins in the temple, and he goes out and he hangs himself. The chief priests take up the money and they say, "It's not lawful for us to put it in the treasury because it's blood money," meaning it's money that was used to betray somebody else's blood. And so they confer together, and they decide to buy a field in which to bury foreigners. For this reason, the field had been called "the field of blood" to this day. So the money that Judas threw back into the temple was used to buy a field to bury people, and it was called "the field of blood" because it was purchased with blood money. Okay, fair enough.

What about the book of Acts? The book of Acts has a different account about Judas dying. It doesn't say anything about him hanging, in fact. And it doesn't say anything about thirty pieces of silver buying this field of blood. What happens in Acts, chapter 1, verse 18 and following, is that Judas had acquired a field with the reward of his wickedness. It sounds like he took the money and he bought a field. "And falling headlong, he burst open in the middle and all his bowels gushed out." So he didn't hang himself. Somehow he fell headfirst. So I don't know if he dived off a cliff or what. But when he hit, his middle opened up—his stomach opened up—and his intestines all gushed out. "This then became known to all residents of Jerusalem so that the field was called…," in their language "Helkama"—that is, "field of blood." Why is it called the field of blood? It's because Judas spilled his blood on it.

Both accounts agree that there is a field connected with Judas's death that's called the field of blood, something connected with Jesus, betraying Jesus, and something connected with him dying, but they do it in different ways. In one way, it's a field bought with blood money; the other, it's a field in which Judas himself had bought that he spilled his blood on, and so it's called a field of blood. So people try to reconcile these traditions. When people notice that there's a discrepancy, of course, you can always come up with a way of reconciling a tradition if you work hard enough at it. And the way that this is typically reconciled is that Judas hangs himself, the rope snaps, he falls down headlong and bursts out and spills his bowels on the field. I'm not quite sure how he would end up falling headfirst but, anyway, that's the way they reconcile it.

Papias also has a story of Judas that's quite interesting. In Papias's account—Papias's account is quite different and even more graphic—this is what Papias said: "Judas went about in this world as a great model of impiety"—this is after the betrayal, "He became so bloated in the flesh that he could not pass through a place that was easily wide enough for a wagon. Not even his swollen head would fit," because he couldn't walk down the street and not even his head would fit down the street he's gotten so bloated. "They say that his eyelids swelled to such an extent that he could not see the light at all and a doctor could not see his eyes even with an optical device so deeply sunken were they in his surrounding flesh. And his genitals became more disgusting and larger than anyone's. Simply by relieving himself to his want and shame, he emitted puss and worms that flowed through his entire body." So he's being punished. "And they say that after he suffered numerous torments and punishments, he died on his own land and that land has been, until now, desolate and uninhabited because of the stench. Indeed, even to this day, no one can pass by the place without holding his nose. This was how great an outpouring he made from his flesh on the ground."

So this seems to be rooted in the idea of Luke, that he fell forth and gushed out on the ground. The reason for how that happened, he'd gotten so enormously fat that when he hit, everything fell out and left this huge stench. So this is evidence of an oral tradition that is continuing on in early Christianity as the tradition continues to be changed with the telling of the story.

There's another interesting oral tradition found in the writings of Papias that is probably the best-known passage in Papias. I think it's probably the most frequently quoted passage in Papias because there's a passage in which Papias informs us who the authors of our gospels were. This is the first time we have any indication from any author who wrote the gospels. He doesn't talk about all four Gospels. He doesn't mention Luke or John in this little fragment we have. But he does mention Mark and Matthew. And the question is, Is he talking about our Mark and Matthew or about other books?

This is what he says: "This is what the elder used to say. The elder" says Papias, "used to say that when Mark was the interpreter of Peter, he wrote down accurately everything that he recalled of the Lord's words and deeds, but not in order. For he neither heard the Lord nor accompanied him. But later, as I indicated, he accompanied Peter who used to adapt his teachings for the needs at hand"—notice, oral tradition, "He used to adapt his teachings about Jesus for the needs at hand, not arranging, as it were, an orderly composition of the Lord's sayings. And so Mark did nothing wrong by writing some of the matters as he remembered them. For he was intent on just one purpose, to leave out nothing that he had heard or to include any falsehood among them." So he writes down the sayings of Peter that Peter rearranges for the occasion, and Mark writes them down as best as he can remember them.

I assume he's talking about our Gospel of Mark. I have no real reason to doubt that. I guess he's talking about our Gospel of Mark, but there's nothing here that makes sure that he's talking about the

Gospel of Mark that we have. And there's nothing that shows us that. But perhaps he is. It's more controversial with the second brief comment that he has about the Gospel of Matthew. About Matthew, he says this, "And so Matthew composed the sayings in the Hebrew tongue and each one interpreted them to the best of his ability." "Matthew wrote down the sayings," presumably the sayings of Jesus, "in the Hebrew tongue and each one interpreted them to the best of his ability." This is often taken as a reference to our Gospel of Matthew, but I don't think he's talking about our Gospel of Matthew. For one thing, our Gospel of Matthew is much more than the sayings of Jesus. It's also narratives of his deeds and his passion. Moreover, Matthew was not written in Hebrew; it was written in Greek originally as linguists have shown beyond any doubt. Now maybe Papias didn't know it was written in Greek. Maybe he thought it was written in Hebrew, or maybe he's talking about a different book actually written by somebody named Matthew. Our Gospel of Matthew, of course, doesn't claim to be written by somebody named Matthew. So I don't think he's referring to our Matthew. I suppose he's referring to our Mark, but it's hard to be completely sure.

In any event, what is clear is that oral traditions about Jesus and the gospels came to be embodied in yet later written accounts. We have other gospels that have been discovered, some in modern times, some very recently, and some throughout the centuries past, other gospels in which Jesus is said to have said and done a wide range of things. We have gospels about what Jesus was like as a five-year old boy—the infancy Gospel of Thomas. We have gospels that talk about what actually happened when Jesus emerged from the tomb— his resurrection—in the Gospel of Peter. We have gospels that contain his secret teachings, the interpretation of which will lead to eternal life in the Coptic Gospel of Thomas. We have gospels in which Jesus gives mystical reflections about how this world came into being as a cosmic disaster when there was a disruption in the divine realm, in the Gospel of Philip and the secret Gospel of John. We have gospels in which Jesus gives a revelation to one of his followers after his resurrection to give them the truth necessary for salvation, including, for example, the Gospel of Mary, one of the Gnostic gospels, a range of gospels from early Christianity that shows that in the oral tradition the sayings and deeds of Jesus came to be changed in the passing of time before the Gospel authors wrote them down.

To sum up, as the fragments of Papias show, oral tradition played an enormously important role in early Christianity both before and after the accounts of Jesus' life were written down by the anonymous authors of our New Testament gospels.

Lecture Nineteen
The Shepherd of Hermas— An Apocalypse

Scope:

One of the most popular writings among the Apostolic Fathers is called The Shepherd, written by a man named Hermas. It is a very long book—longer than any book of the New Testament. In it, the writer narrates a number of visions that inform him about the nature of the Christian Church, its current plight, and its imminent struggles. These visions are invariably interpreted to the author by an angelic companion who has taken the form of a shepherd; hence, the title of the book.

In this lecture, we will consider the overarching themes of the work and its salient message, in particular, a theme that runs throughout its long narrative: the question of whether a Christian can have a "second" chance with God if he or she sins after being baptized. The answer The Shepherd's visions give is clear: A Christian has a second chance to return to God, but no more.

Outline

I.   In the early centuries of Christianity, one of the most popular writings of the Apostolic Fathers was The Shepherd of Hermas.

    A. This is far and away the longest writing of the Apostolic Fathers and is much longer than any book that made it into the New Testament.

    B. The book records a series of visions given to a Christian prophet named Hermas.

       1. There have been long debates over who this Hermas actually was.

       2. Some indication of Hermas' identity is given in the anonymous pamphlet called the Muratorian Canon, a fragmentary text discovered in the 18th century.

       3. The author of the Muratorian Canon translated into Latin an earlier original written in Greek. Most scholars think the anonymous author of the original Greek text was writing in the 2nd century around or in Rome.

4. The Muratorian Canon lists a 24-book canon and confirms 22 of the 27 canonical books of the New Testament as being canonical. The author names some books that he feels should be excluded because of heresy and mentions others that he feels are acceptable, but should, nevertheless, not be included in the canon of Scripture. The Shepherd is one of these because it is not an ancient book whose author was connected with one of the apostles.

5. The Muratorian Canon also indicates that Hermas was the brother of the bishop of Rome, Pius (r. A.D. 140–154).

6. Somewhat later, the church father Origen indicated that Hermas was none other than the companion of the apostle Paul, mentioned in Romans 16:14.

7. It is difficult for us to know who, in fact, Hermas was, other than that he appears to have been an early-2nd-century Christian author.

C. His book is called *The Shepherd* because the visions that he receives are interpreted for him, for the most part, by an angelic figure who comes to him in the guise of a shepherd.

D. The book is best understood as an *apocalypse*.

1. Apocalypses were a popular genre among Jews and Christians in the first two centuries A.D., even though the only one most people today know about is the Apocalypse of John.

2. But we have numerous surviving examples from antiquity, which we will explore more fully in the next lecture.

3. For our purposes here, it is enough to give a simple definition of the genre: An apocalypse is a book that records visions given to an earthly prophet, usually interpreted by a heavenly messenger, containing a number of bizarre and deeply symbolic images that convey heavenly truths to explain earthly realities. An apocalypse is meant to answer such questions as: Why is there suffering in the world? Why are the righteous persecuted? What can be expected to happen in the future of the world?

4. The Shepherd is considered part of sacred scripture and included as part of the New Testament in the Codex Sinaiticus, discovered in the 19th century in the Monastery of St. Catherine at Mount Sinai.

II. The Shepherd of Hermas divides itself into three major sections.
  A. It begins with a section of 5 "visions."
    1. These represent a series of revelations given to Hermas that are meant to instruct him concerning life in this world, especially as it relates to sins against God and the need to repent.
    2. Some of the visions contain more than one revelation.
    3. In the fifth vision, The Shepherd himself appears to Hermas, and he will be the interpreter for the rest of the book.
  B. There follows a section of 10 "commandments."
    1. These are ethical injunctions concerning how to live for God.
    2. They are not just a list of dos and don'ts; some involve visions that come to be interpreted by The Shepherd.
  C. The book ends with the longest section of 12 "parables."
    1. These, too, are symbolic visions of the author, which are interpreted by The Shepherd.
    2. By and large, they concern the Christian Church, its makeup, its problems, and its need to stay faithful to God.
  D. As can be seen, these three sections are not completely distinct from one another.
    1. There are visions and commandments in each of them, for example.
    2. And the longest parable (the ninth) is actually a prolonged exposition of one of the visions (the third) that has to do with a tower that the prophet sees being built out of a variety of stones, which is actually the Church being constructed out of a variety of different kinds of people.

III. To get an idea about the nature of the book, it is perhaps easiest simply to work through the first section, the five visions, to see what the overarching concerns of the author are.

    A. The first vision appears to record an autobiographical recollection.

        1. Hermas, a former slave, sees his former mistress, Rhoda, bathing in the Tiber River, and admires her beauty (ch. 1).

        2. He then has a vision of her looking down on him from heaven, accusing him for his impure thoughts (which comes as a surprise to him, because he was not conscious of having any; ch. 2).

        3. This leads him to self-reflection and repentance for his sins against God (chs. 2–3).

    B. In the second vision, Hermas sees an elderly woman reading a book (ch. 5).

        1. The book contains an account of the sins of his family against God (ch. 6).

        2. An important note is sounded in the vision: There is not much time left for people to repent (ch. 6).

    C. In the third vision, Hermas first sees the elderly woman again (ch. 9).

        1. He is allowed to sit only on her left hand, because her right is reserved for those who have suffered for the faith (ch. 9).

        2. He then sees a tower being built out of a variety of stones by six young men (ch. 10).

        3. The tower, it turns out, is the Church, which is also what the elderly woman represents (ch. 11).

        4. The builders of the Church are angels (ch. 12), and the stones are different kinds of persons who either join the Church or come to be excluded from it because of their sins (chs. 13–14).

    D. In the fourth vision, Hermas sees a terrifying monster that he passes by (ch. 22).

        1. The monster represents a coming time of tribulation for the Church (ch. 23).

        2. Only by remaining faithful to God can Christians survive this coming onslaught (ch. 24).

E. In the fifth vision, The Shepherd comes to Hermas and announces his plans to stay with him and give him commandments from God.

IV. The Shepherd of Hermas is a very long book with some very basic themes.

   A. The visions are meant to be heavenly revelations that provide instruction for Christians living here on Earth.

   B. The overarching message is that they need to be faithful to God and repent of their sins.

   C. Those who refuse to do so will be removed from the Church and will suffer the consequences when the end comes, which will be very soon.

Essential Reading:

Bart D. Ehrman, ed., "The Shepherd of Hermas," in *The Apostolic Fathers*, pp. 162–473.

Clayton Jefford, *Reading the Apostolic Fathers: An Introduction*, pp.134–158.

Supplementary Reading:

James Jeffers, *Conflict at Rome: Social Order and Hierarchy in Early Christianity*.

J. Christian Wilson, *Five Problems in the Interpretation of the Shepherd of Hermas*.

Questions to Consider:

1. Can you think of any reasons why The Shepherd of Hermas might have been eventually excluded from the canon, even though a number of early Christians considered it scriptural?

2. From what you've gathered from this lecture, is there information in The Shepherd that might help us understand the struggles Christians were having at the time of its writing?

Lecture Nineteen—Transcript
The Shepherd of Hermas— An Apocalypse

In the early centuries of Christianity, one of the most popular writings of the Apostolic Fathers was The Shepherd of Hermas. This is far and away the longest writing of the Apostolic Fathers and it's much longer than any book that made it into the New Testament. In fact, this is a very long book. Some people have considered it, in fact, to be interminable.

The book records a series of visions given to a Christian prophet whose name is Hermas. There have been long debates over who this "Hermas" actually was. In the early 3rd century, the church father, Origen, indicated that this Hermas was none other than the companion of the apostle Paul, who is mentioned in Romans 16:14, one of Paul's letters of the New Testament. Paul gives greetings to the Christians who live in the city of Rome and one of the people that he greets is a fellow named Hermas.

It's not quite clear why Origen makes this identification with this Hermas, who is known to Paul. It's possible that this is a way of providing some credentials for the book. At one point in his life, Origen considered The Shepherd, written by Hermas, to be a canonical book and so this is possibly a way for him of providing some kind of apostolic connection for the book, saying this Hermas was the one who was known to the apostle Paul.

Somewhat earlier than Origen, the anonymous pamphlet that's called "The Muratorian Canon" also gives some indication about the authors of the book, and historians have been more inclined to accept the identification of Hermas that's found in this collection of works called "The Muratorian Canon." Let me say something briefly about what "The Muratorian Canon" is to explain this reference to Hermas.

"The Muratorian Canon" is a fragmentary list of the books that its anonymous author thought belonged to the New Testament. We're not completely sure when and where the book was written. It was discovered—this "The Muratorian Canon" itself was discovered—in the 18th century by an Italian scholar of antiquity whose name was Muratori, and so this discovery of this text was named after its discoverer. So it's called "The Muratorian Canon."

The book itself appears to be a 7th- or 8th-century document that's written in Latin. It's terrible Latin, in fact, very difficult to understand because the Latin scribe who made the text, in fact, couldn't write proper Latin and so it's ungrammatical in places. This 7th- or 8th-century scribe is actually translating an earlier original, an original that was written, evidently, in Greek. And the text that we have, this Latin text that we have from the 7th or 8th century, is fragmentary. It begins in the middle of a sentence and it ends in the middle of a sentence. So we don't have the entire collection.

Most scholars think that this collection, this anonymous writer that the scribe is copying, was actually producing his work probably in the late 2nd century, around or in the city of Rome. He lists which books he considers to be part of the canon of the New Testament and it's interesting that he lists 22 of our 27 books. He lists all of the books that eventually made it into the New Testament, except for the books of Hebrews, James, I and II Peter, and III John. All the other of the 27 books, the other 22 books, he lists as being canonical scripture. But, in addition, he lists the Apocalypse of Peter as being a canonical book and a book called The Wisdom of Solomon. And so he had a 24-book canon that was roughly like the canon that eventually became the New Testament, but not completely like the book of the New Testament.

Within his description of the books that belonged in the New Testament, the author—the anonymous author of "The Muratorian Canon"—specifies some books that don't belong in the canon. He names some books that are heretical books that are to be excluded because they contain heresy, but he also mentions a few books that are acceptable in terms of their orthodoxy, but they, nonetheless, are not canonical.

In particular, he mentions The Shepherd of Hermas. The Shepherd of Hermas, he says, is valuable to be read, but it's not to be included in the canon of scripture. He indicates that The Shepherd, in fact, was written quite recently in our own times by a man named Hermas, who was the brother of Pius, who was the bishop of Rome. In other words, one of the early popes, early 2nd-century Pope Pius, had a brother named Hermas and Hermas is the one who wrote The Shepherd of Hermas recently in our own times.

Now, it's possible that this is a historical recollection of who Hermas actually was. And this is why "The Muratorian Canon" excludes The Shepherd of Hermas from its New Testament books, because it's not an ancient apostolic book, as we have seen in an earlier lecture. For a book to be accepted into the canon, it had to be ancient. It had to go back near the time of Jesus, and it had to be written by somebody who was connected with the apostles.

This book, however, comes from the mid-2nd century and is written by somebody who wasn't connected with one of the apostles; he was connected with the bishop of Rome, but that's not good enough. Books had to be written by apostles to be included in the New Testament. In any event, if this identification is correct, then Hermas would have been thriving sometime in the middle of the 2nd century because his brother, Pius, was bishop of Rome between 140–154 A.D.

Whether or not this is the correct Hermas—whether or not the author of "The Muratorian Canon" actually knew who Hermas was—it appears that whoever it was, he was an early- to mid-2nd-century Christian author who was probably not one of the very upper elite of the intellectuals in the Christian church. This book is not particularly gripping intellectually, but at least he was literate and could write in Greek and could write correct Greek and so he was highly educated, even though he's not among the intellectual elite in the church at the time.

He called his book The Shepherd, or at least it's called by others The Shepherd because the visions that the person in the book, the prophet in the book—presumably, the author himself—the visions he receives are interpreted for him by an angelic figure who comes down to heaven to spend time with him, who comes to him in the form of a shepherd. And so, this shepherd is a key figure to the book because this shepherd explains the vision that the prophet Hermas has. And so the book is simply called The Shepherd.

In terms of genre, this book is probably best understood to be an apocalypse, the genre of the apocalypse. Apocalypses were a popular genre among Jews and Christians in the first two centuries A.D., even though the only apocalypse that most people today know about is the one that made it into the New Testament, the apocalypse of John. But in the 1st and 2nd centuries, there were numerous apocalypses that had been written by Jews and Christians. We will

©2005 The Teaching Company Limited Partnership

be exploring some of these other apocalypses and see how the apocalypse genre worked as a genre in the next lecture.

For our purposes here, it's enough to give a simple definition of the genre. An apocalypse is a book that records visions given to an earthly prophet, usually interpreted by a heavenly messenger. These visions contain a number of bizarre and deeply symbolic images which convey heavenly truths to explain earthly realities. The visions are symbolic statements which convey heavenly truths to explain earthly realities, answering such big questions as why there is suffering in the world, why the righteous are persecuted, and what could be expected to happen in the future of the world. Those are the kinds of big questions that apocalypses try to address. And so there's a whole body of literature that consists of these apocalypses from Jewish and Christian antiquity.

Sometimes with my students, my undergraduate students, I explain apocalypses in the following shorthand term, that they are kind of like science fiction theodicies for the oppressed. I call them science fiction because they are the closest things we have in the ancient world to something that would be like science fiction, where there are people who travel in space—in this case, they travel to heaven, which would be outer space for these people. They see other life forms, other forms of higher intelligence, they communicate with these forms of higher intelligence, and they often learn about what's really going on on earth and it puts what's going on on earth in context of the bigger universe.

They're theodicies—the word theodicy is an English word that comes from two Greek words, which means God's righteousness. A theodicy is a way of explaining how God can be righteous if this world is such a miserable place. If this world has so much suffering in it, how can God be righteous if he's in control? I mean, if he's in control, why doesn't he stop the suffering? A theodicy explains why God doesn't stop the suffering, and these apocalypses are theodicies. They explain why there's such pain and suffering here on earth.

So they're science fiction theodicies for the oppressed. Apocalypses, as we'll see in the next lecture, are largely written for people who are experiencing suffering themselves to give them an explanation for why it is they're suffering. And so, even though eventually apocalypses came to be used widely among those who are not particularly oppressed—for example, in our modern context, some of the biggest fans of the apocalypse of John are, in fact, middle-class Americans who are doing just fine by worldly standards and aren't particularly oppressed by anybody or anything. But originally, these books were written for those who are oppressed to explain that their suffering has meaning and it's soon going to come to an end. They serve as important lessons for those who are experiencing oppression.

The Shepherd of Hermas, then, is an early Christian apocalypse and it's one that nearly made it into the New Testament. Even though "The Muratorian Canon" excluded it, there were other people who considered The Shepherd of Hermas to be part of sacred scripture. It was included as part of the New Testament in one of our earliest manuscripts of the New Testament, the famous Codex Sinaiticus. Codex Sinaiticus was discovered in the 19th century by an inveterate discoverer of manuscripts. A man named Constantin von Tischendorf discovered this manuscript at St. Catharine's Monastery on Mount Sinai, and to his surprise and joy, this included not only the books of the New Testament; it also included a major section of The Shepherd of Hermas, considered then to be canonical by the 4th-century scribe of the Codex Sinaiticus.

The Shepherd of Hermas divides itself into three major sections, so it's a large book with three major sections. It begins with a section of five visions, five visions given to the prophet. These represent a series of revelations that are given to Hermas and that are meant to instruct him concerning life in this world, especially as it relates to sins against God and the need to repent. These visions have this constant motif that people sinned against God, especially Hermas and his family, and they need to repent before it's too late.

Some of the visions contain more than one revelation. And so, even though they're categorized into five separate visions in the manuscripts themselves, the first vision has a revelation, but some of the visions have several revelations. In the fifth vision, the shepherd himself appears to Hermas for the first time and we're told that the shepherd, then, will be his interpreter for the rest of the book and that's what happens. The rest of the book is Hermas in company with the shepherd, Hermas receiving some kind of vision and the shepherd discussing with him the meaning of the vision.

So the book begins with five visions. There follows a section of ten commandments—ten commandments, or, actually, ten sets of commandments. This section of the book includes ethical injunctions concerning how to live for God. They're not just a list of do's and don'ts. Some of these commandments involve visions that come to be interpreted by the shepherd, ten sections, each of which is called a commandment, sometimes called a mandate. And so sometimes you've got the division of visions and commandments, or some people call them visions and mandates.

The third section of the book is the longest section by far. It consists of 12 parables, or they are sometimes called similitudes. These are not parables in the sense that we commonly think of where Jesus tells a parable; these, in fact, are also symbolic visions that the author sees, which are interpreted by the shepherd. So they're parables in the sense that the author sees something and it stands for something else. It's a symbolic or an allegorical vision that the shepherd interprets. By and large, these parables concern the Christian church, its makeup, its problems, and its need to stay faithful to God. So these are the three sections: 5 visions, 10 commandments, 12 parables.

As can be seen, even from my short summary, these three sections are not completely distinct from one another. For example, there are visions and commandments in each of the sections. All of the sections have visions, not just the first section, which consists of the visions—another illustration, in fact, that these are not distinct from each other, these sections. The longest parable of the book is the ninth parable. Remember there are 12 parables—the ninth parable is the longest one. It's extremely long. It goes on forever. It is, in fact, a prolonged exposition of one of the visions.

In the third vision, as we'll see in a minute, the author has a vision and he sees these giant men building a huge tower with stones. And there are some stones that fit in the tower and some stones that don't fit in the tower and he doesn't quite understand what this is all about and he gets it explained to him that the stones that fit in the tower are Christians who are upright and do God's will. The ones that don't fit are Christians who have gone off to sin in one way or another and so they don't fit in the tower, and it turns out the tower, in fact, is the church that's being built. And so some people get kicked out of the church because they don't fit because of their wickedness. So that's in the third vision.

In the ninth parable, you have the same vision again, with some slight variations in it, of a tower being built. But this time, the author goes on and on and on about the various kinds of stones. Some stones have cracks, some are rough, some are round, some are too smooth, some don't fit because they're misshapen, some are burned, and he goes on. And each one of these stones represents a different kind of Christian, or a different kind of person in the world. And then the author explains all these things about all of these stones and goes on and on and on. So the ninth parable is closely related to the third vision. My point here is simply that the sections of The Shepherd are closely related to one another.

Now, we won't have time in this short lecture to go through the entire book. Probably if you wanted to go through the entire book, it would take a course of 24 very long lectures. So I think what I'm going to do, instead of trying to get through the whole book, is I'm going to give you an example of what it looks like, how the book works, by dealing specifically with the first section—the five visions that the author has. And this will give us a pretty good sense of what the overarching concerns of the author are.

The first vision is very interesting because it appears to present an autobiographical reflection of the author. The author seems to be talking about something that actually happened to him and it's a very interesting episode, as it turns out. It begins just right off the bat, without much of an introduction. The author says, "The one who raised me sold me to a certain woman named Rhoda in Rome"—and so whoever raised this person, maybe a stepparent or something, sold him into slavery to a woman named Rhoda. Slavery was very common in the ancient world in some parts of the empire, for example, in the city of Rome. Probably something like a third of the inhabitants were slaves and so it's very common—slavery is very common. So anyway, this person, Hermas, was a slave to a woman named Rhoda in Rome.

"After many years, I regained her acquaintance and began to love her as a sister." So he apparently has been set free and he loved her as a sister. I would assume that means within the Christian church. "When some time had passed, I saw her bathing in the Tiber River"—well, now this is getting interesting very quickly—"and I gave her my hand to help her out of the river. When I observed her beauty, I began reasoning in my heart; I would be fortunate to have a wife of such beauty and character." So she apparently is bathing naked in the Tiber River. Some people doubt that this is an autobiographical statement because it seems kind of unlikely that an upper-class elite woman is just out bathing naked in the Tiber River. But some people think it's autobiographical. So he helps her out of the river and he's struck by her beauty and says, "I'd be fortunate to have a wife of such beauty and character." "This is all I had in mind, nothing else," he says. And so he has no other thoughts about anything apart from "I'd be lucky if I had a wife like her." And we find out later, by the way, that, in fact, he's already married. So this Rhoda is standing in contrast to the woman that he's already married to.

"When some time had passed, I was traveling to the countryside glorifying the creations of God and thinking how great, remarkable, and powerful they are." Okay, so he's walking along in the countryside just minding his own business, thinking how great God is, and then, all of a sudden, he falls asleep. I'm not sure how he falls asleep walking, but he apparently does. And the spirit carries him to a deserted place that was impassable. It's steep and there are all sorts of rivers and streams going through it and you can't really walk on it until he comes to level ground. And he bows his knees and he begins to pray to God, confessing his sins. He's very big on confessing his sins in this book.

While he's praying, the sky opens up and he sees the "Woman I had desired." So he sees Rhoda up in the sky looking down on him. And she says, "Hermas, greetings." "I looked at her and I said"—I guess what you would expect him to say—"lady, what are you doing here? She replied to me, 'I have been taken up to accuse you of your sins before the Lord.'" And so she's been snatched up into heaven in order to accuse him before God of his sins. "And he says, 'So now you're accusing me?' 'No,' she said, 'but listen to what I have to say to you.'" It doesn't really make sense; now she says, "No, I'm not accusing you" when she just said, "I was accusing you." "'Listen to what I say' she says, 'The God who dwells in heaven and who, for the sake of his holy church, created, increased and multiplied that which exists, although that which does not exist is angry at you for sinning against me.' I answer, 'Have I sinned against you? in what way? When did I speak an inappropriate word to you? Have I not always thought of you as a goddess?'" He evidently did; when he helped her out of the river, he thought of her as a goddess. "'Have I not always respected you as a sister? Why do you make such evil and foul accusations against me, oh woman?' But she laughed and said, 'The desire for evil did rise up in your heart,'" and she goes on to say, "Well, you say you weren't thinking anything untoward, but, in fact, you were, so I'm accusing you before God for all of this."

So when she finishes accusing him, the skies shut up again and he becomes very upset. He begins saying, "If this sin is recorded against me, how can I be saved? I didn't even do anything. If this is against me, I'm in big trouble." And so he gets all upset. "While I was mulling these things over in my heart and trying to reach a decision, I saw across from me a large white chair"—so he has a vision of the large white chair—that's made of wool, white as snow. And an elderly woman came, dressed in radiant clothes, holding a book in her hands," and she greets Hermas and he greets her. She says, "Why are you sad, Hermas, you who are patient, slow to anger, and always laughing? Why are you so downcast and not cheerful?" and he says, "Well, because this good woman has been accusing me, saying I've sinned against her." And this elderly woman said, "May such a thing never happen to a slave of God. But probably something did rise up in your heart about her." So he probably did do something wrong.

Then she goes on to say, "But, in fact, God is angry with you, not about this, but so that you may convert your household which has acted lawlessly against the Lord and against you, their parents." She goes on to say that "You haven't been strict enough with your children" and so now they've grown up to be sinners. And then she goes through a long discourse explaining how sinful his children are and how he needs to get them to turn back to God. That's the first vision.

So then the second vision comes along and what happens in the second vision is Hermas is walking through the countryside a year later, almost exactly a year later, and the spirit, once again, takes him to this wilderness area. So he has this ecstatic vision of moving into the wilderness area. And when he comes to the place, he bows down to his knees and he begins to pray. When he gets up from prayer, he sees across from him the elderly woman again, who is walking and reading a little book. And so he wants to know what's in this book that she's been reading and then he finds out that these are the words that were written, "Your offspring, Hermas, have rejected God, blasphemed the Lord, and betrayed their parents with a great evil. Yet they have added still more licentious acts to their sins and piled on more evil, and so their lawless acts have gone as far as they can go." And so the words in this book are actually words about his family, saying that they've sinned. And they go on to say that they need to repent because if they don't repent right away, it's going to be too late. And if it's too late, then they're going to lose their salvation. And so in the second vision, Hermas is urged to get his family in line so that they can enter into the kingdom when it comes.

Now the third vision is one that I've mentioned to you already. It's the building of the tower. He sees this elderly lady again and he wants to know what this is all about, all these visions he's having, and she says, "I'll meet you in the field." And he says, "Well, where in the field?" She says, "Pick a part of the field that you want to go to and I'll meet you there." So he finds a place in this field and he waits there for her and then, all of a sudden, he sees an ivory couch set up in the field. On the couch, there is a linen pillow and a piece of fine linen cloth on top. He's astounded and terrified; this couch has appeared out of nowhere.

And then he sees this woman coming with six young men. And she takes him by the hand and sits him down on this couch. And he wants to sit on her right-hand side. And she says, "No, you can't sit on my right-hand side. You have to sit on my left side," and he's upset because he wants to sit on her right side. "Why can't I sit on the right side?" "Well," she says, "the right side is reserved for others who have already pleased God and suffered on behalf of his name."

And it turns out the people who were to sit on her right are those who have experienced floggings, imprisonments, afflictions, crucifixions, and wild beasts for the sake of the name. For that reason, "The right-hand side of holiness is reserved for them and you haven't suffered, so you get the left side." And so he doesn't get the place of honor.

She talks with him for a while and she sends the six men who came with her away and she asks Hermas, "Do you see anything?" He says, "No, I don't see anything." She says, "Don't you see that tower being built?" And he looks and there's this tower being built on the water out of stones. People are bringing stones to the six men who are building this tower. And then he describes some of these stones, that some of them fit together so perfectly you can't even see the joints between them. Other stones are left lying around the tower and not being used in the building. Some of them have a rough appearance, some have cracks, some are broken off, and some are wider rounded and do not fit. So he sees all these stones being used and not used for the tower.

He wants to know what this is, what this all means. And he asks the lady and he says to her, "What good does it do me for me to see these things if you don't tell me what they mean?" And so she tells him. She says, "The tower which you see being built is I, the church, who have appeared to you both now and previously." And then she goes on to describe. So she's the church and she's also the tower. "Why is it being built on water?" "Because a person enters the church only through baptism, through water." "What are the various stones?" "Well, the ones that fit perfectly are the good Christians, especially the apostles and the bishops of the churches." And then she describes these various stones that don't fit into the building of the tower precisely because they are Christians who have sinned and fallen away from the faith and are in danger, then, of not being included in the tower.

The fourth vision is very interesting. In the fourth vision, Hermas is told, "Be strong and don't be of two minds. Be single-minded." And then, all of a sudden, he sees this huge monster. It's a hundred feet long and it's terrible looking and really frightening and it's on the road that he's walking along. He realizes that he'd just been told that he has to be strong in the faith, so he decides he has to walk by this horrible monster.

As he walks by, the monster lies down and doesn't move and just sticks out its tongue like a snake sticking out its tongue. And he walks by without any problem. Then, 30 feet later, he meets a young woman who says, "Have you seen anything on the road?" He says, "Well, there's this monster on the road." And she said, "Yes, that represents the tribulation that is soon to come against you and your family against this world. If you remain faithful though, you'll be able to pass by this affliction without suffering." And so, it's a sign of the suffering. And then, when she finishes, she disappears and then he says that he turned around quickly because he thought he heard a noise. He thought the monster was coming after him. So he wasn't all that faithful at the end, as it turns out. The fifth vision, then, is simply that the shepherd appears, turns up and tells Hermas that he is now going to be his interpreter for the rest of the commandments and the parables.

Well, this is at least to give you an idea of the book. The Shepherd of Hermas is a very long story, with some very basic themes. The visions are meant to be heavenly revelations that provide instruction for Christians living here on earth. The overarching message is that people, Christians, need to be faithful to God and repent of their sins before it's too late because the tower is going to be completed, and when it's completed, then that will be it. So people need to be ready for the coming of the end.

Those who refuse to do so will be removed from the church and will suffer the consequences when the end of time comes, which will be very soon.

Lecture Twenty
Apocalypses in Early Christianity

Scope:

The Shepherd of Hermas is thoroughly imbued in apocalyptic thought; this gives us an opportunity to consider the importance of apocalypticism for the early Christian movement. In this lecture, we will consider the major tenets of apocalypticism, as found in both Jewish and Christian sources; we will see how Jesus himself proclaimed an apocalyptic message; and we will note how this apocalyptic view of the world both continued in the preaching of Jesus' followers (such as Paul and the author of Revelation) and came to be modified as Christians realized that the apocalyptic expectation of the imminent end of the world had not transpired and probably would not transpire. This "failure of the end" forced Christians to reconsider some of the basic aspects of their proclamation, away from an anticipation of an imminent end to a determination to accommodate to a world that was to be here for the long haul.

Outline

I. We saw in the preceding lecture that The Shepherd of Hermas is an example of an early Christian apocalypse.

    A. Apocalypses were a common genre in early Christianity and Judaism.

    B. Their basic function was to explain earthly realities through visions of heavenly truths.

    C. In this lecture, we will explore more fully what the genre entailed and consider a couple of other examples.

II. It is important to differentiate the genre *apocalypse* from the worldview called *apocalypticism*.

    A. *Apocalypticism* was a worldview widely shared among Jews and Christians around the beginning of the Christian era.

        1. Apocalypticists were dualists who maintained that the current evil age was soon to be overthrown by God, who would bring in his good kingdom in the near future.

2. There were many apocalypticists—for example, Jesus and Paul—who never wrote an apocalypse.

B. The term *apocalypse* refers to a specific genre of revelatory literature that conveys an apocalyptic message.

C. These *revelations* could be of two different types.

    1. Some apocalypses contain visions of the future of the Earth (usually in highly symbolic language); this is the *historical* type.

    2. The earliest example of a historical apocalypse is the book of Daniel, which contains a number of visions.

    3. In Daniel 7, for example, Daniel has a symbolic vision of horrible beasts that take over the earth, but are destroyed by the Son of Man. An angelic interpreter tells Daniel that the four beasts represent the four kingdoms of the Babylonians, the Meads, the Persians, and the Greeks. The ten horns on the fourth beast represent the ten kings of the Seleucid Empire. The Son of Man represents the saints of the Most High, who will inherit the Earth, when God brings his kingdom to his saints and earthly kingdoms are destroyed.

    4. Other apocalypses contain visions of the heavenly realm (again, in symbolic language). Here, the idea is that what happens on Earth is a reflection of what happens in heaven; this is the *heavenly vision* type.

    5. Some apocalypses combine the two types, as happens, for example, in the New Testament book of Revelation, where the visionary, John, sees the heavenly realm and has explained to him the future course of what will happen on Earth.

III. A number of specific features can be found in most apocalypses (not all apocalypses have all these features, but most have most of them).

A. Most apocalypses are pseudonymous, written in the names of famous religious persons of the past.

    1. We have apocalypses written in the names of Peter, Enoch, and even Adam!

    2. The ploy of pseudonymity was particularly useful for the historical type of apocalypse, because the "future" predictions were, in fact, already past at the time of writing.

    3. As it turns out, both The Shepherd and the Apocalypse of John do not share this particular feature of most apocalypses.

  B. Apocalypses contain a series of highly symbolic visions that are "mediated" by a heavenly messenger, who explains their meaning.

  C. There are often *violent repetitions* in the visions—that is, repetitions of the same sequence of events over and over again, which "violate" any literal, chronological reading.

  D. The visions often move from disaster to triumph to show that even though things will get much worse, in the end, truth, justice, and God himself will prevail.

  E. The motivation of these apocalypses is to encourage those who are suffering and to urge believers to hold on till the end.

IV. The best known apocalypse from Christian antiquity, of course, is the book of Revelation.

  A. The book of Revelation contains a series of revelations given to a prophet named John, who has been exiled to the isle of Patmos.

    1. John has a vision of the throne of God, who is holding a scroll fastened with seven seals. This represents the future course of Earth's history.

    2. The Lamb of God breaks the seals. As each seal is broken, a catastrophe hits the Earth. The breaking of the last seal sets off a chaotic series of catastrophes.

    3. Finally, an antichrist appears who makes war with Christ in heaven. Christ wins and the evil forces are purged from Earth.

    4. Christ reigns for a thousand years and there is a final judgment, in which all against God are judged, and God brings into existence a new heaven and Earth, where there is no suffering.

    5. It would be a mistake to rip Revelation out of its context—as is usually done—and claim that it is a blueprint for our own future.

B. Revelation was written in its own historical context of Christian persecution and Christian apathy and is meant to address those concerns.

C. The symbolic visions of the book indicate that it was meant for Christians in the Roman Empire.

    1. This can be seen clearly, for example, in the vision of the whore of Babylon in chapter 17, who is described in such a way as to make it certain that the text is referring to the ancient city of Rome.

    2. And it can be seen in other symbols, such as the number of the Antichrist, 666, which appears to be a reference to the Emperor Nero (the letters of whose name add up to 666!).

V. But there were other apocalypses that were popular in the early Church as well, including the Apocalypse of Peter.

A. Written in the name of Simon Peter, this book was thought by some Christians to belong to the canon of Scripture.

B. This is clearly a heavenly vision type of apocalypse.

C. It is, in fact, the first Christian account that we have of a guided tour of heaven and hell, a forerunner of Dante's *Divine Comedy.*

VI. Even though The Shepherd of Hermas is the only apocalypse among the Apostolic Fathers, it was the kind of book that enjoyed considerable popularity among Christians in the first two centuries of the Common Era.

Essential Reading:

Bart D. Ehrman, *The New Testament: A Historical Introduction to the Early Christian Writings*, chapter 28.

Christopher Rowland, *The Open Heaven: A Study of Apocalyptic in Judaism and Early Christianity.*

Supplementary Reading:

David Aune, *The New Testament in Its Literary Environment.*

John Collins, *Apocalypse: Morphology of a Genre.*

Questions to Consider:

1. How does understanding how apocalypses worked as a genre affect the interpretation of the book of Revelation? Should it be seen as a prediction of what is still to happen in the future?

2. What kind of book written today would be the closest thing to ancient apocalypses?

Lecture Twenty—Transcript
Apocalypses in Early Christianity

We saw in the preceding lecture that The Shepherd of Hermas is an example of an early Christian apocalypse. Apocalypses were a common genre in early Christianity and Judaism. Their basic function was to explain earthly realities through visions of heavenly truths.

In this lecture, we will explore more fully what the genre entailed and consider a couple of other examples from early Christianity. To begin with, it's important to differentiate the genre apocalypse from the worldview called apocalypticism. Apocalypticism was a worldview widely shared among Jews and Christians around the beginning of the Christian era. As we've seen already, apocalypticists were dualists who maintained that the current evil age was soon to be overthrown by God who would bring in his good kingdom in the near future.

Apocalypticists believed that there were forces of good and evil in the world, with God, of course, being over all that is good and God having a personal opponent, the Devil, over all that is evil. Good versus evil—the world was originally created good, but something happened to corrupt the world. So apocalypticists were dualists in the sense that they thought, in the present there are two forces that are doing battle, not just among themselves but also with people. So, the people align themselves with the forces of good or the forces of evil and everybody has to choose between good or evil.

Apocalypticists, by and large, did not maintain that this had been an eternal struggle between good and evil. This is one thing that differentiates apocalypticists from, say, those who were dualistic in other religious traditions—for example, in Eastern religions where, in some Eastern religions, you have an eternal battle of good and evil.

Apocalypticists were Jews or Christians who believed that God had originally created the world, so that the good and evil in the world now does not go back into eternity, because, at one point, there was only God and he created all things and he created all things good. But something happened so that forces of evil came into the world and, at this point, there are battles now between good and evil. But just as there is not evil in eternity past, so there will not be evil in eternity future. There's evil only now in the present time because God will intervene in the course of history, overthrow the forces of evil, and set up his good kingdom on earth, and that will be an eternal kingdom, and so we're living in a kind of interim period in which there is both good and evil in the world.

This is how apocalypticists explained suffering. I mentioned, in the previous lecture, that apocalypses are a kind of theodicy, a kind of explanation for how it is God can be righteous if there's so much suffering. In particular, apocalypticists were troubled by the idea that those who are righteous suffer. It would make sense if people who were wicked suffer because then the forces of good would be punishing them for their evil, but the problem is when good people suffer. Why is it that people who are completely innocent suffer? Why is it that babies suffer? Why is it that people who are righteous, adults who try and follow God and obey his law, why do they suffer?

Apocalypticism explained that the reason there is innocent suffering in the world is because there are forces of evil opposed to God, who are opposed to God's people, who are creating the suffering. This is the worldview, then, that scholars have called apocalypticism.

There were a number of apocalypticists—in other words, people who held to an apocalyptic worldview—who never wrote an apocalypse. An apocalypse is a literary genre. Not everybody who was an apocalypticist wrote an apocalypse. For example, we have no evidence to suggest that Jesus ever wrote an apocalypse—even though he was an apocalypticist—and no evidence that Paul, the apostle Paul, ever wrote an apocalypse. The term "apocalypse" refers to a specific genre of revelatory literature—a specific genre of revelatory literature that conveys an apocalyptic message. So anybody who wrote an apocalypse was an apocalypticist, but not all apocalypticists wrote apocalypses. So, that's the difference between the worldview and the genre.

Apocalypses, these revelations—apocalypse is the Greek word which is translated into Latin as "revelation," so that apocalypse and revelation are equivalent terms—these revelations could be of two different types, so the genre divides itself into two major types of apocalypse. Some apocalypses contain visions of the future of the earth, visions of what will happen here on earth, usually in highly symbolic language. Scholars have called this type of apocalypse—

where the future of the earth is seen—they've called this type a historical type of apocalypse.

One of the best examples of a historical type of apocalypse is the first apocalypse that we have—the earliest that we have—which turns out to be The Book of Daniel in the Hebrew Bible, the Old Testament. The Book of Daniel is a story of this person, Daniel, who allegedly is taken into exile during the Babylonian captivity in the 6th century B.C., and it's about his life in Babylon. But it includes a number of visions; starting in Daniel 7, it includes a number of visions allegedly given to this Daniel, 550 years before the Christian era.

In Daniel 7, for example, we have a vision of Daniel, and this vision in Daniel 7 corresponds to a historical type of the apocalypse. Daniel has this vision of the sea being stirred up by the winds of heaven and out of the sea there comes a sequence of dreadful beasts, one after the other. These are horrible beasts that come up out of the sea and take over the earth one after the other. The final beast is especially awful, with terrible grinding teeth and feet of iron that stamp out all that is living, especially the saints of the Most High.

And then Daniel has a vision after seeing this fourth beast, which, by the way, has 10 horns and then it has a little horn that uproots three of the previous horns, so these are highly symbolic visions. He then sees one like a Son of Man coming on the clouds of heaven. And the beasts are destroyed. The fourth beast is punished and taken out of power and this one like a Son of Man is given authority over the earth forever and ever. So this one like a Son of Man inherits, then, the eternal kingdom.

This is a symbolic vision because then an angelic interpreter comes and tells Daniel what the vision means. It turns out these four beasts represent four kingdoms that are going to come on earth. And it doesn't take too much for an interpreter to realize what these four kingdoms are—scholars today are fairly unified. The first beast that comes out of the sea represents the Babylonians, allegedly during Daniel's day. The second is the kingdom of the Medes. The third is the kingdom of the Persians. The fourth is the kingdom of the Greeks—the kingdom of the Greeks, brought by Alexander the Great who conquered that part of the world. These are all world empires.

The ten horns on this fourth beast represent the kings of the Seleucid Empire. This Seleucid Empire was the empire that ruled in Syria in the wake of Alexander the Great's conquering. And so, this is a vision that there will be four kingdoms on earth prior to the coming of the one like the Son of Man who is interpreted as being another kingdom. But this time, instead of being a fierce beast out of the sea, this is one that comes from heaven. Well, who is this one like a Son of Man?

Well, according to the angel's interpretation of the vision, this one like a Son of Man—this human one, as opposed to these grotesque beasts—this one that actually has human form, is none other than the saints of the Most High, who will inherit, then, the earth when the beasts are taken out of power. In other words, God will bring his kingdom to his saints when the earthly kingdoms are destroyed. So, it's a historical vision because it's giving a historical sequence of what's going to happen in the future. That's a historical type of apocalypse, Daniel 7.

There are other apocalypses that contain visions of the heavenly realm itself, again in highly symbolic language. So a prophet is taken up to heaven and sees what's happening in heaven. Here, the idea is that what happens on earth is a reflection of what happens in heaven, so the earth is a kind of shadow of the reality in heaven or a reflection of what's taking place in the heavenly realm.

Scholars have called this second type of apocalypse a "heavenly vision" type of apocalypse. Now, there are some apocalypses that combine the two types. For example, in the New Testament Book of Revelation, as we'll see in more detail in a minute, the prophet, John, is taken up into heaven where he sees the heavenly realm and he has explained to him the future course of what will happen on earth. And so, in some senses, the book of Revelation in the New Testament is a combination of the two traditional types—the historical type and the heavenly vision type of apocalypse.

Apocalypses of both types have a number of specific literary features in common. Just as short stories and novels and limerick poems and epics and every other genre of literature have specific literary features that make them that kind of genre, so too were the apocalypses. There are specific literary features that are found in the apocalypses that make them apocalypses. It's not that every apocalypse has every one of these features, it's that most of these features are found in most of the apocalypses.

To begin with, most apocalypses that we have from Jewish and Christian to antiquity are pseudonymous; they're pseudonymous writings, written in the names of famous religious persons of the past. In other words, whoever's actually writing the apocalypse is claiming to be some famous religious person from antiquity. We have apocalypses that are written in the name of Paul—we have an apocalypse of Paul. We have an apocalypse of Peter. We have an apocalypse of Enoch. If you remember, Enoch was a person from the Hebrew Bible, the Old Testament, who was seven generations removed from Adam, who didn't die; he was so righteous that God took him up into heaven without dying.

Well, we have apocalypses allegedly written by this person Enoch. We even have an apocalypse allegedly written by Adam—as in Adam and Eve fame. And so these are people who are claiming to be these people who are seeing the future, of course, of the earth.

Daniel appears to be a pseudonymous writing. Daniel, allegedly, is written by a character, Daniel, who is taken into exile during the Babylonian captivity in the 6th century. But in fact, it is almost certain that the book of Daniel was written in the 2nd century, 400 years later, by somebody during the Maccabean Revolt, which I've referred to earlier, when Antiochus Epiphanes was making life so miserable for so many Jews. This author is writing to explain that the end is coming very soon and Antiochus will be taken out of power by God himself.

This ploy of pseudonymity, of writing in somebody else's name, was particularly useful for the historical type of apocalypse for a reason you could figure out if you thought about it for a while. If somebody is living in the 2nd century B.C. and he wants to show that the suffering that the people of God are currently experiencing is soon to end, what this person could do is write an apocalypse pretending to be somebody who lived a long time ago. And this person who lived a long time ago would predict things that are going to happen.

Now, the reader who's reading this thinks it really is this person from a long time ago who's predicting things are going to happen, and the reader knows those things have happened. Of course they've happened—the person writing them is living after they've happened, just pretending to be somebody who lived a long time ago. But then the author continues to predict things up to his own day, and you'll note when you get a historical type apocalypses like this, the predictions get more and more detailed as you get closer to the person's own day. They get to be very detailed, in fact. And then he continues to predict what's going to happen after his day.

Now, the reader doesn't know that he's predicting things that are going to happen after his day because he doesn't know when this person's day is. The person thinks that this person is living in great antiquity. And so, the predictions of what's to be in the future are of the same character as all the other predictions for the reader. So it looks like they're just as likely to come true as the things that were predicted that, in fact, were past. And so this is a way of convincing readers that the end is coming soon because when you predict the end, that prediction has the same value as predictions of things that, for the writer, are already past.

And so this idea of pseudonymity turned out to be quite useful. That's why Daniel claims to be by somebody in the 6th century. It's actually written in the 2nd century. And it traces the course of history up to its own time and then indicates that the fourth beast and its 10 horns are going to be taken out of power when one like a Son of Man is given the—if one of the horns, the final horn, is in fact Antiochus Epiphanes's, the enemy of the Jews in the day of the author's writing and it's predicted that he's going to be taken out of power, then the reader naturally thinks that 400 years ago somebody saw all that's happening in our day as coming true and has indicated to us that, in fact, the end is near.

So apocalypses tend to be pseudonymous. Now, having said that, I have to point out that our two most familiar apocalypses for this course—The Shepherd of Hermas and the apocalypse of John— appear not to be pseudonymous, as it turns out. Hermas is not writing in the name of some famous person from the past, unless Hermas was a famous person in his own congregation and somebody later is pretending to be Hermas, but that seems unlikely.

And the apocalypse of John is written by somebody named John, but he doesn't claim to be any particular John. He doesn't claim to be John, the son of Zebedee, the disciple of Jesus. So it may be pseudonymous. It may be somebody's claiming to be that John, but, if so, he's not making a very strong claim to be that John; he just calls himself John.

So first characteristic of most of apocalypses—usually, they're pseudonymous. Secondly, apocalypses contain a series of highly symbolic visions that are mediated by a heavenly messenger who explains their meaning. All these apocalypses have highly symbolic visions that are given. Third, these highly symbolic visions often are violently repetitive. Now, when I say they're violently repetitive, I don't mean that the visions are always about violence, although they often are. When you read the book of Revelation in the New Testament, these visions of the coming catastrophes hitting the earth are extremely violent—massive destruction of humanity on earth.

But when I say that they're violently repetitive, what I mean by that is that you can't trace the events that are narrated on a strict chronological line because the chronology doesn't work. What happens is the author sort of writes around and around the problem, so he keeps repeating disasters that are continually going to happen. He doesn't mean this to be a kind of linear development. Let me give you and example of why I know that that's true.

In the book of Revelation, there is a series of catastrophes that hit the earth. One set of catastrophes happens when there's an event that takes place in heaven where a scroll is being opened up and each of the seals is being broken off this scroll. It's sealed with a number of seals and when a seal is broken, then a catastrophe hits the earth. And the sixth seal gets broken and the author sees that there's a great earthquake. The sun becomes black as sackcloth, the full moon becomes like blood, the stars of the sky fall to the earth as the fig tree drops its winter fruit when it's shaken by a gale, the sky vanished like a scroll, rolling itself up, and every mountain and island was removed from its place. Well, you think this is the end. The sun's gone, the moon's gone, the stars are falling down, the skies turn black, and the whole earth is in this huge disruption. You think this is it. Well, this is not it, this is just chapter 6. We have another 16 chapters to go. Well, how could there be anything that happened after that? Well, because it's not meant to be a kind of chronological timeline of things that are going to happen. There are repetitions, which violate the literal meaning of the text, and that's why I call them violent repetitions in these visions, repetitions of the same sequence of events over and over again, which violate any literal, chronological reading.

Another characteristic of apocalypses, generally, is that these visions tend to move from disaster to triumph. This is in order to show that even though things will get much worse in our age, in the end, truth, justice, and God will prevail. Finally, the motivation of these apocalypses seems to be fairly consistent, whether reading the Jewish or the Christian apocalypses. The motivation of the apocalypses appears to be to encourage those who are suffering and to urge believers to hold on to the end. Don't give up the faith, even if you're suffering for it because the suffering is soon going to come to an end when God intervenes and brings in His good kingdom to earth.

The best-known apocalypse from Christian antiquity, of course, is the book of Revelation, which came into the New Testament. The book of Revelation records a series of visions given to a prophet named John who has been exiled, apparently for Christian activities, to the isle of Patmos. The book of Revelation begins by John being given a revelation—a vision of Jesus himself in heaven. It continues with the prophet actually going up to the heavenly realm.

In chapter 4, the prophet looks up to the sky and he sees there's a window in the sky and he sort of shoots up through this window and he's up, then, in the heavenly realm and he sees the throne of God himself and he sees God on the throne. In God's hand is a scroll that is sealed with seven seals. He's very upset because this scroll is sealed with seven seals and there's nobody who's worthy to break the seals. And so, he gets upset because he wants to know what's in the scroll. What's in the scroll that nobody can open is, in fact, the future course of earth's history.

But then he sees a lamb next to the throne of God, the lamb that was slain, obviously a reference to Christ who, in the Gospel of John, is talked about as the Lamb of God who takes away the sins of the world. Angelic beings inform the prophet that the lamb is worthy to break the seals. The lamb receives the scroll from God on the throne and begins to break the seals. And he breaks the seals one at a time. As he breaks a seal, a catastrophe hits the earth after each seal. When he breaks the seventh seal, we're introduced to seven angels who have trumpets, and each angel blows his trumpet, and as he blows a trumpet, another set of disasters hit the earth.

When the seventh angel blows the seventh trumpet, we're introduced to seven angels who have bowls—huge, immense bowls—of God's wrath, which they pour out on the earth, and more disasters hit the earth, one at a time. Finally, when all hell has broken out on earth, there appears an antichrist figure who does war against Christ in heaven. Christ brings forth the heavenly armies to attack the antichrist figure on earth and, of course, without much of a battle at all, Christ wins, and then we're introduced to the future of what's going to happen after the forces of evil are destroyed.

The evil forces are, in fact, taken and thrown into a lake of eternal fire for eternal torment. The earth is purged of all evil and there's a thousand-year reign of Christ on the earth. After a thousand years of utopia on earth, then there's a final judgment in which all that is against God is judged and God brings a new heavens and a new earth into existence—a new heavens and a new earth in which there'll no longer be any suffering.

It's important to recognize that Revelation, like other apocalypses of Christian antiquity, was written in its own historical context—a context of Christian persecution and Christian apathy, near the end of the 1st century, when some Christians were experiencing severe suffering and others had grown complacent. And the book of Revelation is meant to address those concerns.

It would be a real mistake to rip the book of Revelation out of its own context, as is usually done, and pretend that, in fact, it's written for our context. This normally happens when people think that the book of Revelation is providing us with a blueprint for our own future of things that are going to transpire sometime soon in the 21st century. In fact, the book of Revelation is not meant to be a blueprint for the future of our situation; the book of Revelation was written for its own situation at the end of the 1st century. The symbolic visions of the book indicate that it was meant for Christians living in the Roman Empire. Let me give you one example of this.

At one point in the book, in chapter 17, the prophet is given a vision that is the vision of what's called "the great whore of Babylon." The prophet goes out in the wilderness and he sees a woman who is seated on a wild beast that's made of scarlet—a scarlet beast. The beast has seven heads and 10 horns. This sounds kind of like what you get in the Book of Daniel, a beast with 10 horns. The woman is dressed in purple and scarlet and bedecked with many jewels. She holds a cup in her hand that is filled with the abomination and impurities of her fornication, it says. And on her forehead is written a name that is called a mystery: "Babylon the Great, Mother of Whores," and the words, "abominations."

And the woman, as it turns out, is drunk—drunk with the blood of the saints and the blood of the witnesses to Jesus. Well, the prophet sees this and can't make heads or tails of it. And so, as happens in The Shepherd of Hermas and other early apocalypses, an angelic figure comes to interpret the vision. And the angelic interpreter leaves no doubt concerning who, in fact, this whore of Babylon is. Babylon, by the way, was seen as the city in antiquity that was the enemy of Israel because the Babylonians conquered ancient Judea and destroyed Jerusalem, destroyed the temple. So Babylon was a nickname for the enemy of God's people.

Well, as it turns out, this woman also represents a city. We're told that this woman is seated on this beast with seven heads and the angel says the seven heads represent the seven mountains on which the woman sits. Moreover, the 10 horns represent 10 kings. Well, kings of what? They are the kings of a city. What city? What is the city that was built on seven mountains? Well, as any student of the ancient world knows, Rome is the city built on seven hills. And at the end of the angel's interpretation, he says that, "the woman you saw is the great city that rules over the kings of the earth."

This whore of Babylon is none other than the city of Rome, that has committed abominations against the earth, fornicated with the kings of the earth—in other words, engaged in economic transactions that are abominable and against the will of God. She's drunk with the martyrs of Jesus because Rome had started persecuting Christians, especially under Nero—The Neronic Persecution. And so this woman, in fact, is a vision of Rome. Babylon is the code name, then, for Rome, the current enemy of God.

So the book of Revelation is to be read as a book that was speaking to its own day of the situation that was transpiring in the Roman Empire, and the author's message, as the message of most apocalypses, is that the people of God need to hold on because God will soon intervene and overthrow the Roman Empire and bring in his good kingdom.

Apart from the book of Revelation, there were other apocalypses that were very popular in the early church, including, as we've seen, The Shepherd of Hermas, which was included by several authors as part of the canon of the New Testament. And another book that was also considered canonical by some Christians in the early centuries is this other apocalypse, which in some parts of the church nearly made it into the canon, the Apocalypse of Peter. The Apocalypse of Peter is a book which is very different from the book of Revelation because it's not giving a future sketch of what's going to happen to earth. It's a sketch of what happens when people go to heaven and hell. In the Apocalypse of Peter, the apostle, Simon Peter, is given a guided tour of heaven and hell by Jesus himself, and he sees the torments of the damned and the blessings of the righteous.

Of particular interest to most readers are the torments of the damned. People are punished for the sins that they have committed. For example, those who have blasphemed against God are hanged by their tongues over unquenchable flame; women who have plaited their hair in order to be attractive to men, so they commit a fornication, are hanged by their hair over eternal flame. The men who have committed fornication with them are hanged by their genitals over eternal flame. There are people who chew their tongues and are tormented with red-hot irons and have their eyes burned out. Those are those who have slandered God.

There are others who have done deeds in deception in their lives. They have their lips cut off and fire enters into their mouths and into their entrails. There are people who are dressed in rags and filthy garments and they suffer unceasing torture—these are those who grew rich and trusted in their riches and despised the widows and the orphans. There's another place where men and women are up to their knees in muck. We're told that those are people who lent out money at interest. So the bankers among us—take heed. The Apocalypse of Peter, then, is designed to show that in the afterlife God will resolve the problems of evil by rewarding the faithful and punishing the wicked.

Well, to sum up, even though The Shepherd of Hermas is the only apocalypse that we find among the Apostolic Fathers, just as the book of Revelation is the only apocalypse in the New Testament, The Shepherd was the kind of book that enjoyed considerable popularity among Christians in the first two centuries of the

Common Era. It's a book in which a mortal prophet has a vision of heavenly realities that help make sense of our mundane life, our life of suffering, our life of pain here on earth.

Lecture Twenty-One
The Letter to Diognetus—An Apology

Scope:

The final writing of the Apostolic Fathers to be considered is an anonymous book called the Letter to Diognetus. This represents one of the earliest surviving instances we have of a Christian *apology*. The word *apology* in this context does not mean saying that one is "sorry." It comes from the Greek word *apologia* and refers to a reasoned "defense" of Christian claims against their cultured despisers.

The Letter to Diognetus is an intellectual defense of Christianity that argues for its moral and doctrinal superiority in the face of opposition to it by the pagans who made up the majority of the ancient Roman world. In this lecture, we will examine the letter's arguments that Christianity is not only a valid religion but, in fact, the one superior religion to be adhered to by all, rather than persecuted as an aberrant faith.

Outline

I. To this point, we have considered nine writings of the Apostolic Fathers. In this lecture, we deal with the final one, a literary gem known as the Letter to Diognetus.

    A. This book is unique among the work of the Apostolic Fathers in that it is an *apology* for the Christian faith.

        1. The term *apology*, in this context, refers to a reasoned defense of a philosophical or religious tradition (the Greek word for "defense" is *apologia*).

        2. Apologies became a popular literary form among Christians starting in the second half of the 2nd century, as that was when the Christian Church had both the need and the ability to defend itself.

        3. The Church needed to defend itself because of the increased notice it was receiving from the world at large and the Roman government in particular (in terms of persecution).

4. It was able to defend itself because a number of intellectuals had begun to convert to the faith who could argue for Christianity's innocence before the state, on the one hand, and its moral and religious superiority, on the other.

5. Christianity grew from about 20 followers of Jesus right after his death to about 5% of the Roman empire (or three million people) by the early 4th century.

6. Christianity's defenders included Tertullian in North Africa, Origen in Alexandria, Justine Martyr in Rome, and others.

B. We have already seen the context of persecution of Christians in the 1st and 2nd centuries.

1. Christians were out of favor among the general populace because they were known not to worship the state and local gods and because they were suspected of committing social improprieties.

2. Jews, of course, also did not worship the state gods, but they were tolerated because they held to ancient traditions of their own.

3. Christians, on the other hand, were known not to hold to ancient traditions but to subscribe to a relatively new faith.

4. That is part of the reason that some Christians, such as the author of the Letter of Barnabas, were so intent to claim the ancient traditions of the Jews for themselves.

5. This was a ploy used by a number of apologists, as well, including the most famous of them all, Justin Martyr.

6. As it turns out, it is not the ploy used by the anonymous author of the Letter to Diognetus, who defends the faith using other arguments.

II. Even though it is a stylistically superior work, the Letter to Diognetus was not well known throughout antiquity.

A. It is never mentioned, let alone quoted, by any other early Christian author.

B. In fact, it remained unknown until a manuscript containing its text was discovered by a young cleric among some papers used to wrap fish in a fishmonger's shop in Constantinople in 1436.

C. The manuscript was transcribed by scholars several times over the course of the next couple of centuries.

D. Unfortunately, the manuscript itself, which was eventually deposited in the municipal library of Strasbourg, was destroyed by fire during the bombing of the city in the Franco-German war in 1870.

III. Given the fact that the book is not mentioned by other early Christian authors, it is difficult to say much about it.

    A. Its author is anonymous.

    B. The recipient of the letter was someone named Diognetus, which literally means "born of Zeus."

        1. Given that he is called "most excellent," he may have been a Roman official of some kind or a person of high status (possibly the tutor of Marcus Aurelius?).

        2. Or his name may simply be a cipher for an imaginary reader, much like the recipient of the New Testament books of Luke and Acts, Theophilus ("beloved of God").

    C. Scholars dispute the date of the work, but given its apologetic concerns and somewhat unsophisticated theology, it may be best to date it to the middle or late 2nd century.

IV. The theme of the book is expressed already at the outset (ch. 1).

    A. Diognetus wants to know about the nature of the Christian religion, about why Christians don't accept the gods of the pagans, yet don't worship in the same way as the Jews.

    B. The book tries to answer these questions one at a time, beginning with the question of Christian views of pagan gods (ch. 2).

        1. Here, the author attacks pagan idols as being no more than the material that they are made of (2:2–4).

        2. This is a kind of polemical attack found commonly in Jewish and Christian writings, for example, in Isa. 44:9 ff.

    C. The letter then appeals to "common knowledge" that the distinctive features of Judaism, such as Sabbath observance, circumcision, and kosher food laws, are both ridiculous and superstitious (chs. 3–4).

D. Next, the author argues for the innocence and superiority of Christians.

    1. They live in socially innocuous and common ways (ch. 5).

    2. But they are morally superior to everyone else (ch. 5).

    3. They are to the world what the soul is to the body: that which gives it life (ch. 6).

    4. Their religion was not "dreamt up" but came from the one true God himself (ch. 7).

    5. Thus, the Christian understanding of God is superior to anything imagined by pagan philosophers (8:1–4).

    6. The author concludes with some long reflections on how much God has loved the world and patiently endured its ungodly behavior, but he will soon enter into judgment with all those who refuse to accept his revelation in Christ (10:7–8).

V. In sum, the Letter of Diognetus is an early example of Christian apology, in which the unknown author, a member of a persecuted minority in the empire, makes the audacious claim that his religion is, in fact, superior to everything else the empire has to offer and should be adopted by all, rather than subjected to imperial disfavor and opposition.

Essential Reading:

Bart D. Ehrman, ed., "Epistle to Diognetus," in *The Apostolic Fathers*, vol. 2, pp. 122–159.

Clayton Jefford, *Reading the Apostolic Fathers: An Introduction*, pp. 159–169.

Supplementary Reading:

Henry Meecham, *The Epistle to Diognetus*.

Robert M. Grant, *Greek Apologists of the Second Century*.

Questions to Consider:

1. From a "pagan's" point of view, why would it make sense to try to stamp out the Christian religion?

2. Why would the defense mounted by the Letter to Diognetus probably not prove to be persuasive to a pagan or Jewish audience?

Lecture Twenty-One—Transcript
The Letter to Diognetus—An Apology

To this point, we've considered nine of the Apostolic Fathers. In this lecture, we will deal with the final one, a literary gem known as the Letter to Diognetus. This book is unusual among the Apostolic Fathers in that it is an apology for the Christian faith. The term "apology," in this context, doesn't mean saying, "I'm sorry."

Christian intellectuals did not apologize to Romans for being Christian in the sense that we normally use the word "apology." The term "apology" in this context refers to a reasoned defense of a philosophical or religious tradition. It comes from the Greek word for defense, *apologia*, which means "defense." So this would be a reasoned defense written by a Christian intellectual in order to defend Christianity against its culture despisers.

Apologies became a popular literary form among Christians, starting in the second half of the 2nd century, as that was when the Christian church had both the need and the ability to defend itself. It needed to defend itself because of the increased notice that it was receiving from the world at large, and the Roman government in particular, in terms of persecution. We've seen already that Christians were persecuted sporadically throughout the years of the early church by official authorities so that we only know of a few Roman emperors who were involved with persecution—the emperor Nero being the first one with the persecution of Christians in Rome in the year 64—and then, we know about possibly there were persecutions under Domitian at the end of the 1st century, but we don't know this for a fact.

We do know there were persecutions under the emperor Trajan in the early 2nd century and we know there were persecutions under Marcus Aurelius in the mid-2nd century and persecutions became more frequent, then, at the end of the 2nd century, not just by imperial authorities but also by local authorities in various places throughout the Roman Empire within the provinces.

Christianity, then, began to need to defend itself because of its increased notice. It was able to defend itself in this period, in the second part of the 2nd century, because a number of intellectuals had converted to the faith. These intellectuals could argue for

Christianity's innocence before the state, on the one hand, and its moral and religious superiority on the other.

There were not very many Christian intellectuals in the early decades of the church. As you know, Jesus himself was a lower class peasant from Galilee. He was a rural person who didn't have a high rhetorical training of any kind. His earliest disciples were all lower class peasants from Galilee. Soon after Jesus' death, there were, occasionally, people who were intellectually inclined who converted, such as the apostle Paul, but Paul must have been one of the real exceptions. Paul's letters are difficult. He was obviously a very smart man and it's an interesting question to ask how many of Paul's readers would have been able to make sense of his letters.

When you read Galatians, it turns out it's a very difficult letter to understand, even among people who have spent 20 or 30 years trying to study Galatians. I have friends who write books on Galatians who have studied that book for 20, 30 years, and they still disagree about what it means. It's a very complicated book. The idea that Paul's readers could have just read it once and known exactly what he was talking about really sort of defies belief. I think that, probably, Paul was engaged in intellectual exercises that most of his readers couldn't follow. In any event, Paul was an exception to the rule that most people in the early church were not among the intellectual class.

By the end of the 2nd century, though, as Christianity is increasing in size, there are people converting to the faith who are intellectuals. How quickly was Christianity expanding in this period? It's very difficult to say how quickly Christianity grew. Let me give you the basic numbers that most historians think are at least not completely problematic. In other words, these are the least problematic numbers that have been advanced by historians.

Most people would agree that Jesus' followers started out as a group of disciples in Jerusalem after his death. And, according to our earliest tradition, we're talking about 11 men and a handful of women, so, say something like 20 people, right after his death. By the beginning of the 4th century—about 300 years later—there are reasons for thinking that Christianity made up something like 5 percent of the empire, that Christianity, by the early 4th century, made up something like 5 percent of the empire. By the end of the 4th

century, Christianity had exploded onto the scene. It exploded onto the scene because the Roman emperor himself, Constantine, converted to Christianity. Once the emperor converted to Christianity, Christianity was no longer a persecuted religion, but a favored religion and it became a very popular thing for people to become Christian. So by the end of the 4th century, probably half of the entire empire was Christian. So there's an explosion of conversions in the 4th century.

But prior to that, we move from there being something like 20 followers of Jesus after his death to being something like 5 percent of the empire. Now, the empire—it's difficult to come up with an accurate estimate of the demographics of the period, but most scholars put the empire's population at around 60 million people. So we went from 20 people around the year 30 to maybe something like 3 million people at the beginning of the 4th century.

People crunch the numbers in different ways, but the short story is that you don't have to have had massive conversions to Christianity in order to go from the small beginnings to the rather large outcome at the beginning of the 4th century. What you need is a steady rate of growth. One scholar has estimated that if you calculate a rate of growth of about 40 percent growth every decade—a steady stream of growth of about 40 percent per decade—then you would get to the necessary numbers at the beginning of the 4th century. So, you don't need to have some kind of massive evangelistic rally where thousands of people convert at one time in order to get the larger numbers by the 4th century; you just need steady growth, 40 percent every decade. That's an interesting number, by the way, because that's the percentage of growth rate that the Mormon Church has experienced since its founding in the 19th century. It has grown and continues to grow at about 40 percent per decade.

So, Christianity is growing, and here, in the late end of the 2nd century, it's probably growing, say, 40 percent a decade; it goes up and down, but it's not a completely steady state. It goes up and down, but there are enough people converting that some of the people converting are real intellectuals. These real intellectuals both see the need to convince others that Christianity is harmless and should not be persecuted and they have the ability to do so because they are, after all, trained rhetorically and can write effective responses to the situation of oppression that Christianity was facing.

These intellectuals include people like Tertullian in North Africa, a man named Origen in Alexandria, Justin Martyr in Rome, and several other people that we'll see in the course of this lecture and the next.

Christianity, of course, faced a context of persecution in its first two centuries. As we saw in a previous lecture, Christians were unpopular among the general populous because they were known not to worship the state and local gods, and also because—as we'll see in the next lecture—Christians were largely suspected of committing social improprieties. Now, that might seem strange to think that Christians, in fact, were committing social faux pas and were widely regarded, in fact, as being immoral, but that is the case. They were regarded as immoral and unethical, as we'll see in the next lecture.

The main problem with the Christians, though, is they did not worship the state gods and most people thought that if you didn't worship the gods, the god would punish you, so that if you were experiencing any suffering, it was because the gods were angry at not being worshiped. Christians didn't worship the gods and, therefore, Christians were to blame.

Jews, of course, also did not worship the state gods, but they were, by and large, tolerated in the Roman world because the Jews held to ancient traditions of their own. Their religion was founded on ancient traditions. That's part of the reason why Christians, such as the author of the Letter of Barnabas, were so intent to claim the ancient traditions of the Jews for themselves. The Christian authors who wanted to claim that they were the true heirs of the promises of Israel were doing so because they were living in a world that did not respect invention, but did respect antiquity.

This was a ploy that was used by a number of apologists, as well, the ploy of claiming that Christianity was, in fact, true Judaism. We see this, in particular, in the most famous of all Christian apologists, Justin Martyr. Justin Martyr wrote several books in the middle of the 2nd century. He lived in Rome. His several books, in one way or another, all defend Christianity against charges against it. One of Justin Martyr's favorite claims is that Christianity must be true because Christianity fulfills the prophecies of ancient prophets. That shows that it's given by a divine supernatural being. Because, otherwise, how could you have prophecies 800 years before the fact that came true in Jesus, if God weren't directing affairs on earth? And so, he has a number of arguments that will be familiar, even to modern Christians today, because these arguments continue to be used.

For example, as Justin Martyr points out, Jesus was born of a virgin. Well Isaiah 7:14 predicts that there will be a child born of a virgin. And this one will be called "God is with us." Justin argues that Jesus was born of a virgin, and therefore Jesus, 800 years after Isaiah, fulfilled the prophecy, which shows that God was at work not just in Isaiah, the Jewish prophet, but also in Jesus himself. Jesus, then, and his followers, fulfilled the predictions of scripture, or Isaiah 53— which Justin also takes to be written 800 years before Jesus—Isaiah 53, which talks, in Justin's opinion, about the crucifixion of Jesus. How could Isaiah, 800 years before Jesus' death, know how he was going to die? Because for Justin, God inspired Isaiah and sent Jesus to fulfill his prophecy. So this religion is divine from beginning to end. And so Justin's books—we have three of his books that survive today—are not just about fulfillment of prophecy but they're largely taken up with this issue of how Jesus fulfilled the prophecies of the Jewish prophets.

As it turns out, this ploy of using fulfilled prophecy to demonstrate the truthfulness of Christianity is not used by the anonymous author of the Letter to Diognetus. This author, in fact, defends the faith by using other kinds of arguments, so even though proof from prophecy was very common among Christian apologists, it's not used by this particular author.

Even though The Letter to Diognetus is a stylistically superior work—it's written in very good Greek, as opposed to most early Christian writings—this book was not well known throughout antiquity. As it turns out, the Letter to Diognetus is never mentioned, let alone quoted, by any other early Christian writer. In fact, the Letter to Diognetus remained completely unknown—we didn't even know it existed—until a manuscript containing its text was accidentally discovered in 1436. It's a somewhat peculiar story and I don't have all the details. I've tried to track them down, but I don't have them all.

But there was a young cleric who was in a fishmonger's shop in Constantinople, apparently buying some fish, and fish were being wrapped up in old scraps of paper and other writing materials that were just thrown out. And so, they're wrapping up the fish, and he noticed that some of the papers being used to wrap fish, in fact, had writing on them that looked to be quite ancient. So he pulled this paper out and he noticed that, in fact, it contained some ancient writings, and it turns out that it was a manuscript that contained this Letter to Diognetus, found in a fishmonger shop in Constantinople in 1436.

This manuscript, once it was recovered, was transcribed by scholars several times over the course of the next couple of centuries. So scholars took it and copied out its text so that we have copies of the text. Unfortunately, the manuscript itself, which this fellow found in 1436, was eventually deposited in the Municipal Library of Strasbourg, where it was destroyed by fire during the bombing of the city in the Franco-German War in 1870. So this is a manuscript we didn't know existed. It was found and it existed for 444 years until it was destroyed again. So we still don't have the manuscript. But, luckily, we do have the copies made of the manuscript by scholars over those four centuries.

Given the fact that the book is not mentioned by any other Christian author, it's rather difficult to say very much at all about it. Its author is anonymous, so the author doesn't tell us who he is. He does name the recipient of his letter though. It's a man named Diognetus. Now, the name Diognetus literally means someone who is born of Zeus. Diognetus means born of Zeus, which presumably means that the recipient is a pagan, a non-Christian worshiper of Zeus—at least his parents wanted him to be. And it's clear when one reads the Letter to Diognetus that, in fact, this person is a pagan that the author is trying to defend Christianity to.

Diognetus is called "most excellent Diognetus" in the letter. So he may, in fact, be some kind of Roman official, or at least a person of high status. As it turns out, there was a Diognetus who was the tutor of Marcus Aurelius—the Emperor Marcus Aurelius—and so Diognetus is not a completely rare name in the ancient world, but being a tutor of Marcus Aurelius, that's about the time it looks like this book was probably written. It may be this author is writing this letter to the tutor of Marcus Aurelius.

Now, I should say with these apologies, frequently apologies were written by Christians directly to the Roman emperors. But there's nobody who really thinks that the Roman emperors were sitting down reading Christian apologies as if they had nothing better to do with their time. And so, probably, these apologies are meant to be open letters that are sent to somebody important—theoretically, sent to somebody important—but actually serving as open letters. And that may be the case here with the Letter to Diognetus, possibly the tutor of Marcus Aurelius.

Or it may be that his name is simply a cipher for an imaginary reader. We have instances of this in early Christian literature. The best-known instance of this involves the New Testament books of Luke and Acts. Whoever wrote Luke and Acts—again, these books are anonymous—addressed the books to somebody named Theophilus, most excellent Theophilus. Some people think Theophilus was an actual person, again, maybe a Roman official of some kind. Other people thought that Theophilus, in fact, is just a cipher for an imaginary reader. The name "Theophilus" means "Beloved of God." And it may be that this author of Luke and Acts is writing his book for Christians who are beloved of God and just addresses it to somebody and he makes up the name because this lends credibility to his writing because it's being addressed to somebody allegedly important. So, just as in the case with Luke and Acts, it may be that the Letter to Diognetus is addressed not to a particular person, but is meant to be a book openly read.

Scholars dispute the date of the Letter to Diognetus. But given its apologetic concerns and the theology in it, which by later standards would be somewhat unsophisticated—even though it's written in elegant Greek, its theology is somewhat unsophisticated—it may be best to date the letter sometime to the middle or to the late 2nd century.

I want to spend the rest of the lecture actually looking at some of the things that this anonymous author says in defense of Christianity. The theme of the book is stated already at its outset, and so this is how the book begins: "Since I see, most excellent Diognetus, that you are extremely eager to learn about the religion of the Christians and are wishing to discover which god they obey and how they worship him so that they despise the world and disdain death, neither giving credence to those thought to be gods by the Greeks nor keeping the superstition of the Jews, I welcome this eagerness of yours and ask that I may be allowed to speak in such a way that you derive special benefit by hearing." And so this author begins by saying, "I hear you want to understand something about the Christians; I'll tell you about the Christians, both why they don't worship many gods like pagans do, and also why they don't follow the superstitions of the Jews."

And so, the first two chapters, then, are taken up in showing how Christians are different from both pagans and Jews. First, the author deals with the question of Christian views of the pagan gods, where this author engages in a kind of standard polemic against the polytheists of his environment, where he says—if this is actually sent to somebody who himself is a devout pagan, it's a little bit hard to explain because this person is quite avid in his opposition to the pagan gods and says some rather unkind things about those who worship the pagan gods, as we see in chapter 2—"Consider the true nature and form of those you call and consider to be gods, not only with your eyes but with your mind. Is not one of them a stone, like that which we walk on? And another, copper, no better than utensils forged for our use? And another, wood, already rotted? And another, silver, needing someone to guard it to keep it from being stolen? And another, iron, being eaten away by rust? And another, pottery, no more attractive than that which is fashioned for the most disreputable purposes?"

In other words, pottery, just like a chamber pot you have in your house, that's the stuff that you make your gods out of, or wood, or iron. And so he says, "These are all destructible matter. How can you possibly say that these are gods? They're made by the coppersmith, by the sculptor, by the silversmith, by the potter, and these crafts people could have shaped these gods into some other shape if they wanted to." "What is so special about these things as god? These are the things that are worshiped by you. Could they not have been made by human hands and the utensils similar to all the others? Aren't these gods deaf and blind and lifeless and unable to perceive and unable to move? Are they not all rotting? Are they not all decaying? These are what you call gods. These are what you serve. These are what you worship. In the end, these are what you become like." So, this is a rather vicious argument against the pagan gods. They're like other things that are made by human hands.

In attacking the polytheistic religions as worshiping idols, I should point out that probably this author and other opponents of idol worship are not really giving the polytheistic religions their due. Most pagans didn't really think that this statue of the god was a god. This statute might have been the means by which god manifested himself into the world or a physical representation of the god. But most pagans didn't really think that this statue itself is the god. I mean the god is somewhere else and the statue represents god.

This way of polemicizing against idols, though, is common in both Jewish and Christian authors. As far back as the Book of Isaiah, we get Jewish polemic against worshiping idols. Isaiah has this very interesting passage in Isaiah 45 where he insists that the idols, in fact, are nothing and that they're simply made by ironsmiths and carpenters and he has this really interesting passage about how this carpenter cuts down a cedar tree and he uses part of the cedar tree for fuel for his fire so he can warm himself and he uses this fuel to bake his bread with, and so half of the cedar tree burns in the fire. And the other part of it, he makes into a god and then he bows down to it and says, "Save me, for you are my god." Half of it is used for his fire to bake his bread, and half of it he considers his god. It's just ridiculous because this, in fact, is a piece of wood. It's not God.

This author of the Letter to Diognetus, again, takes this kind of standard polemic and applies it to his current situation. The Christians don't worship pagan idols because it's silly to worship pagan idols. Moreover, the author goes on to say that Christians are not Jews, and so in the beginning of chapter 3, we have: "I suppose you especially long to hear about why Christians do not worship like the Jews." Well, that would be a natural question for a polytheist in the ancient world. "So you worship only the one god, the God of Israel, so you must be Jewish." This author wants to say, "No, we're not Jewish either. We don't worship the many gods that you do, but we also don't worship the God of the Jews because," he says, "those who suppose they are performing sacrifices of blood and fat and whole burnt offerings and therefore to be bestowing honor on God by these displays of reverence seem no different to me from those who show the same honor to the gods who are deaf, one group giving to gods who cannot receive the honor, the other thinking that they can provide something to the one who needs nothing. You think God needs your sacrifices the way Jews sacrifice to God? Why would God need a sacrificial religion? He's in no need of blood and fat and smoke. Why, then, sacrifice to him? And I do not think you need to learn about the Jewish anxiety over food, their superstition about the Sabbath, their arrogance over circumcision and the pretense they make of fasting and their celebration of the new moon—ridiculous matters and unworthy of argument."

So, he's making fun of the Jewish religion as being highly superstitious, and on that point, probably he would have his pagan reader agreeing with him, because Jews, throughout the empire, were mocked for their religious practices. Circumcision—cutting the foreskin off your baby boys—what kind of barbarism is that? Not being able to eat shrimp or pork—what kind of religious observation is that? Not working one day of the week? Jews took the seventh day off. Everybody else worked. There was no such thing as weekends in the ancient world. This author, as many other authors, thought that this was a superstition and, in addition, Jews were thought to be lazy. They didn't work one day out of seven.

And so the author is assuming, I think, that his reader is going to agree that Jews are superstitious. So, on the one hand, you have pagans who worshiped false gods who aren't really gods and then you've got Jews who are superstitious, and over against that, then, he sets the Christians. He indicates that Christians did not learn their religion from any human means and you can't understand it by any human means. Christians are like everyone else in the world in that they live in the world, but they are superior to the world.

According to this author, what the soul is to the body, this is what Christians are in the world. And so he likens Christians to the soul that is found within people's body. He indicates that the soul lives throughout the body, but it doesn't belong to the body. It's separate from the body, just as Christians live in the world, but they don't really belong in the world; they're a different essence.

The soul, which is invisible, is put under guard in the visible body. Christians are known to be in their world, but their worship remains invisible; it's secret. The flesh hates the soul, just as the world hates the Christians. But the soul is the thing that benefits the body. It's what gives the body purpose. It's what gives the body life. So the soul is imprisoned in the body, but it benefits the body. Christians are hated by the world, but they benefit the world. The soul, which is immortal, dwells in a mortal tent. Christians temporarily dwell in perishable surroundings, but await that which is imperishable. God has appointed them to such a position and it would not be right for them to abandon it.

This author goes on to indicate that the religion that the Christians follow was not a dreamt up religion; it came, in fact, from the one true God himself. He indicates, as well, that this God of the Christians, who has given such a superior religion to the world, is far above anything that non-Christian pagan minds can imagine.

He points out, for example, that pagan philosophy comes up with ideas of God that are completely unsatisfactory. For example, some philosophers say that God is fire. Others say that he's water or some other element. In fact, God is far beyond fire, water, or the other elements. This God—the one true God—has created the world itself, and he's given people an opportunity to repent. This author insists that people need to repent because the end is coming soon and if they don't repent, then they will be tormented by eternal fire.

And so, this is a defense of Christianity, written by a Christian intellectual who's trying to reason with his reader to try and show that this Christian religion is superior to other things in the religious world of his day in the Roman Empire.

And so, let me sum up. The Letter to Diognetus is an example of Christian apology—Christian defense—in which the unknown author, who is a member of a persecuted minority in the empire, makes the audacious claim that his religion is, in fact, superior to everything else the empire has to offer, whether pagan or Jewish, that Christianity, therefore, should be adopted by all, rather than subjected to imperial disfavor and opposition.

Lecture Twenty-Two
Apologetics in Early Christianity

Scope:

The consideration of the Letter to Diognetus in the preceding lecture takes us into the interesting realm of Christian apologetics: that is, the intellectual defense of Christianity against those who found it to be a baseless and even harmful superstition. In this lecture, we will consider some of the charges leveled against Christianity in the first two centuries—for example, that it promoted atheism (because it didn't acknowledge the gods) and flagrant immorality (Christians were accused, among other things, of infanticide and cannibalism!). We will then see how Christians mounted arguments against these charges and went even further to maintain that only followers of Christ could hope to escape the fires of hell and inherit eternal life with God in heaven.

Outline

I. In the preceding lecture, we began to see how Christians started writing apologies for the faith in the mid-2nd century.

    A. An apology is a reasoned "defense" (Greek: *apologia*) of the faith against its cultured despisers.

    B. Christians needed to defend their faith because they were a persecuted minority in the Roman Empire.

    C. We can get a fuller sense of the charges widely leveled against the Christians from some of these apologies, especially the *Octavius* written by Minucius Felix.

        1. Minucius Felix was a Christian intellectual living in Latin-speaking North Africa in the second half of the 2nd century.

        2. His work, the *Octavius,* records an imaginary conversation that took place between a pagan named Caecilian and a Christian named Octavius about the nature of the Christian religion.

        3. In it, Caecilian describes in graphic detail some of the charges of moral impropriety leveled against the Christians, namely that they engaged in sexual license, including incest, infanticide, and cannibalism (*Octavius*, chap. 9).

4. These charges might seem incredible to us today, but they were believable in a world that knew Christians to form a secret society that met under the cover of darkness, where "brothers and sisters" greeted one another with kisses and ate the flesh and drank the blood of the "son" of God!

5. On top of all this, Christians were widely considered to be atheists—literally, "without the gods"—in that they rejected the gods otherwise worshiped by pagans in the empire.

II. To get a fuller sense of how Christian intellectuals defended themselves against such charges, we can consider the apology written by Athenagoras, a Christian philosopher from Athens.

A. Called the "Plea Regarding the Christians," this apology was written in A.D. 177.

B. Like many apologies, it is addressed to the reigning Roman emperors (Marcus Aurelius and Commodus).

1. It is unlikely that emperors ever read such literature.

2. It may be best to consider such writings to be "open letters" to the all-powerful rulers or even "in-house" literature, providing Christians themselves with ammunition for their battle against their opponents.

C. The apology begins with a statement of the Christians' innocence and unjust suffering.

D. It continues with a plea that Christians be punished for actual crimes against the state, not for their name (ch. 2).

1. This sounds like a reasonable request, but it must be remembered that the name *Christian* actually meant something to both pagans and Christians themselves.

2. In particular, anyone who claimed this name refused to worship the state gods, and that was widely known to be a problem.

E. Athenagoras then names the three charges typically associated with the name of *Christian*: atheism, Thyestian feasts (that is, cannibalism), and Oedipean intercourse (that is, incest) (ch. 3).

F. He proceeds to show that the charges are without foundation, one by one.

G. It is not true that Christians are atheists.
1. Atheists were rare in the ancient world.
2. There were certain groups that were called "atheists" including the Epicureans, who believed that, at death, the body's atoms disperse so there is no afterlife.
3. Minucius Felix points out that unlike other "atheists" of the ancient world, Christians were not complete materialists but distinguished God from matter (ch. 4).
4. This might be a reference to the Epicureans who believed the gods were made up of atoms like the rest of the universe.
5. Moreover, Minucius Felix continues, Christians actually have more than one "God," even though God is "one," because God has a Son who is also worshiped.
6. In addition, Christians worship the Spirit as divine and acknowledge the existence of other supernatural beings.
7. It is true that Christians do not worship these divine beings through animal sacrifices, but that, in fact, shows the superiority of their religion (ch. 10).
8. Moreover, other peoples in the empire are allowed to worship their own gods: Christians alone should not be isolated as worthy of punishment (ch. 14).

H. It is also not true that Christians engage in grossly immoral acts.
1. Athenagoras suggests that pagans who make this charge against Christians must be thinking about the activities of their own gods (ch. 32)!
2. In fact, Christians are highly moral, not allowing even the *thoughts* of immoral activities, let alone indulgence of the activities themselves (ch. 33).
3. Far from engaging in infanticide and cannibalism, Christians don't even watch gladiatorial contests or expose their children (ch. 35).

I. In short, none of the charges against the Christians can be held up to scrutiny; therefore, Christians should not be punished by the state.

III. There were other stock arguments used by other apologists throughout the 2nd and 3rd centuries.

    A. Some others argued that Christianity is proved to be true by the fact that Christ fulfilled prophecies made about him hundreds of years before he was born.

    B. Yet others argued that there should be a strict separation of Church and state, that the state apparatus should not be involved with matters of personal religion.

        1. This latter was an argument that most people in the ancient world would have found nonsensical.

        2. It's worth noting that as soon as the Roman emperor became Christian, theologians stopped making this argument!

IV. But it wasn't until this conversion of the emperor that the need for Christian apologies ceased, in the early years of the 4th century.

Essential Reading:

Bart D. Ehrman, ed., *After The New Testament: A Reader* pp. 51–94.

Robert M. Grant, *Greek Apologists of the Second Century.*

Supplementary Reading:

Arthur Droge, *Moses or Homer: Early Christian Interpretations of the History of Culture.*

Robert Wilken, *The Christians as the Romans Saw Them.*

Questions to Consider:

1. How might a pagan have argued against Athenagoras's claim that Christians should not be persecuted simply for their "name"?

2. How might different people living in different countries today react to the apologists' insistence that the state not be involved with matters of religion?

Lecture Twenty-Two—Transcript
Apologetics in Early Christianity

In the preceding lecture, we began to see how Christians started writing apologies for the faith in the mid-2nd century. An apology is a reasoned defense from the Greek word, "apologia," a defense of the faith against its cultured despisers. Christians needed to defend their faith because they were a persecuted minority within the Roman Empire.

We can get a fuller sense of the charges widely leveled against the Christians from some of these apologies, especially one that is called the *Octavius*, written by Minucius Felix. Minucius Felix was a Christian intellectual living in Latin-speaking North Africa in the second half of the 2nd century. His work, the *Octavius*, records an imaginary conversation that took place between a pagan named Caecilian and a Christian named Octavius, about the nature of the Christian religion.

Now this form of writing would have been very familiar to people in the ancient world because frequently in ancient philosophical discourses a treatise would be set up as a conversation between two or more individuals who would be talking about some issue of importance, and so you find similar ways of setting up conversation, for example, in the writings of Plato, the dialogues of Plato, or in Plutarch or in other philosophically oriented authors.

And so the *Octavius* is using this common form of a conversation to write an apology because one of the conversationalists will be a pagan who's trying to attack Christianity intellectually and a Christian who's trying to defend Christianity intellectually. And, of course, as happens in Plato's dialogues, where Socrates is confronting somebody else on some issue or another, Socrates of course always wins. Well, that's because Plato is writing it, and Socrates was his teacher and his key figure. So of course he makes Socrates win all of these discussions. Well, that's what happens in the *Octavius* by Minucius Felix. Minucius Felix himself is a Christian, and so he stages this conversation between the Christian and the non-Christian and the Christian seems to get the better of the argument.

In the course of their discussion back and forth, we find a graphic and vivid description of some of the charges that are leveled against

Christians by pagans in the 2nd century. These charges will sound surprising to many Christians today, but they were widely believed in antiquity.

Christians, according to the charges spelled out by Caecilian, Christians engaged in sexual license together, including incest, infanticide, and even cannibalism. Let me read you several passages from Minucius Felix's book the *Octavius*, where Caecilian is talking, where he says, "The Christians recognize each other by secret marks and signs. Hardly have they met when they love each other, throughout the world, uniting in the practice of a veritable religion of lusts. Indiscriminately they call each other brother and sister, thus turning even ordinary fornication into incest by the intervention of these hallowed names." So what is that about? They greet one another with secret signs. They call one another brothers and sisters and then engage in incest.

Well, Christians of course did call one another brothers and sisters because they understood that they all belonged to the new family of faith. They greet one another with signs—well, that's probably a reference to the circumstance that Christians met in secret and didn't let non-Christians join them. How do you know if everybody present in the room is a Christian? Well, there may have been some kind of secret handshake or some such thing, as is sometimes described by other Christian authors. And what is the business of committing incest? Well remember, Christians greet one another with a kiss and they have, as part of their ritual service during their worship, a kiss of greeting—a peace kiss. This has been taken to an extreme by pagan authors who know that these brothers and sisters are getting together in secret societies and kissing one another. And they draw the conclusion that in fact they are committing incest.

The author goes on to say that, "It is also reported that the Christians worship the genitals of their pontiff and priest, adoring, it appears, the sex of their father." Worshiping the genitals of the priest—what is that about? That may be a reference to when somebody is being blessed by the priest, he kneels down before the priest and the priest puts his hand on his head. To an outsider, it looks like then the person kneeling is adoring the genitals because the face is right in front of the priest's genital area. And so they claim that's what the Christians are engaged in, is genital worship.

He then goes on and gives probably the most gory aspect of his description, one that has become most famous among scholars, "To turn to another point," Caecilian says, "the notoriety of the stories told of the initiation of new recruits is matched by their ghastly horror. A young baby is covered over with flour, the object being to deceive the unwary. It is then served before the person to be admitted into their rites. The recruit is urged to inflict blows upon it. They appear to be harmless because of the covering of flour. Thus, the baby is killed with wounds that remain unseen and concealed. It is the blood of this infant—I shutter to mention it—it is this blood that they lick with thirsty lips. These are the limbs they distribute eagerly. This is the victim by which they seal their covenant. It is by complicity in this crime that they are pledged to mutual silence. These are their rites, more foul than all sacrilegious combined. And so they engage in infanticide and cannibalism as an initiation rite." What is this all about? Well, Christians were known to engage in a ritual in which they ate the flesh and drank the blood of the Son of God.

That seems to be interpreted in a rather perverse way here by an outsider who doesn't really understand what it means to eat the flesh and drink the blood of the Son of God. The flesh is represented by the flour, which is of course made into bread, and so this represents the bread. The blood of course comes from the infant, and so he imagines if they're eating an infant, they have to kill it first. And so there must be a ritual sacrifice of this infant and then an eating of it. And so this is what Christians do when they are initiated into the religion, probably referring to the First Eucharist that people are allowed to participate in after they've been baptized, and so it's an initiation ritual. And so they don't understand that in fact this is a meal in which they commemorate the death of Jesus by eating bread and drinking wine together.

He goes on, "We all know too about their banquets. They're on everyone's lips everywhere, as the speech of our early Caecilian testifies. On a special day, they gather for a feast with all their children, sisters, mothers—all sexes and all ages. There, flushed with a banquet after such feasting and drinking, they begin to burn with incestuous passions. They provoke a dog tied to the lamp stand to leap and bound towards a scrap of food which they've tossed outside the reach of the chain. By this means the light is overturned and extinguished and, with it, common knowledge of their actions. In the shameless dark with unspeakable lust, they copulate in random unions, all equally being guilty of incest, some by deed, but everyone by complicity."

And so they have these nocturnal feasts. And so this activity that's being described is sometimes talked about in shorthand in some early sources as "putting out the lights" or "extinguishing the lights." And the idea is you're eating outside, and you have this big festival, so, according to him, everybody is getting drunk. And then the light is provided by torches that are on stands, literally, burning torches. And they have dogs who are leashed to these torches. And then when it comes time, they take a piece of meat and throw it beyond the reach of the dog's chain so the dog runs after it and, in so doing, knocks over the light. And so it turns everything dark and then they're free to engage in random copulation. And so that's called "extinguishing the lights" or "putting out the lights."

And so this author knows that these Christians are engaged in such activities because Christians are known to worship in the dark. Remember, we saw earlier that Christians would often come together before it was light to have their worship services. They engage in a ritual kiss. They call one another brothers and sisters, and so this is the kind of wild activity that Christians are engaged in according to Caecilian in Minucius Felix's the *Octavius*.

This is the kind of charge that many pagans took quite seriously. They might seem incredible to us in a world where many people who are Christian consider themselves to be more moral than other people, and Christianity of course is a religion based to a great extent on high ethical values, so these charges against Christians might seem credible, that anybody would think such a thing. But they were in fact believable in a world that knew that Christians met in secret society under the cover of darkness where brothers and sisters covered one another with kisses and ate the flesh and drank the blood of the Son of God.

Now on top of all of these kinds of ethical charges of immorality against the Christians, Christians were widely considered to be, as I pointed out earlier, atheists; that is, they were without the gods in that Christians rejected the gods that were otherwise worshiped by pagans in the empire. Christian apologists then had to defend themselves against charges such as this, to show that Christians were not an immoral group that committed incest and infanticide and cannibalism, that, in fact, Christians were highly moral and that they were not atheists. They in fact did worship god, but they thought there was only one true God. This was the burden then of the apologists, to attempt to defend themselves against the charges widely leveled against them.

To get a fuller sense of how Christian intellectuals proceeded in writing their apologies, we would do well to consider one particular instance—an apology written by a man named Athenagoras, who was a Christian philosopher from Athens. Athenagoras wrote a book called Plea Regarding the Christians in about the year A.D. 177, so in the second half of the 2nd century. Like many apologies, Athenagoras's is written to address the reigning Roman emperors. In this case, his book is written to address Marcus Aurelius and Commodus, who were joint emperors for a time during the 2nd century.

I should indicate, as I pointed out in the previous lecture, that it's unlikely that these emperors actually read such literature. Even if Athenagoras meant for them to read this literature, it's unlikely that they ever did so. It may be best to consider this apology of Athenagoras to be a kind of open letter to the all-powerful rulers of the state, or even to be in-house literature providing Christians themselves with ammunition for their battle against their opponents. This is what happens today, by the way. There continued to be Christian apologists—people who tried to defend Christianity intellectually and show that on intellectual grounds, Christianity is superior to every religion and to atheism. And so there are still apologists today, especially among evangelical Christians.

But these apologists in fact aren't writing for people to convince them that Christianity is right. Usually they're writing for Christian insiders, who are given ammunition then with which to approach their non-Christian friends. And so, even today, popular apologists are defending the faith for insiders, rather than for outsiders.

So we turn to the apology of Athenagoras, written in the year 177. The apology is called *Plea Regarding the Christians*—a plea regarding the Christians. And it begins by the author addressing his two imperial readers: "To the Emperors Marcus Aurelius Antoninus and Lucius Aurelius Commodus, conquerors of Armenia and

Sarmatia and, what is more important, philosophers." Okay, so he's acknowledging that these two emperors are philosophers, and if they're philosophers, they'll of course literally be lovers of truth, which is what the word "philosopher" means, somebody who loves the truth. And if they love the truth, then of course they will be open to the truth, as this author will be laying it out.

This author begins with a statement that Christians are completely innocent and have suffered unjustly at the hands of society. He points out that there are a wide range of religions throughout the Roman Empire but most of them experience equal rights before the law, that Christians alone are isolated as worthy of suffering, and this doesn't seem fair. If there's a wide range of religions, why is Christianity pointed out as being anything distinctive that deserves to be oppressed?

This author points out that it doesn't make sense to punish Christians for simply having a name—the name "Christian." But instead, if there's to be any punishment, the punishment should be for actual crimes. And so he says, for example, in chapter 2: "If the accusation goes no farther than a name, and it's clear that up to today the tales about us rest only on popular and uncritical rumor, and not a single Christian has been convicted of wrongdoing, then it's your duty, illustrious kind and most learned Emperors, to relieve us of these calamities by law." In other words, you should pass a law that there should be no persecution of Christians. "For," he says, "with us, the mere name appears to be of more weight than legal proof. Is this legally satisfying that just by being called something we're worthy of punishment? We should not be hated and punished because we are called Christians. For what has a name to do with our being criminals?—rather should we be tried on charges." And so he's insisting that they be tried not for the name but on charges.

If you remember, I've discussed the earlier incident with Pliny the Younger during the reign of the Emperor Trajan, where Pliny would interrogate somebody to ask if he or she was a Christian. And if they said yes or no, he would bring in a statue of the emperor and ask them to perform a sacrifice to it. If they wouldn't, if they refused to perform a sacrifice, then he would know this person is a Christian. And since he was a Christian, or she was a Christian, he would order them to be killed.

So on one level, that's being killed simply because you have the name "Christian." This author is claiming having a name shouldn't kill you. It should be for doing something that's illegal. This shows by the way, that being a Christian was not illegal, because he's able to argue on these grounds. In fact, the Christians are being persecuted not because they happen to be called "Christian" but because of what being called "Christian" really meant. What it meant was, you didn't worship the state gods. And so I'm not sure that this particular argument would hold much sway with polytheists who were intent on persecuting the Christians.

Athenagoras goes on to name the three charges that are typically associated with the name "Christian," chapter 3: "Three charges are brought against us: atheism, Thyestean feasts"—that means cannibalism—"and Oedipean intercourse" from Oedipus, meaning incest." If these are true," says the author, "then spare no class. Proceed against our crimes. Destroy us utterly. But if these charges are inventions and unfounded slanders, they arise from the fact that it is natural for vice to oppose virtue"—a clever little line.

So try us to find out whether we're guilty of atheism and cannibalism and incest. If you find that we're not guilty, well, then, that would make sense because, of course, for Athenagoras, we're virtuous, and who is opposed to those who are virtuous? those who are filled with vice. And so you're punishing the wrong people. It's a clever way of putting it.

He goes on to take these charges apart, one by one, in order to show that they, in fact, don't hold up. To begin with, it's not true that Christians are atheists. Now, as I've indicated in an earlier lecture, what we think of as atheists didn't really exist very often in the ancient world. There are very few people who would come out and say there is no God. There were certain groups who were called atheists, however. There was a group of philosophers that are sometimes called atheists, who were the Epicurean philosophers.

Epicureans have a bad reputation in the modern world because it's thought that Epicureans were out just for their own pleasure—that they were hedonists. But that's not really true about the ancient Epicureans. The ancient Epicureans thought that when a person dies, their atoms in their body go back to be redistributed among the atoms in the universe. In other words, people's bodies dissolve, and you return back to a disparate state in which the atoms are no longer coherent to a body and soul. So there's no afterlife for the Epicureans.

The Epicureans thought, therefore, since there's no afterlife, you should enjoy life in the here and now. But they were not hedonists. They didn't urge that you engage in wild licentious pleasure, because with wild pleasure comes a lot of pain. You should try, in fact, to foster the simple pleasures in life. And so you should eat well, but you shouldn't eat too much. You should drink good quality wine, but don't drink too much wine. Don't get drunk; you get drunk, you get a hangover. And so that's pain. You don't want pain, so don't get drunk. You should engage in interesting conversation with groups of friends and family. And so these were the kinds of pleasures that the Epicureans believed in.

The Epicureans believed that there were gods, but the gods are like us, made up of atoms. And the gods will eventually also disperse; their atoms will disperse. They live much, much longer than humans do, but their atoms eventually disperse. But the gods are not involved with human affairs. The gods have their own things to be worried about. They're also enjoying their existence, and so they don't interact with humans. And so, since the Epicureans thought that the gods didn't interact with humans, they were sometimes called atheists. Christians too were sometimes called atheists. Christians are atheists because of course they don't believe in the traditional gods; they are without the gods.

Athenagoras wants to argue that in fact Christians are not atheists, and he comes up with a number of arguments to try and show that Christians are not atheists. He begins by saying, "Is it not mad to charge us with atheism when we distinguish God from matter and show that matter is one thing and God another and that there's a vast difference between them?" Now this might be kind of a slight reference to the Epicureans, who were called atheists, because the Epicureans thought that the gods are made up of atoms, just as humans are made up of atoms, just as everything in our universe is made up of atoms.

But Christians don't think that. Christians differentiate between God, on the one hand, and matter, on the other hand, so don't lump us with those atheistic Epicureans. Our teaching affirms that there is one God who made the universe, being himself uncreated. So we believe in God. But more than that, we also think that God has a son. The Son of God is his word in idea and in actuality, for by Him and through Him were all things made, the father and son being one. So you have God the Father and you have God the Son. But in addition, we say that the Holy Spirit himself, who inspires those who had prophecies is an effluence from God. So we also have a Holy Spirit.

Who then would not be astonished to hear those called atheists who admit God the Father, God the Son, and God the Holy Spirit and who teach their unity and power and their distinction and rank? So we don't have three gods, but we have three persons who are distinct from one another who are all God. So how can we be atheists?

Moreover, he says, "We affirm to a crowd of angels and ministers whom God has appointed to several tasks. We have supernatural beings. We have a God in three persons. How could we possibly be called atheists?" And so this is his argument against the initial charge.

The author wants to go on then and argue that Christians do not worship their divine beings that they have through animal sacrifices the way pagans worshiped their divine beings. This, though, doesn't show that Christians are atheists because they don't perform sacrifices to the gods; this simply shows that Christianity is superior. Are we to think that the creator of heaven and earth needs sacrifices of animals? What would he need them for? Pagans seemed to presuppose that the gods are satisfied when they have offerings made to them. Well, what kind of god is it that needs satisfaction by the burning of an animal? And so Athenagoras concludes that Christians, in fact, are not atheist at all and that they have a superior form of Christian worship.

He moves on then later in his book, in chapters 31 and 32 and following, to take up the moral charges against the Christians, that they engage in these wild licentious activities. He starts out on kind of a sarcastic note by saying, "It's nothing surprising that our accusers should invent the same tales about us that they tell of their own gods." This is a clever remark because "You accuse us of incest. Well, what about the myths of the Roman gods and the Greek gods? Had they wanted to judge shameless and indiscriminate intercourse as a frightful thing, they should have hated Zeus. For it's in the myths, Zeus had children from his own mother Rhea and his daughter, Kore, and he married his own sister. You want to talk about incest, you look at Zeus, the king of the gods. So you're charging us with the things that your own gods are guilty of."

He goes on to say, "We, however, do not commit incest at all." What he tries to argue is that Christians don't engage in immoral activities because Christianity is rooted in a very strict code of morality. According to the Christian ethical code, it's wrong to engage in immoral activities; it's wrong even to harbor the thought of immoral activity.

So he says, for example, "But we on the contrary are so far from viewing such crimes as incest with indifference that we're not even allowed to indulge a lustful glance." And so he quotes Jesus that, "The law says don't commit adultery. I say to you, don't even lust after a woman in your heart." "So we go beyond moral, we don't even entertain lustful thoughts." He then refers to the kiss of the Christians where the kiss is part of the Christian worship, and he points out that according to the scriptures somebody should not kiss a second time. This, in fact, is not found anywhere in scripture. He quotes it as if it's found in scripture, but he's trying to emphasize that we have a very chaste kiss during our worship services. And it happens only once, so we're not engaging in these incestuous activities.

Moreover, as far as the charges of infanticide and cannibalism go, he wants to show once again that Christians not only don't engage in these activities; they don't engage in activities that pagans engage in that could lead them to the same charges, or similar charges. For example, it was common, of course, in the Roman Empire for people in large cities to go watch the gladiatorial contests, where men would be pitted against one another to fight, and sometimes, of course, men would die. And this was considered to be entertainment. Christians refused to even watch gladiators contend against one another. This shows that they're not interested in killing, let alone killing one another.

With respect to killing, this author points out that it's common in the ancient world to expose children. If a child is born and the parents don't want the child, they leave the child in a public place, hoping that somebody will pick it up. The person picking it up by the way may be picking it up because they're going to need a future slave in ten or fifteen years, and so they'll raise the child to be a slave sometimes. Christians don't do that. Christians don't expose their children.

So Christians are not engaged in these accusations against them of incest and murder and cannibalism. In fact, Christians have a highly moral religion. In short, for Athenagoras, none of the charges against the Christians can be held up to scrutiny and, therefore, in his view, Christians should not be punished by the state.

I should point out that there were other stock arguments used by other apologists, including the Letter to Diognetus, throughout the 2nd and 3rd centuries. Some argued, as I pointed out in the previous lecture, that Christianity is proved to be true by the fact that Christ fulfilled prophecies made about him hundreds of years before he was born.

There are others who argue that there should be a strict separation of church and state. This is very interesting. To the best of my knowledge, this is the first time anybody made this argument, that the church [sic state] should not be involved with affairs of religion, that the state apparatus should not be interfering with one's personal beliefs and practices. This argument was one that most people in the ancient world would have found to be nonsensical because of course the state is involved in the worship of the gods because the gods made the state great.

It's also worth noting that Christian apologists made this argument of separation of church and state until the state became Christian. Once the emperor converted to Christianity, then the apologists stopped making those arguments. In fact, everybody stopped making those arguments.

It wasn't until this conversion of the emperor—the Emperor Constantine specifically—that the need for Christian apologies, the need itself, actually ceased in the early years of the 4th century. That was when Christians no longer needed to defend the faith and intellectuals among the Christians could then turn their minds to other things and begin to work seriously on the various theological issues that still needed to be resolved; and that occupied Christian thinkers all the way down to the Middle Ages.

Lecture Twenty-Three
The Apostolic Fathers as a Collection

Scope:

In this lecture, we will begin to wrap up the series by considering several of the key overarching issues that have emerged from our study of the Apostolic Fathers, especially as these relate to the emergence of Christianity as a world religion. How is it that Christianity became the kind of religion that it did? Why did it shift so radically away from the teachings of the historical Jesus himself? What kind of religion had it become by the middle of the 2nd century, some 120 years after Jesus' death?

In particular, we will consider what the Apostolic Fathers can tell us about the three pillars of the emerging Christian Church: the canon of Scripture, the creed to be confessed by all Christians, and the clerical hierarchy within the Church.

Outline

I. We have covered a broad range of material in these lectures on the Apostolic Fathers. I can begin summarizing what we have discovered by stressing the wide diversity one finds in this collection of authors.

   A. The books themselves deal with a wide range of issues.
      1. 1 Clement is an attempt of the church of Rome to reverse an ecclesiastical coup in the church of Corinth.
      2. 2 Clement is a sermon encouraging its hearers to rejoice in the salvation they have received.
      3. The Letters of Ignatius are written in haste to several congregations of Asia Minor, urging them to avoid false teachers and to adhere to the authority of their bishop.
      4. The Letter of Polycarp is addressed to the Christians of Philippi, giving them advice about how to live in community together.
      5. The Martyrdom of Polycarp is an eyewitness account of the arrest, trial, and death of the bishop of Smyrna.
      6. The Letter of Barnabas is focused on the relationship of Christianity to Judaism, arguing that the Jewish religion is and always has been a colossal mistake.

7. The Didache is a Church order that gives instructions about how to live, how to perform Christian rituals, and what to do about wandering prophets who were taking advantage of the communities they visited.

8. The fragments of Papias contain apocryphal accounts of the sayings and deeds of Jesus and his followers.

9. The Shepherd of Hermas is an apocalypse that describes visions of the author that are meant to encourage believers in their lives on Earth and to urge them to repent before the end arrives.

10. The Letter to Diognetus is an apology that defends Christianity against the charges of its cultured critics and argues that the Christian religion is, in fact, superior to all others.

B. These books are of different genres: several letters, a sermon, a martyrology, a Church order, a fragmentary commentary, an apocalypse, and an apology.

C. They come from a range of dates, from the end of the 1st century (1 Clement) to, probably, near the end of the 2nd (the Letter to Diognetus).

D. How, then, does it make sense to collect these works together into a body of writings and circulate them as "the" Apostolic Fathers?

II. Even though this collection was made in relatively modern times, there is evidence of some movements toward collecting some of these works together from the earliest of times.

A. The Letters of Ignatius, for example, were evidently collected first by none other than Polycarp.

B. Some biblical manuscripts contain a couple of these works.

C. And Codex Constantinopolitanus, for example, contains 1 and 2 Clement, the Didache, the Epistle of Barnabas, and the Letters of Ignatius.

III. Nonetheless, most of these writings were unknown and unread throughout most of the history of Christianity.

A. In the early centuries of Christianity, some of these works were regarded as Scripture (for example, The Shepherd and the Letter of Barnabas).

B. Eventually, however, the canon of the New Testament was formed without them.

C. Most of them were forgotten for centuries, through the Middle Ages and even the Reformation.

    1. Even though some of them were known in the 16th century, Protestants and Catholics were not particularly interested in them.

    2. Protestants were completely obsessed with Scripture (*sola Scriptura*) and Catholics were more interested in the later "great" theologians, such as Jerome and Augustine.

D. In the 17th century, however, interest shifted to a concern for what the earliest Christian writings outside the New Testament had to say.

    1. In part, this shift was fueled by the discovery of new manuscripts, such as Codex Alexandrinus, which contained 1 and 2 Clement, in 1627.

    2. In part, it was generated by a concern on all sides to show the antiquity of their particular theological and ecclesiastical views.

    3. Nowhere is this concern more evident than in the debates between the famous scholar James Ussher and John Milton over the legitimacy of the Church hierarchy.

    4. The debates, which raged in Britain in the 1640s were over the legitimacy of the church hierarchy.

    5. When the Reformation came to Britain, bishops and archbishops remained extremely powerful in the Church of England.

    6. The widely popular Calvinist movement—especially as embodied by radical Puritans—resented this power. They wanted the church to abandon its hierarchical system, which they saw as a corruption of the teaching of the apostles.

    7. The advocates of the established church argued that ecclesiastical offices were supremely endowed with apostolic authority.

    8. John Ussher was an archbishop and brilliant scholar, whose name was tarnished when he tried to claim that the world had begun in 4004 B.C.

9. Ussher held that the episcopacy was a divinely ordained institution. He included as evidence for his claim certain so-called "Letters of Ignatius" that Milton argued were forgeries.

10. Eventually, Ussher was vindicated on the grounds that his evidence also included the seven Letters of Ignatius that were known to be authentic.

IV. Largely as a result of these debates, there developed an interest in collecting the earliest non-canonical writings together.

    A. The first collection was made by a French scholar, Cotelier, in 1672.

    B. Various collections were made at the end of the 17th and throughout the 18th and 19th centuries.

    C. Different scholars had different criteria for deciding which books to include in the collection.

        1. Some thought that any works, forged or genuine, associated with the early non-canonical authors should be included.

        2. Others maintained that only genuine works produced by those who were actually companions of the apostles should be included.

        3. Both criteria are problematic on historical grounds: On the one hand, why would the forgeries be useful? But on the other hand, what if none of the authors was actually a companion of the apostles?

    D. The question of criteria continues to be debated today: If, for example, the oldest non-canonical writings are to be collected together, should this include early Christian apocrypha, such as the Gospel of Thomas?

    E. Probably the best solution is to include the earliest proto-orthodox writings from after the New Testament period, which are traditionally found in the collection.

V. In significant ways, then, this collection is similar to, but different from, the writings that make up the New Testament.

    A. The New Testament, too, is an ad hoc collection of writings of different genre, dates, authors, and emphases.

    B. But it is an *ancient* collection.

C. And it is seen as an *authoritative* collection.

D. By contrast, the Apostolic Fathers is a modern and merely useful collection of early Christian writings from proto-orthodox circles.

Essential Reading:

Bart D. Ehrman, ed., "General Introduction," in *The Apostolic Fathers*, vol. 1, pp. 1–16.

Clayton Jefford, *Reading the Apostolic Fathers: An Introduction*, pp. 1–10.

Supplementary Reading:

L. W. Barnard, *Studies in the Apostolic Fathers and Their Background*.

Simon Tugwell, *The Apostolic Fathers*.

Questions to Consider:

1. What do you see as the historical function of having such a disparate group of writings collected together and given a name (the Apostolic Fathers)?

2. If a 1st-century writing from, say, the apostle Paul were to turn up, do you think it should be included in the New Testament? Or could it be included in the Apostolic Fathers instead?

Lecture Twenty-Three—Transcript
The Apostolic Fathers as a Collection

We've covered a broad range of material in these lectures on the Apostolic Fathers. I can begin summarizing what we've discovered by stressing the wide diversity one finds in this collection of authors. The books themselves, as we've seen them, deal with a wide range of issues from early to mid-2nd-century Christianity. So I'll give you actually a summary of the things that we've looked at to this point to refresh your memory and to set up what I want to do in the rest of this lecture.

The first book we looked at was First Clement. First Clement is a letter written by the church of Rome to the Christians in the church of Corinth that attempts to reverse an ecclesiastical coup that had taken place there. We don't know what this coup was all about exactly. We don't know who ousted whom, but it does appear that people who had been appointed presbyters either by the apostles or their successors in Corinth had been removed from office and a group of upstarts, at least in the opinion of the author of First Clement, had taken their place as rulers of the church. The book of First Clement is meant to reinstate the presbyters to their place of authority and urges the people who are reading the letter not to engage in acts of jealousy, but to strive for unity, which can come only when the properly appointed authorities are in power.

The letter of Second Clement is a sermon. It's not a letter at all, even though it's called the letter of Second Clement, It's a sermon, probably the first sermon from outside the New Testament to survive. This sermon is based on an interpretation and exposition of an Old Testament text, Isaiah, chapter 54, in which the anonymous author encourages his hearers to rejoice in the salvation that they have received And so it's a celebration of the salvation that they've received in Christ and an exhortation for them to stay faithful to the salvation.

Next, we considered the letters of Ignatius. These are letters that were written in haste to several congregations of Asia Minor by Ignatius of Antioch, the bishop who had been arrested for Christian activities and was being sent to Rome in order to face the wild beasts. En route, he wrote seven letters. These letters urged their hearers to avoid false teachers and to adhere to the authority of the bishop. In addition, we saw Ignatius's letter to the Romans sent to the Christians in Rome urging them not to intervene with the proceedings against Ignatius when he arrived in town because Ignatius, in fact, wants to be martyred by being thrown to the wild beasts.

The letter of Polycarp is addressed to the Christians of the church of Philippi. These Christians of Philippi have asked Polycarp for some advice about some practical issues in the church involving false teaching and possibly a case of embezzlement of funds. Polycarp provides them with advice about how to live in community together. The martyrdom of Polycarp is written several decades after the letter of Polycarp. The martyrdom of Polycarp is an eyewitness account of the arrest, trial and death of the Bishop of Smyrna, Polycarp. And so as I've indicated previously, Polycarp is rather well known to us because we have a letter sent to him by Ignatius, a letter sent by him to the Philippians and then a book written about him, specifically about his execution and death. This martyrologe is the first martyrologe—first account—of a martyrdom we have from outside the New Testament in early Christianity, and it's designed to show that Polycarp's death was in conformity with the gospel, meaning that he emulated Christ in his death, as the readers should do as well.

The letter of Barnabas is focused on the relationship of Christianity to Judaism. It's actually written anonymously, although it's been attributed to Paul's companion, Barnabas. The thesis of the letter is that the Jewish religion is, and always has been, a colossal mistake. Jews have misunderstood their religion from the very beginning because the covenant—the agreement—that God made with the Jews was broken as soon as it was made. Moses smashed the two tablets of the covenant when he came down off of Mount Sinai, and the covenant was never restored to the Jews. As a result, they completely misunderstood the laws that God gave Moses, thinking that they are to be interpreted literally to guide their worship and life together, when, in fact, these laws were meant to be taken figuratively. For Barnabas, the Old Testament, in fact, is a Christian, not a Jewish book.

The Didache is a book that was discovered in relatively modern times, near the end of the 19th century. It is unlike the other books of the Apostolic Fathers in that it is a church order that gives instructions to its readers about how to live together as Christians—

how to perform their Christian rituals, such as baptism and the Eucharist—and what to do about wandering prophets and apostles who appear to have been taking advantage of the various communities that they visited.

We also considered the fragments of Papias, a shadowy figure from the early 2nd century, who wrote a five-volume work on An Exposition of the Sayings of the Lord. These expositions contained apocryphal accounts of the sayings and deeds of Jesus and his followers. Unfortunately, we have these accounts only in snippets as they're quoted by later Christian authors.

We then looked at The Shepherd of Hermas, a very long apocalypse that describes visions of the author, which are interpreted to him by an angelic mediator who comes to him in the guise of a shepherd. These visions are meant to encourage believers in their life in the here and now and to urge them to repent before the end of all things comes. Finally, we looked at the letter to Diognetus. This is an apology that defends Christianity against the charges of its cultured critics and argues that the Christian religion is in fact superior to all others.

It should be clear upon this review of what we've covered in this course, these books of the Apostolic Fathers are of different genres. Some of them are letters; one of them is a sermon; another is a martyrologe. They include a church order, a fragmentary commentary on scripture, an apocalypse, and an apology. Moreover, they're diverse, not only in terms of genre but also in terms of date for they come from a range of dates from the end of the 1st century. First Clement is usually thought to have been written around the year 95 or 96 or so, although it's just a guesstimate, but there are pretty good reasons for thinking that's about when it was written; whereas, with the letter to Diognetus, we're probably dealing with something written in the second half of the 2nd century. We're not sure exactly when because, as I've indicated previously, it's hard to date ancient writings unless they make some reference to external events, and the letter to Diognetus does not refer to anything specific that allows us to pinpoint its date. But it does look like it was written probably in the second half of the 2nd century and possibly Second Clement is also written at about that time, making them probably the latest among the Apostolic Fathers. So we're dealing with books that are spread out over something like 80, 90 years.

How then does it make sense to collect these books together into one body of writings and circulate them together as the Apostolic Fathers? Even though this collection was made in relatively modern times, as we'll see, there's evidence that there was some movement toward collecting some of these works together and circulating them as a group from even the ancient world. I'll give you a couple of examples of how some of the Apostolic Fathers were circulating together and being seen as a group of writings.

The letters of Ignatius are the most obvious example because, as we've seen, the letters of Ignatius were collected by none other than Polycarp himself. The Christians in Philippi had asked Polycarp for a collection of Ignatius's letters, and he sent a collection to them, which would have included the letters that Polycarp had written to Smyrna, where Polycarp was—so the letter of Polycarp and the letter of the Smyrnians—and would have included the four letters that Ignatius wrote while he was in Smyrna. So that's four of the other letters. So at least six of the seven letters of Ignatius were collected already sometime in the early 2nd century.

It's also worth noting that we have Biblical manuscripts that contain several of these works as a group, for example, Codex Alexandrinus, discovered in the early 17th century. A 5th-century manuscript of the New Testament also contains 1 and Second Clement. The manuscript called Codex Sinaiticus, discovered in the 19th century, contains both The Shepherd of Hermas and Barnabas, apparently again as parts of the New Testament scripture. So sometimes several of the Apostolic Fathers are combined with books of the New Testament and considered scriptural.

And we have one manuscript, which is called Codex Constantinopolitanus, which is written in the year 1096. We know it's written in the year 1096 because the scribe actually adds a note indicating when he was doing his writing. Constantinopolitanus, written in 1096, contains First and Second Clement, the Didache, the letter of Barnabas, and the letters of Ignatius. This shows that some of these works that we today call Apostolic Fathers were in circulation together in the Middle Ages.

Nonetheless, most of these writings were unknown and unread throughout most of the history of Christianity, and, I might add, most of them are unknown and unread by most Christians today. Most Christians have never heard of these books, even though they're extremely important for understanding the development of Christianity after the New Testament period. But, in fact, they continue to be widely unknown.

In the early centuries of the church, I should point out though, that some of these books were considered to be scripture. In other words, these were very important books for some Christians early on. Clement of Alexandria, for example, considers The Shepherd of Hermas and the letter of Barnabas to be scripture. And we've seen some Biblical manuscripts contain some of these works of scripture.

Eventually though, when the canon of the New Testament came to be finalized, which was sometime probably—it's hard to put an exact date on when to say the canon of the New Testament was finalized because there was never a vote that was taken in the early church to decide these 27 books and only these 27 books. There was no ecumenical council, no worldwide council that decided the matter. But by the 5th century, at least, most Christians in most places agreed on our 27 books. When that happened, these 27 books of course did not include any of the writings that we now call the writings of the Apostolic Fathers.

As a result, most of these books came to be forgotten for centuries through the Middle Ages and even down into the Reformation. Even though that was the case, some of these books were known in the 16th century during the Protestant Reformation. And now just to give a brief historical background: As you know, in the early 16th century, Martin Luther broke with the Roman Catholic Church, leading to what we call the Protestant Reformation. The Reformation was called "Reformation" because Protestants did not understand that they were starting a new religion. They understood that they were reforming the church. There are a lot of important aspects to the Protestant Reformation. The one that is of most importance for us in this present context is the importance that the Protestants put on the writings of scripture as opposed to their Catholic opponents.

Protestants came to believe that the Catholic Church was run too much by traditions that had developed after the New Testament period, that the dogmas and the doctrines that developed after New Testament times had become as authoritative as the writings of scripture themselves. Martin Luther was quite insistent that the only authority—the only final authority—for all Christian faith and practice was scripture itself, that scripture was the Word of God, or contained the Word of God and that the later developments within Christianity are traditions which have no authoritative bearing. In Luther's term, the authority for all Christian practice and belief is *sola Scriptura*, scripture alone.

This naturally led Protestants to become more avidly trained in Biblical studies. And one can make the case that the discipline of Biblical studies goes back all the way to the Reformation, the development of Biblical studies in the modern sense. The critical engagement with these texts is a Reformation project.

What happened to the Apostolic Fathers during the Reformation? Well you might think that early on in the Reformation, Protestants and Catholics would be interested in seeing what church fathers wrote in the period right after the New Testament. You might think that that would be of some interest for both Protestants and Catholics because Protestants then could claim that the Christian Church hadn't developed in any significant way like it did in the Middle Ages, by the time right after the New Testament, and Roman Catholics could point to developments within the Apostolic Fathers as leading to what happened in the Middle Ages. So you would think that the Apostolic Fathers would become a battleground in the early 16th century with Luther's Reformation, but, in fact, that didn't happen.

It didn't happen because the Protestants in the 16th century were far more interested in what scripture itself had to say, and anything after scripture was considered to be non-authoritative and so of little interest. The Roman Catholics, on the other hand, were not particularly interested in the earliest church writings because they were interested in the later great theologians of the church, like Jerome and Augustine. These figures were the ones who are the beginnings of theology for Catholic theologians, not their predecessors, who were thought to be rather naïve and unsophisticated in their theological affirmations. And so in the 16th century, the Apostolic Fathers simply were not an issue to any extent at all in the debate between Protestants and Catholics.

That actually started to change in the 17th century. There was a shift of concern in the 17th century toward what the earliest Christian writings outside the New Testament had to say. In part, this shift toward an interest in later writings—later than the New Testament—

this shift happened in part because of new manuscript discoveries, in particular the discovery of Codex Alexandrinus in the year 1627. As you know, Codex Alexandrinus is this 5th-century manuscript that was discovered and given by a church authority, Cyril Lucar, who was the patriarch of Constantinople, to the King of England. It was to be given to King James, but James died before the gift was actually delivered and so it arrived during the reign of King Charles I.

This manuscript of the New Testament contained within it, First and Second Clement, and it got people interested in some of these early writings then because here was this new manuscript that had turned up. And so manuscript discoveries explained some of the shift in the 17th century. Another explanation for the shift of interest was a concern on all sides, both Protestant and Catholic, and various forms of Protestant, to show the antiquity of their particular theological and ecclesiastical views.

Christians began to see that it would be important to show that their views, even if they're not found in the New Testament, nonetheless have antiquity to them and people could appeal to the Apostolic Fathers to show the roots of what later developed within Christianity. There were debates over the importance of the Apostolic Fathers for deciding ecclesiastical issues in the 17th century.

Nowhere is this concern more evident than in the debates that took place between one of the most famous scholars of the 17th century, a man names James Ussher, and one of the most famous authors in the English language, John Milton, author of *Paradise Lost*. This debate took place decades before Milton wrote *Paradise Lost,* when he was just a young man. It was the debate between James Ussher, an archbishop, and John Milton, who stood over against the Church of England as being himself a Puritan. The debate was over the legitimacy of the church hierarchy.

The debate raged throughout England actually in the 1640s throughout Great Britain in the early 1640s. When the Reformation hit England, British bishops and archbishops remained enormously powerful, even though they were no longer Catholic bishops and archbishops, but were bishops and archbishops in the Church of England. And the widely popular Calvinist movement, especially as it was embodied by the radical Puritans, resented the power that the bishops and the archbishops had in the Church of England. And so there were debates then between the bishops and archbishops on the one hand, and the radical Puritans on the other.

There were, in fact, petitions that were submitted to parliament in 1640 by the Puritans. These petitions were designed to force the church to abandon its Episcopal system. The Puritans wanted to turn the church into a Presbyterian model, where there would be elders in the church who would make decisions and you wouldn't have powerful bishops and archbishops. And there were a lot of pamphlets that went back and forth in the 1640s by representatives of both sides of this debate. This was in an age when pamphleteering was really quite a phenomenon, where, when you wrote a pamphlet, you would actually say what you thought of your intellectual opponent, and you would call him names. And so it is really quite delightful reading some of these pamphlets going back and forth in the 1640s.

On the one side of these debates then you have Puritan scholars, who saw the formation of the church hierarchy to be a later corruption of the teaching of the apostles. On the other side, you had advocates of the established church, who argued that ecclesiastical offices were supremely endowed with apostolic authority. James Ussher wasn't originally a part of this back and forth, but he did get dragged into the affair. He was an Irish ecclesiastic of Armagh and an extraordinary scholar, one of the most brilliant scholars of his age. I should say that Ussher's name has been tarnished in the years ever since because of a particular intellectual project that he pursued.

By comparing all of the genealogies of the Bible, who begat whom and how long this person lived and then that person begat so and so, and then that person lived so many years, and then begat so and so and lived so many years. He added up all the numbers of the genealogies, and wherever there were gaps, he appealed to Babylonian and Assyrian and Egyptian records, and he tried to calculate the number of years from the time of Jesus backwards to the time of creation, and he decided that creation occurred in the year 4004 B.C.—in fact, on October 23, at noon.

So this is where the idea came about that the world started in the year 4000 B.C., and so that probably wasn't his best academic endeavor. And it certainly has left his name to be tarnished, as people today think this is a bit of a ridiculous activity. But in his day, in fact, it was a fairly important achievement, just that science hadn't developed anything like it has till now. In any event, he was a remarkably erudite historian. He could read all these sources in their original languages—Greek, Latin, Hebrew, et cetera. But he was also an archbishop. He was an archbishop in the Church of England.

In a tractate that was published in 1641, Ussher urged Biblical and post-Biblical reasons for thinking that the episcopacy was the divinely ordained institution. He included in his account references to early church fathers, such as Ignatius. Ignatius of course argues there should be only one bishop over all the churches. Well, Ussher points to this and says, "See, right after the New Testament, each church has a bishop" and so this is a very ancient institution.

There was a problem though. It involves a problem I haven't mentioned in this course of lectures about Ignatius. The problem was that the seven letters of Ignatius were not the only letters that were known by Ignatius in the 17th century. In the 17th century, the additions of Ignatius had 13 letters—13 letters. And some people had come to suspect that these 13 letters had been forged because a number of them seemed to reflect events that happened well after Ignatius's day.

This is where John Milton comes in. John Milton answered Ussher's tractate, which favored the episcopacy. Milton was a Puritan, and he was a 32-year old. And this is only his second piece of published prose, so it's very early in his life. Nobody had ever heard of him before, so he was seen as this young upstart who is taking on the tradition of none other than the great Ussher himself. But Milton's view was that the textual tradition of Ignatius was so corrupt that the voice of the historical figure of Ignatius could no longer be heard. In other words, he thought that this collection of Ignatius's letters was filled with forgeries. And so you can't quote it to see what Ignatius really thought.

And so just to quote from Milton's pamphlet, "In the midst therefore of so many forgeries, where shall we fix to dare say this is Ignatius? To what end then do they cite Ignatius as authentic for episcopacy when they cannot know what is authentic in Ignatius?" And so he attacks Ussher for quoting Ignatius when, it turns out, we have all these forgeries. You can't quote forgeries.

Well, as it turns out in this back and forth, Ussher actually had an ace up his sleeve that he didn't tell Milton about. It's a rather long story that I will condense. Ussher had noted that even though there are 13 letters of Ignatius floating around, the church father Eusebius quotes only seven of them. And, moreover, the seven that he quotes seem to have passages that could be taken out that seem to be referring to things in later times. So if you take out these passages and you just have the seven letters, that might be authentically Ignatius.

So Ussher went on a hunt trying to find manuscripts of Ignatius with just the seven letters and without the false additions to the letters. And as it turns out, he found two manuscripts that were in Latin which contained the letters of Ignatius without the passages that looked like they had been stuck in later. Eventually, scholars found other manuscripts. And Ussher's case was vindicated, and, in fact, Ignatius wrote only seven letters and these are the letters from Ignatius himself. I give you this account of James Ussher and John Milton in order to explain some of the ferment that was being raised in the middle 17th century over the writings of the Apostolic Fathers, in this case, the writings of Ignatius, but the other Apostolic Fathers were beginning to get interesting as well.

This all resulted in a monumental event in the year 1672, not in England, as it turns out, but in France. There is a French scholar named Cotelier, who in 1672 published our first edition of the Apostolic Fathers. Cotelier included in his edition the writings of Barnabas, Clement, Hermas, Ignatius and Polycarp, including the martyrdoms of Polycarp and Ignatius. And he included everything that had to do with these authors. So he included not just First and Second Clement but he included everything that was even forged in the name of Clement down into the Middle Ages. So it was a very long book that included authentic materials and forged materials having to do with these five church fathers—five of our Apostolic Fathers.

That started the movement to collect the Apostolic Fathers, and there were a number of movements through the 17th and 18th centuries. There have always been disagreements among scholars concerning this collection of Apostolic Fathers. What should it include? Should it include any work connected with one of these fathers, whether the work is forged or not? That's what Cotelier did. Well, you might think so, but what's the use of having Ignatius forgeries if you want to know what Ignatius said? So that doesn't quite make sense.

Other people maintained that you should have only genuine works that are written by people who really were companions of the apostles. And so some collections of the Apostolic Fathers include only the writings of Clement, Ignatius and Polycarp, since those three were more likely actually companions with the apostles. But the problem with that view is, what if these three actually were not companions of the apostles historically? Well, then you don't have a collection any longer.

So what most historians have concluded today is that this collection should include the writings of the early church fathers from, say, the early to mid-2nd century. Would you include all the Christian writings from that time period? What about things like the Gospel of Thomas? The Gospel of Thomas was written at about the same time. Shouldn't it be an Apostolic Father? Well the problem with the Gospel of Thomas is that it's not proto-orthodox. And all the other writings are proto-orthodox.

So, what many scholars have concluded today is that the best way to proceed is to have a group that you call the Apostolic Fathers that includes the earliest proto-orthodox writings from after the New Testament period. And so that is what gives us the collection of writings that I've been talking about in these lectures. The 10 writings of the Apostolic Fathers that we've discussed sometimes numbered 11 because, as I've mentioned, there's one author named Quadratus from whom we have one sentence that some people include as one of the Apostolic Fathers because he's a proto-orthodox author living soon after the New Testament.

In significant ways then, the collection of the Apostolic Fathers is similar to, but different from the collection of writings that make up the New Testament, because the New Testament also is an ad hoc collection of writings of different genres, different dates, different authors, and different emphases. On the other hand, the New Testament is an ancient collection, not a relatively modern one, and the New Testament is seen as an authoritative collection, whereas most people ascribe no authority to the collection of the Apostolic Fathers.

By contrast, the Apostolic Fathers then is modern, and it's merely a useful collection of early Christian writings from proto-orthodox circles. It's a collection though that is extremely valuable for understanding proto-orthodox theology, practice, ethics, ritual, social structure, reactions to persecution, relationship to the outside world. Without these books, our knowledge of the early Christian church is seriously impoverished. The Apostolic Fathers, therefore, are extremely valuable and precious writings to anyone who is interested in knowing about the history of early Christianity.

Lecture Twenty-Four
The Apostolic Fathers and Proto-orthodoxy

Scope:

In this final lecture, we will look back at what we have covered in the course to consider the historical significance of the Apostolic Fathers. We will stress that the collection of these writings into a corpus of literature is a modern invention: Unlike the New Testament (an ancient collection of books), the writings of the Apostolic Fathers, for the most part, circulated separately from one another over the centuries. But they are nonetheless significant as a group of writings: They cohere, in some rather basic ways, as the writings of those Christians whose views were eventually to "win out" in the struggle over what the Christian religion was eventually to become, when the Church throughout the world became the "Catholic" Church, with theological views and ritual practices that became standard throughout the Middle Ages and down to today.

Outline

I. We saw in our last lecture that the Apostolic Fathers is a useful collection of writings because it contains the earliest records of the proto-orthodox movement.

   A. *Proto-orthodoxy* is a term used by historians to refer to the kind of Christianity that ended up as victorious by the 3rd Christian century.

   B. Before that time, in the 2nd and early 3rd centuries, there were many different Christian groups with a wide range of belief and practice, scattered throughout Christendom.

   C. The story of the victory of proto-orthodoxy is a long and intriguing one.

   D. Older historians simply assumed that the orthodox view had always been the dominant one.

   E. Many historians have come to see, instead, that it was simply one view—the one that happened to win out.

   F. The older view of the relationship between heresy and orthodoxy is sometimes called the Eusebian view because it was first popularized by Eusebius, the father of church history.

1. One of the values of Eusebius' work is that he often quotes sources that have not survived.
2. The Eusebian view of church history holds that the truth was communicated through Jesus to his apostles, who communicated it to the bishops they appointed, who, in their turn, communicated it to their successors.
3. Sometimes heretical offshoots would arise, such as Marcionism and Gnosticism,
4. Orthodoxy goes back to Jesus; heresy is always a secondary corruption of orthodoxy, which is the view held by the majority.

G. The Eusebian model was exploded by Walter Bauer's book of 1934 entitled *Orthodoxy and Heresy in Earliest Christianity*.

1. This book claims that Eusebius gave a slanted version of what really happened in early Christianity: what was later called heresy was the *original* form of Christian faith.
2. According to Bauer, early Christianity is best understood as represented by pods of believers in different regions believing different things, as for example, Gnosticism in Egypt, and Marcionism in Asia Minor.
3. Christ, as far back as can be traced, is characterized by wide-ranging diversity. Eventually, one of these groups managed to assert its authority over other Christian groups and grew to become the majority view, claiming that it had always been the majority view.
4. It is no accident that the form of Christianity that took over the world is the form that was prevalent in Rome in the 2nd century.
5. Bauer hypothesized that the reason why the Roman Church was so intent on reinstating the original presbyters in Corinth was because the Roman Church believed the new Corinthian presbyters were heretics.
6. The Roman Church was the largest of the Christian churches and wealthy. It began using its influence and wealth to ensure that other churches and individual converts followed its beliefs and practices.

7. After the Roman emperor converted to the Christianity of the Roman Church, other churches were outlawed.

8. Christians writing about church history then made it appear that the Roman Church had always been favored by the majority.

9. Bauer's understanding of early Christianity appears to be basically correct.

H. The victory of the proto-orthodox involved three developments, each of which played a significant role in the struggles to determine the shape of the Christian religion: the canon, the clergy, and the creed.

II. We can already see the beginnings of the formation of the New Testament canon within the writings of the Apostolic Fathers.

A. Even before these writings (or simultaneously with some of them), within the pages of the latest writings of the New Testament, we can see a movement toward a new canon of Scripture.

1. Christians, of course, had always had a canon, in that Jesus and his followers, as Jews, revered the writings of Jewish Scripture as canonical.

2. By the end of the 1st century, some Christians were considering the sayings of Jesus and the writings of his apostles also as canonical.

B. Some of the Apostolic Fathers show that the New Testament was beginning to be conceived of as a sacred collection of books.

1. Some writings, such as The Shepherd of Hermas, do not quote earlier texts.

2. But with Ignatius, we find that the preaching of Jesus was seen as sharing equal importance with the Jewish Scriptures.

3. And with the Letter of Polycarp, we see how extensively early Christian writings were sometimes accepted as canonical authorities.

C. Some of the writings of the Apostolic Fathers were themselves accepted as Scripture.

D. As time progressed, proto-orthodoxy applied several criteria to writings to decide which books should belong in Scripture and which should not.

E. The decisions were not finally reached, however, until the end of the 4th century or so.

F. But even before the decisions were finalized, this movement to establish a set canon of Scripture proved important for the victory of proto-orthodoxy, because these books were authoritative accounts of what to believe and how to act.

III. So, too, within the Apostolic Fathers, we can see the movement to establish a Church hierarchy.

A. The earliest Christian communities were charismatic (that is, run by the spirit; cf. 1 Corinthians).

B. But as problems arose, including the problem of "false teaching," it became clear that leaders were needed who could run the churches.

C. We see a movement in this direction already in the Didache, around A.D. 100.

D. At about the same time, we see the importance of having the *right* leaders in 1 Clement.

E. But it is especially with Ignatius, and his insistence on establishing a single bishop over every church, that we see the real movement toward a Church hierarchy.

F. This movement would continue until we reach the Church structure that proved so effective in dealing with heresy and schism—each church with its own bishop and some regional bishops especially powerful, with the bishop of Rome seen as head of the entire Church.

IV. We also see, within the writings of the Apostolic Fathers, the movement to establish correct theological beliefs, which would eventuate in the familiar Christian creeds that have come down to us.

A. From its beginning, Christianity insisted that right belief was necessary for salvation—as opposed to nearly all other religions of the Roman world.

B. In the Apostolic Fathers, we see a concern for those who embrace the wrong belief, for example, in the docetists encountered by Ignatius and Polycarp.

C. To help counter false teaching, certain beliefs were confessed by Christians, for example, when they were baptized.

D. Sometimes, these creeds took on a paradoxical character because of the false beliefs they were attempting to counter.

E. We can see the paradoxical character of these statements of faith already in the time of Ignatius.

F. Eventually, such paradoxes would lead to the orthodox understandings of Christ and the Trinity.

    1. Christ was both fully human and fully divine.

    2. The Trinity makes up one God, who is manifest in three persons.

V. In sum, the Apostolic Fathers are our earliest witnesses outside the New Testament for proto-orthodoxy—the kind of Christianity that came to be dominant and ended up determining the shape of the Christian religion for all time.

Essential Reading:

Bart D. Ehrman, ed., *After the New Testament: A Reader in Early Christianity*, pp. 193–234, 309–316, 317–342, 405–436.

———, *Lost Christianities: The Battles for Scripture and the Faiths We Never Knew*.

Supplementary Reading:

Harry Gamble, *The New Testament Canon: Its Making and Meaning*.

Jeroslav Pelikan, *The Christian Tradition*, vol. 1.

Questions to Consider:

1. In what ways other than those mentioned in the lecture do the Apostolic Fathers seem to adumbrate later developments within Christianity (for example, the retention of Jewish Scripture, the opposition to Jews, and so on)?

2. In your opinion, is it important to know how and why, historically, Christianity became the kind of religion it did? Why or why not?

Lecture Twenty-Four—Transcript
The Apostolic Fathers and Proto-orthodoxy

We saw in our last lecture that the Apostolic Fathers is a useful collection of writings because it contains the earliest records of the proto-orthodox movement. Proto-orthodoxy is a term, as we've seen, that is used by historians to refer to the kind of Christianity that ended up as victorious by the late 3rd Christian century. Prior to that time, in the 2nd and early 3rd centuries, there were many different Christian groups with a wide range of beliefs and practices scattered throughout Christendom.

Proto-orthodoxy represents the point of view that eventually won out. We call it proto-orthodoxy because it's the view before it went out. These views eventually became dominant within early Christianity. Older historians simply assumed that the orthodox view of Christianity had always been the dominant view, and I want to spend some time in this lecture showing where that perspective came from and why modern scholars by and large don't agree with it.

The older view of the relationship of heresy and orthodoxy is sometimes called the Eusebian view. The relationship of heresy and orthodoxy, in other words, between the various kinds of early Christianity, theologically is sometimes called the Eusebian view because it was first popularized by Eusebius, the Father of Church History. If you recall, Eusebius wrote a 10-volume work called the *Ecclesiastical History,* or *The Church History* in the early 4th century.

His book was designed to sketch the history of Christianity from its beginnings with Jesus up to Eusebius's own day, up to about the time of the conversion of the Emperor Constantine. And so Eusebius's *Church History* has been a gold mine of information for historians because it provides us with a sketch of what was happening in Christianity's formative 300 years.

One of the values of Eusebius's work is that, in it, he not only gives us an indication of what happened in those three centuries, he often will quote sources, direct quotations of primary sources, many of which no longer survive. So in many instances, Eusebius is our only access to previous Christian authors whose works have been destroyed or disappeared over the years. And so, as I said, it's a gold mine of information for historians.

Historians in the 20th century though, especially in the 20th century, came to realize that Eusebius cannot be taken as an objective outside viewer of the phenomenon of Christianity. Eusebius had a particular point of view and that point of view determined how he told the story. Now, when historians came to this conclusion about Eusebius, it's not that they blamed Eusebius and said Eusebius is unlike every other historian because other historians are objective and Eusebius is not objective. No, most historians realized that doing history is a subjective affair, just as every human activity is a subjective affair because all of us are subjects. We're not objects; we're human beings. We have views and priorities and values. We have beliefs, we have disbeliefs, we have loves, we have hates—all of the things that make humans human. And Eusebius was a human and his entire worldview affected how he told his story.

One of the things his worldview affected was the way he told the story of the struggle among early Christians to decide what to believe and how to act, in other words, the struggle between different forms of Christianity, some of which Eusebius would call heresy and others of which he would call orthodoxy. The Eusebian model for understanding the relationship of heresy and orthodoxy works like this: According to Eusebius, Christianity started out as an orthodox religion, meaning Christianity had one point of view that was promulgated by Jesus himself, told to his apostles and passed on by his apostles to the bishops who founded the churches throughout the Roman world. And so part of the deal with this understanding of the relationship between heresy and orthodoxy is that it involves apostolic succession, that the truth is communicated by Jesus to the apostles, who communicate it to the bishops they appoint over the churches, who communicate it to their successors, who communicate it then to their churches. So if you wanted to know what Jesus and the disciples taught, you simply followed the apostolic line back through the bishops and the major churches.

According to this view, Christianity started out as an orthodoxy, as the correct teaching given by Jesus himself to his apostles. But according to this model, there would occasionally come along somebody who was either possessed by a demon or was willful or had hate in his heart who developed a kind of heretical offshoot from the original orthodoxy of Christianity.

This would happen, for example, when Marcion came along, and Marcion corrupted the true teaching of orthodoxy by teaching that there's not one God, but there are two gods. This happened when Judaizers came along and said, "Despite what Jesus taught, you really do have to keep the law." This is what happened when various Gnostic groups appeared—a group that believes in 30 gods, for example, one group of Gnostics. That's a wicked offshoot off of orthodoxy—or a group that believes there are 365 gods, another wicked offshoot off of orthodoxy.

The basic idea then is that the reason you have diversity of Christianity, according to Eusebius, is because you have offshoot from the original true faith that is held and has always been held by the majority of Christians. So orthodoxy, by definition, goes back to Jesus. It's the original form of Christianity. It is the true form of Christianity, and any other teaching of Christianity is a wicked, demonically inspired offshoot. So heresy, by definition, is always secondary to orthodoxy and is a corruption of orthodoxy. Heresy is always a secondary corruption of orthodoxy.

What did Eusebius think was orthodoxy? Well, of course it was the point of view that he himself had, that the majority of people in his world had, and he argued that this is the point of view that most Christians had always had and that other points of view—alternative points of view—were wicked offshoots from this original orthodoxy.

This point of view, the Eusebian model for understanding the relationship of heresy and orthodoxy in early Christianity, was exploded in a very important work that was written in 1934 by a German scholar named Walter Bauer. Bauer was an important figure in 20th-century Christianity, at least in the field of scholarship. Bauer was a very impressive scholar who, among other things, produced the standard Greek-German dictionary. It was a dictionary of the New Testament in Greek that became the standard tool in Germany for Biblical scholars studying the New Testament that then came to be translated into English and is now the standard tool still for English scholars. So when my graduate students are learning Greek and they want to read the New Testament, they have to buy Bauer's Lexicon. Even though he wrote this thing now many, many decades ago in the early 20th century, it's still the standard work, as it's been revised over the years.

A much more controversial work than Bauer's Lexicon though was a book that he published in Germany in 1934, called *Orthodoxy and Heresy in Earliest Christianity*. The point of this book was to explode the Eusebian model and to show that Eusebius, in fact, gave a slanted version of what really happened in early Christianity. It agrees with Eusebius that early Christianity had a very large range of diverse perspectives. But it disagrees with Eusebius with regard to the question of how it is that there ended up being an orthodoxy. For Eusebius, there had always been an orthodoxy, there had always been a majority, and the other points of view were heresies that split off from orthodoxy. That's not Bauer's understanding at all.

In Bauer's 1934 classic, he argued that in some regions of Christianity, what was later called heresy was in fact the original form and the majority form of Christian faith. In some regions throughout the Roman world, what later came to be called heresy was in fact the original and majority view of Christians in the region.

The way Bauer gets to this point of view is by going region by region throughout the Roman world wherever we have sources available to us from the ancient church, for example, in Egypt or in Eastern Syria or in Asia Minor or in Rome. And he would take writings that come from that region to explore them in order to see what they can tell us about the relationship of various theological views in the earliest period. And what he found was that, in many instances, the earliest form of Christianity attested to in our sources is a form of Christianity that later got branded as a heresy. For example, the earliest forms of Christianity that you can find in records of Egypt are Gnostic. The earliest forms of Christianity you can find in Palestine are Jewish. The oldest forms of Christianity you can find in parts of Asia Minor are, in fact, Marcionite.

How does one explain that the earliest form of Christianity in these regions—if you just date our sources and look and see what they say - the earliest forms appear not to be orthodox but to be heretical. Doesn't this call into question the very terms orthodoxy and heresy? Because if orthodoxy means correct belief, well, then everybody believes the correct belief, and if you're in one region and this is the only belief of Christianity, this would be seen as the correct belief. Moreover, if orthodoxy means the majority opinion, well, then, if you're in Asia Minor and the majority opinion is Marcionite, then isn't that orthodoxy? So doesn't it even call into question the very terms that are being used?

According to Bauer, the way to understand the relationship of the diversity of early Christianity is quite at odds with the understanding of Eusebius. According to Bauer, early Christianity is best understood as represented by pods of believers in different regions believing different things. Now there are some regions where you have different points of view represented within the same church, but you also have some regions that are characterized by one way of understanding the religion—Gnosticism in Egypt, Marcionism in Asia Minor, for example.

According to Bauer, Christianity as far back as we can trace our sources, is found with this wide-ranging diversity, not with one big orthodoxy that splinters are coming off of, but of a number of Christian groups, all of which are fighting for converts. Eventually, one of these Christian groups manages to assert its authority over other Christian groups and it starts to grow and it starts to acquire more converts and it acquires more converts and it starts growing and growing and growing until finally it becomes the majority view throughout the empire.

That point of view that ends up conquering then rewrites the history, claiming that it had always been the majority view all the way back to Jesus and his apostles. The winners write the history. And the winners decide which books survive. So the books representing alternative claims by and large get lost until they just happen to turn up in relatively modern times.

What is the one form of Christianity that ended up taking over the Christian world? Well, for Bauer, it's not an accident that it's the form of Christianity that is predominant in the city of Rome. In the city of Rome, there is a form of Christianity. This form of Christianity in the city of Rome emphasized that there is only one God, that Jesus is his son and Jesus is both human and divine, that the world is a good place created by God that's become corrupt, but that the world itself is inherently good. In other words, it stood over against the Marcionites who thought there were two gods, or the Gnostics, who might believe in multiple gods, or who thought that the creation was evil. The church in Rome didn't think so.

The church in Rome in the 2nd century, having its own perspective and claiming that its perspective went back to Jesus, just as all the other groups claimed that their perspectives went back to Jesus, this one group in Rome started asserting itself over other churches, and we see evidence of that happening already in the 1st century. Bauer points to the letter of First Clement, where the Roman Church tries to reinstate the presbyters in the church in Corinth. Why was the Roman Church so intent on getting the other presbyters back into office? Bauer hypothesizes that it's not just because there's been a coup, it's because there's been a coup of people who have a different perspective from the people that they displaced, that the new presbyters have a different understanding of Christianity and the Roman Christians are not going to abide by it, that the new presbyters are heretics, possibly Gnostic, for example, and the Roman Christians cannot have the valuable church of Corinth go over to the Gnostics, and so they write a letter that insists that the original presbyters be put back into office, be put back into place. Why? because the original presbyters hold to the Roman point of view. And so it goes.

Rome starts using its influence. Rome is located in the capital of the empire. Rome is the largest of the Christian churches. It's a wealthy church and it uses its wealth wisely, Bauer thought. For example, it uses its wealth in order to convince other churches that they ought to follow the Roman Christian way. How do they do that? They promise that they'll give the other churches alms for distribution among the poor if they elect the right bishop. They use their money to set free slaves. Slaves, out of gratitude then, naturally joined the church. Which form of the church do they join? the one that set them free, which is the rich church, the one that's in Rome, and so forth and so on.

There are a number of historical, cultural, and economic factors that lead to the dominance of Roman Christianity until it starts spreading itself and acquiring more converts. The victory of orthodoxy then is the victory of a Roman form of Christianity. And what form of Christianity does the Roman emperor convert to when the Roman emperor converts to Christianity? He converts to Roman Christianity. What happens to the other forms of Christianity? Eventually they come to be outlawed and they eventually disappear and then Christians writing the history of the conflict rewrite it to make it appear that this form of Christianity had always been the majority opinion.

This is a very interesting book and a very influential book. It didn't have as big of an impact in English-speaking scholarship until relatively recent decades. It wasn't translated into English until 1971 and a lot of scholars of the early church were maybe a little bit too lazy to read it in the original German, and so it didn't really start making its huge impact in the English-speaking world until the 1970s and following. But now, I would say that this understanding, even though it might be wrong in a lot of its details, appears to be right in its general understanding of things. Bauer's understanding might be wrong in a lot of its details. Early Christianity appears to have been remarkably diverse. And only one form of Christianity emerged as triumphant, and it emerged as triumphant developing into the orthodoxy that became standard Christianity down through the ages.

I should emphasize that most scholars think that Bauer got a lot of things wrong and he used several arguments, such as the argument from silence, to far too great a degree. If Bauer would find a location at which there was no Christian material, he would wonder why is there no surviving Christian material from these early years. Well, his conclusion would be, because the earliest Christian materials were heretical and so they got destroyed. That's why they don't survive; whereas, if they had been orthodox, there would be no reason to get rid of them. It's a plausible argument, but it's an argument from silence, and so you don't really know if that's the explanation or not.

In any event, Bauer's view continues to assert a strong influence today. It asserts its influence over my use of the term proto-orthodoxy. I don't speak of orthodoxy in this context when referring to what's happening in the first three centuries of Christianity because I don't think this view is the majority view everywhere yet. It becomes the majority view at the end of the 3rd century or so and so I call representatives of this later dominant view proto-orthodox.

As scholars have come to see over the years, the victory of the proto-orthodox party involved three developments, each of which played a significant role in the struggles to determine the shape of the Christian religion. These three developments are ones that we have covered sporadically throughout the course of these lectures, and I want to end this course of lectures by reviewing for you these three key issues that we've already addressed that led to the victory of the proto-orthodox.

These three issues are the canon, formation of the canon, the development of the Christian clergy, and the rise of the Christian creed: the canon, the clergy, and the creed. These are three weapons used by the proto-orthodox in their battles against other understandings of the faith. The formation of the canon of scripture is one of the most important. Christians were fighting it out over what to believe. Some Christians were saying there are multiple gods, some saying there is one God, some Christians saying Jesus was man but not God, some saying he was God but not man, some saying he was both at the same time, some Christians saying the creation was good, some saying the creation was wicked, some saying Jesus' death is what brings salvation from sin, some saying it is Jesus' secret teachings that bring eternal life—different groups with different points of view.

How are these points of view to be negotiated? Well, the Christian canon is one way to negotiate various points of view because, by canonizing certain books as authorities, you can eliminate certain perspectives, depending on which books you give sacred authority to. Even before the writings of the New Testament, of course, we can see a movement toward a new canon of scripture, even before the formation of the canon itself. Even before the last writings of the New Testament itself were produced, we see a movement toward a new canon of scripture.

As we've seen, Christians started out with a canon of scripture in that they were Jews who revered the Jewish scriptures, just as Jesus had done. But, by the end of the 1st century, Christians are considering the sayings of Jesus and the writings of his apostles as canonical. The problem is that there were lots of writings by lots of Jesus' apostles. And so you have gospels not only allegedly written by Matthew, Mark, Luke and John but also a gospel allegedly written by Thomas and a gospel allegedly written by Peter and a gospel allegedly written by Mary. Who is to decide which books are included and which ones are not?

You can see this movement. You can see this movement toward deciding which books to be included and not to include in the writings of the Apostolic Fathers. Some of the writings of the Apostolic Fathers, like The Shepherd of Hermas, strikingly do not quote earlier texts. The Shepherd of Hermas, as large as it is and as long as it goes on simply does not quote earlier texts. But other writings, like the letter of Polycarp, quote earlier Christian authorities extensively. So in the letter of Polycarp, just line after line is alluding to or quoting earlier Christian writings. Eventually, some of the writings of the Apostolic Fathers themselves came to be considered as authoritative. But as time progressed, proto-orthodox Christians were feeling compelled to decide which books to include and which to exclude and they used several criteria to get them there. They wanted to know: Do we include the Gospel of Thomas? Do we include the Gospel of Peter? Do we include the Gospel of Philip? What about the Gospel of Mary? What about the Gospel of Truth?

Proto-orthodox applied the criteria we've discussed already, that a book had to be ancient, it had to be apostolic, it had to be widely used, and it had to be orthodox for it to be accepted. There were debates that went on for decades—in fact, for centuries. As you know, it wasn't until the end of the 4th century that finally an orthodox writer, Athanasius, the bishop of Alexandria, listed our 27 books and only our 27 books as being the authoritative canon of scripture. So the other gospels were excluded, as were the other acts, epistles, and apocalypses which were seen to be problematic from a theological point of view.

So, too, within the Apostolic Fathers we can see a movement to establish the church hierarchy—the clergy. It's one thing to have a collection of books, but it's another thing to interpret the books. Who is going to tell you how to interpret the books? You need to have authorities – living authorities—who can tell you how to interpret the books of scripture, hence the need for having a clergy that can run the show. As we've seen, Christian communities started out as charismatic communities run by the spirit, as we saw in the instance of Paul's church in Corinth, as evidenced in I Corinthians.

Members of the congregation were given different spiritual gifts, different charismata, and the community was to function as a unit as the spirit works through each individual member. This, of course, led to a good deal of chaos, which caused Christians then to think that maybe what we need are church leaders. We see this movement already in the Didache around the year 100 A.D., where the Didache instructs its readers that even though you have these itinerate prophets running around, you should elect bishops and deacons.

We see the same move in First Clement, which presupposes that there's a board of elders or presbyters, both in the Corinthian Church and in the Roman Church and this board of elders is to be followed. We see it even more in the writings of Ignatius, who insisted that there's to be one bishop over the church, only one bishop over every church, thus leading to what eventually became a church hierarchy. This movement toward a hierarchy would continue until we reached the church structure that proved so effective in dealing with heresy throughout the church, where each church had its own bishop, and some regional bishops, especially of the larger churches, had jurisdiction over churches in their area. And eventually one bishop, the bishop of Rome, was seen to be the head of the whole church, or, as he came to be known, the Pope. So you have the canon, you have the clergy, and you have the creed.

Within the writings of the Apostolic Fathers already, we see the movement to establish the correct theological beliefs, which would eventuate in the Christian creeds that have come down to churches today. From its very beginning, Christianity insisted that right belief was necessary for salvation, as opposed to nearly all the other religions of the Roman world, for which belief was not all that important.

In the Apostolic Fathers, we see a concern for those who embraced the wrong belief, for example, in the Docetists, who are encountered by Ignatius and by Polycarp. To help counter false teachings, certain beliefs were to be confessed by all Christians. For example, when they were baptized, Christians were told what they ought to confess. Sometimes these creeds of what Christians confessed took on a paradoxical character. They took on a paradoxical character because proto-orthodox Christians were opposing different groups simultaneously. They were opposing groups that said Jesus was a man, but he's not God. They were also opposing groups that said Jesus was a god, but not man. They had to oppose both groups, which means that they had to affirm at the same time, yes, Jesus is God, and he's also man, in opposition to the groups that deny one or the other statement.

But that means Jesus is both God and man. How can he be both God and man? Well, he's both God and man because it's a paradox. This paradoxical set of affirmations that Christians end up making can be found in one of our earliest creedal fragments from the writings of Ignatius, who says, "There is one physician, both fleshly and spiritual, born and unborn, God come in the flesh, true life in death, from both Mary and God, for subject to suffering and beyond suffering, Jesus Christ our Lord." So even though he's one, he's both flesh and spirit; he comes from both God and he comes from Mary; he's both life and he's in death. And so this is a paradoxical affirmation of who Jesus is.

Eventually, these paradoxes would lead to the orthodox understandings of Christ and the trinity. This movement in proto-orthodoxy to correct belief that develops by the opposition to various points of view leads to the paradoxical affirmations of traditional Christian theology in which Christ is fully human and fully divine. If he's both God and man, does that mean he's half of each? No. He's completely man and he's completely God, not half of each. Well, how can he be completely God and completely man at the same time and still be just one person? Well, he's one person, but he has two natures—the divine nature and a human nature. But how can one person have two natures? These are the kinds of debates that transpired in orthodoxy after the 4th and 5th century. As Christians tried to figure it out, the doctrine of the trinity develops, the doctrine of the trinity that teaches there's one God who is manifest in three persons. Jesus is completely God. The Holy Spirit is completely God. God the Father is completely God. Oh, then you've got three gods? No, we have one God. Well, how can you have one God if there are three of them? because the three are three different persons within the trinity. The trinity is one in number and yet it's distinct in character, so that the three together make up the one God. This becomes the basis then for Trinitarian understanding, and the best theologians have always considered this to be a paradoxical affirmation that can't be understood intellectually because on the logical level, it can't make sense, but that's why it's been called a mystery, because it can't be made sense of from rational, logical ways of thinking. But it nonetheless becomes an absolutely central affirmation within Christianity, the doctrine of the trinity.

Let me sum up this lecture and then all of our lectures. The Apostolic Fathers are our earliest witnesses outside the New Testament for proto-orthodoxy with respect to the development of the canon and the clergy and the creed. This form of Christianity came to be dominant and ended up determining the shape of the Christian religion for all time.

Understanding the rise of proto-orthodoxy means understanding Christianity in its earliest formation, which means understanding some of the foundation stones of all of modern Western civilization. For this reason, if for no other, the Apostolic Fathers demand our attention as little known but highly significant writings that helped to shape not just the religion but also the culture and society as they have come down to us in the West today.

Timeline

4 B.C.? ....Jesus' birth

A.D. 14–37..................................Emperor Tiberius

26–36 ....Pilate as Governor of Judea

30?..Jesus' death

33?..Conversion of Paul

37–41 ....Emperor Caligula

41–54 ....Emperor Claudius

50–60 ....Pauline Epistles

50?–110.......................................Ignatius of Antioch

54–68 ....Emperor Nero

62–113 ....Pliny the Younger

65?..Gospel of Mark

66–70 ....Jewish Revolt and destruction of the Temple

69–79 ....Emperor Vaspasian

70–156 ....Polycarp of Smyrna

79–81 ....Emperor Titus

80–85?...Gospels of Matthew and Luke, book of Acts

81–96 ....Emperor Domitian

90–95?...Gospel of John

95?..Clement of Rome

95?..Book of Revelation

96?..1 Clement

98–117 ....Emperor Trajan

100?..The Didache

100–165 ....Justin Martyr

100–160? ....Marcion

110–140? ....The Shepherd of Hermas

120–140? ....Papias

130–200 ....Irenaeus

135? ....Epistle of Barnabas

140–160? ....2 Clement

155? ....Martyrdom of Polycarp

160–225 ....Tertullian

180–190? ....Letter to Diognetus

d. 190 ....Melito of Sardis

249–251 ....Emperor Decius

260–340 ....Eusebius

285–337 ....Constantine (emperor, 306–337)

300–375 ....Athanasius

303–312 ....The "Great Persecution"

312 ...."Conversion" of Constantine

325 ....Council of Nicea

Glossary

Adoptionism: The view that Jesus was not divine but was a flesh-and-blood human being who had been adopted by God to be his son at his baptism.

Apocalypse: A literary genre common in ancient Judaism and Christianity, in which a mortal prophet is given visions either of the heavenly realm or the future fate of the Earth and is told how these visions can explain the mundane realities faced by the Church.

Apocalypticism: A worldview held by many ancient Jews and Christians that maintained that the present age is controlled by forces of evil but that these will be destroyed at the end of time, when God intervenes in history to bring in his kingdom, an event thought to be imminent.

Apologists: Group of 2nd- and 3rd-century Christian intellectuals who wrote treatises defending Christianity against charges leveled against it.

Apology: Literally "defense," used as a technical term for a reasoned defense of the faith against its opponents.

Apostle: From a Greek word meaning "one who is sent." In early Christianity, the term designated emissaries of the faith who were special representatives of Christ.

Apostolic succession: The doctrine espoused by members of the proto-orthodox community that their version of the Christian faith could be traced through a series of Christian leaders all the way back to the apostles themselves.

Baptism: The Christian practice that became an "initiation" ritual in which a person was made a member of the community through immersion in (or sprinkling of) water.

Bishop: The Greek word for bishop literally means "overseer." Originally, bishops were simply the leaders of the local churches; by the early 2nd century, bishops were beginning to receive greater power to make all the authoritative decisions in the church.

Canon: From a Greek word that literally means "ruler" or "straight edge." The term is used to designate a recognized collection of texts;

the New Testament canon is, thus, the collection of books that Christians have traditionally accepted as authoritative.

Catechumenate: A term that refers to the period of instruction in the rudiments of the Christian faith undertaken by converts who were preparing for baptism.

Charismatic community: A religious community that is organized not under the leadership of individuals but in which every member has a "gift" (Greek: *charisma*) of the Spirit that enables the community to function together.

Chiliasm: From the Greek word for a "thousand," *chiliasm* refers to the belief that there would be a literal 1,000-year reign of Christ on Earth (also called the *millennium*).

Deacons: From a Greek word that literally means "ministers," deacons were leaders in the Church who were predominantly concerned with the physical well-being of its members (for example, they had charge of alms collection and the like).

Dead Sea Scrolls: First discovered in 1947 in caves near the west shore of the Dead Sea, these are Jewish writings that contain a number of copies of the Hebrew Bible, commentaries, rules for how the community was to live together, and other important documents.

Deutero-Pauline Epistles: Letters of the New Testament that claim to be written by Paul but appear to have been written instead by his followers in the next generation; these include Ephesians, Colossians, 2 Thessalonians, 1 and 2 Timothy, and Titus.

Docetism: The view that Jesus was not a human being but only "appeared" to be; from a Greek word that means "to seem" or "to appear."

Doctrine of the two paths: A form of ethical instruction found in both the Didache and the Letter of Barnabas, in which readers are told that they have the choice of following either the path of light (or life) or darkness (death), depending on how they choose to live.

Ebionites: A group of 2nd-century adoptionists who maintained Jewish practices and Jewish forms of worship.

Eucharist: From a Greek word that literally means "giving thanks," this is a technical term that refers to the commemoration of Christ's death in a periodic sacred meal (the Lord's Supper), as instituted in the Last Supper.

Gnosticism: A group of ancient religions, closely related to Christianity, that maintained that sparks of a divine being had become entrapped in the present, evil world and could escape only by acquiring the appropriate secret *gnosis* (Greek for "knowledge") of who they were and how they could escape. This *gnosis* was generally thought to have been brought by an emissary descended from the divine realm.

Heresy: Any worldview or set of beliefs deemed by those in power to be deviant; from a Greek word that means "choice" (because "heretics" have "chosen" to deviate from the "truth"; see **orthodoxy**).

Judaizing: Any approach to Christianity that insists that followers of Jesus continue to keep the Jewish Law.

Manual of Discipline: One of the documents of the Dead Sea Scrolls, which like some of the early Christian texts, contains the doctrine of the two paths.

Marcionites: Followers of Marcion, the second-century Christian scholar and evangelist, later labeled a heretic for his docetic Christology and his belief in two Gods, the harsh legalistic God of the Jews and the merciful loving God of Jesus—views that he claimed to have found in the writings of Paul.

Martyr: From the Greek word for "witness," a Christian martyr is anyone who bears ultimate witness to Christ, that is, by dying for him.

Martyrology: A literary text that describes the trial and execution of a martyr or a group of martyrs, such as the Martyrdom of Polycarp.

Monepiscopacy: The teaching, first found in the Letters of Ignatius, that there should be one and only one leader of the Church—the bishop—who makes all the important administrative decisions and provides all the important theological and spiritual guidance.

Muratorian Canon: An 8th-century manuscript, copied probably from a 2nd-century original, that lists the books that its author considered to belong to the New Testament canon. This is probably our earliest surviving canon list.

Orthodoxy: Literally, "right opinion"; a term used to designate a worldview or set of beliefs acknowledged to be true by the majority of those in power. For its opposite, see **heresy**.

Paganism: Any of the polytheistic religions of the Greco-Roman world; an umbrella term for ancient Mediterranean religions other than Judaism and Christianity.

Pesher: A method of interpretation found in some of the biblical commentaries among the Dead Sea Scrolls, in which a text was cited, followed by an explanation of its contemporary relevance ("this is what it means").

Pope: From a word related to "papa," this refers to the bishop of the church of Rome, understood to be the head of the entire Christian Church.

Presbyters: From a Greek word that literally means "elders," these were the official leaders of local Christian congregations.

Proto-orthodoxy: A form of Christianity endorsed by some Christians of the 2nd and 3rd centuries (including the Apostolic Fathers) that promoted doctrines that were declared "orthodox" by the victorious Christian party in the 4th and later centuries.

Torah: From a Hebrew word that means something like "law" or "guidance," the term *Torah* refers either to the Law given by God to Moses or to the five first books of the Hebrew Bible, allegedly written by Moses: Genesis, Exodus, Leviticus, Numbers, and Deuteronomy.

Trinity: Key doctrine of orthodox Christianity that maintains that the godhead consists of three persons, Father, Son, and Holy Spirit, who are all equally God, even though there is only one God.

Biographical Notes

Athanasius: Athanasius was a highly influential and controversial bishop of Alexandria throughout the middle half of the 4th century. Born around A.D. 300, he was active in the large and powerful Alexandrian church already as a young man, appointed as deacon to the then-bishop, Alexander. He served as secretary at the important Council of Nicea in 325, which attempted to resolve critical issues concerning the nature of Christ as fully divine, of the same substance as God the father, and co-eternal with the father.

As bishop of Alexandria from 328–375, Athanasius was a staunch defender of this Nicene understanding of Christ and a key player in the development of the orthodox doctrine of the Trinity, in which there were three distinct persons (Father, Son, and Spirit) who were nonetheless one God, all of the same substance. This defense created enormous difficulties for Athanasius in the face of powerful opposition, to which he reacted with a show of force (even violence). He was sent into exile on several occasions during his bishopric, spending nearly 16 years away from Alexandria while trying to serve as its bishop.

Author of numerous surviving works, Athanasius is also significant for his role in determining which books should be accepted in his churches as sacred Scripture. In A.D. 367, in his 39th annual "Festal Letter," which like all the others, set the date for the celebration of Easter and included pastoral instruction, he indicated that the 27 books that we now have in the New Testament, and only those 27, should be regarded as canonical. This decree helped define the shape of the canon for all time and helped lead to the declaration of other books, such as the Gnostic gospels and the like, as heretical.

Athenagoras: Not much is known about the 2nd-century Christian apologist Athenagoras, as he is scarcely mentioned in the writings of other church fathers. The few references to him that survive indicate that he was a Greek philosopher who lived in Athens. His best known work is his Christian "Apology" ("Defense"), addressed to the emperors Marcus Aurelius and Commodus, probably written in 177. In it, he defends Christians against charges of atheism and crass immorality involving incestuous orgies and ritual cannibalism and tries to demonstrate the superiority of the Christian faith to all others.

Among his notable contributions to Christian theology is his indication that Christians worship three who are God (the Father), the Son, and the Holy Spirit; eventually, such reflections led to the formation of the classical doctrine of the Trinity.

Barnabas: We are not well informed about the historical Barnabas. He is mentioned both by the apostle Paul (Gal. 2:13; 1 Cor. 9:6) and the book of Acts (Acts 9:27; 11:22–26) as one of Paul's traveling companions, and it appears that he was originally a Hellenistic Jew who converted to faith in Christ, then became, like Paul, a traveling missionary who spread the faith. The book of Acts goes so far as to consider him one of the apostles (Acts 14:4, 14).

The Epistle (or Letter) of Barnabas discussed in this course is attributed to him, but modern scholars are reasonably sure that he could not have written it. The book appears to have been written some time around A.D. 130 or 135, some 60 years or so after the historical Barnabas would have died. The book was attributed to him, then, by Christians who wanted to advance its authoritative claims as being rooted in the views of one of the most important figures from the early years of Christianity.

Clement of Rome: Clement of Rome is another figure about whom we do not have much information. Tradition indicates that he was the second or third bishop of Rome (the disciple Simon Peter having been the first). He may be mentioned in The Shepherd of Hermas as the "foreign correspondent" for the Roman church (prior to becoming bishop?). He is allegedly the author of both 1 and 2 Clement, but it is clear that these two books were written by two different persons, and in neither book is Clement ever mentioned, let alone named as the author.

Diognetus: Diognetus is the unknown recipient of the apology known as the Letter to Diognetus. Literally, his name means "born of Zeus." Because he is called "most excellent" in the letter, there are some scholars who think that he must have been some kind of Roman official. There is known to have been a tutor of the emperor Marcus Aurelius by this name, and thus, some have argued that this is the intended recipient of the letter. It is also possible, however, that the name is meant merely as a cipher for anyone among the pagans who is interested in knowing about the Christian religion and for seeing that, far from being a danger to Roman society, it is, in fact, the one superior religion in the world.

Eusebius: Eusebius of Caesarea is one of the most important figures in the history of the early Church. Born around A.D. 260, he was trained by some of the leading Christian scholars of his time and was to become the first author to produce a full history of Christianity up to his own day, in a book called the *Ecclesiastical* (or *Church*) *History*. Eusebius was quite active in the politics of the Church and empire; ordained bishop of the large and important church of Caesarea in 315, he was active at the Council of Nicea and the theological disputes in its aftermath, originally opposing but later accepting the creedal statements about Christ that were to become orthodox. He died around A.D. 340.

Eusebius was a prolific writer, but it was his *Ecclesiastical History* in particular that made a significant impact on subsequent generations—down to our own day. This chronological sketch of early Christianity provides us with the majority of our information about the spread of Christianity throughout the Roman world, the persecution of the early Christians, the conflicts between what Eusebius considered to be orthodoxy and heresies, the development of Church offices and structures, and so on. Of particular value in this 10-volume work is Eusebius's frequent citation, often lengthy, of his sources, so that through his account, we have access to the writings of his Christian predecessors, which otherwise, have been lost to history. Thus, even though Eusebius puts his own slant on the history that he tells, it is possible to use the sources he cites to gain significant insight into the conflicts and developments that transpired in the Christian Church of the first three centuries, up to his own day.

Hermas: The author of The Shepherd is known to us only through the autobiographical references scattered throughout his work. It appears that he had been raised as a slave in the household of a woman named Rhoda, but that he had been set free while still young. He evidently then married and raised a family, in or around Rome.

In The Shepherd, Hermas recounts a number of symbolic visions that he received in which he was given instruction concerning the current state of the Christian Church and the need for people to repent in view of the imminent end to be brought by Christ. These visions are interpreted to him by angelic mediators, in particular, one that comes to him in the guise of a shepherd, hence the name of the book. This is the longest writing we have from the first two centuries of the Christian Church.

Ignatius of Antioch: Ignatius is one of the most interesting figures from the early 2nd century. We know little of his life, except that he was bishop of the major church in Antioch, Syria, and had been arrested for Christian activities and was sent to Rome under armed guard to face execution by being thrown to the wild beasts in the Roman arena. En route to his martyrdom, Ignatius wrote seven surviving letters to churches that had sent representatives to greet him. In these letters, he warns against false teachers, urges the churches to strive for unity, stresses the need for the churches to adhere to the teachings and policies of the one bishop residing over each of them, and emphasizes that he is eager to face his violent death so that he might be a true disciple of Christ.

One of the letters Ignatius wrote was to the bishop of the city of Smyrna, Polycarp, who may have been the one who collected the other letters together. Within a couple of centuries, other Christian authors forged other letters allegedly by Ignatius; throughout the Middle Ages, these forgeries were circulated with the authentic letters and were not recognized for what they were until scholars undertook an assiduous examination of them in the 17th century.

Justin Martyr: Justin was an important figure in the mid-2nd-century church of Rome. Born of pagan parents (c. A.D. 100), evidently in Samaria, he undertook secular philosophical training before converting to Christianity when he was about 30. He began to teach the philosophical superiority of Christianity to secular learning, first in Ephesus and then in Rome, where he established a kind of Christian philosophical school in mid-century.

Justin is the first prominent Christian *apologist*, that is, one who defended the Christian faith against the charges of its cultured (pagan) despisers and strove to show its intellectual and moral superiority to anything that the pagan (or Jewish) world could offer. Three of his major works survive, usually known as his First Apology (a defense of Christianity addressed to the emperor Antoninus Pius and his sons, including Marcus Aurelius, around A.D. 155); his Second Apology (addressed to the Roman Senate around A.D. 160); and his Dialogue with Trypho, an account of his conversion and subsequent debate with a (possibly fictitious) Jewish rabbi, Trypho, over the superiority of Christianity to Judaism, based largely on an exposition of key passages in the Old Testament.

Justin's defense of Christianity led to political opposition; he was martyred on charges of being a Christian around 165.

Marcion: Marcion was one of the most infamous "heretics" of the 2nd century. Tradition indicates that he was born and raised in Sinope, on the southern shore of the Black Sea, where as a young man, he acquired considerable wealth as a shipping merchant. His father was allegedly the bishop of the Christian church there, who excommunicated his son for his false teachings. In A.D. 139, Marcion went to Rome, where he spent five years developing his theological views, before presenting them to a specially called council of the Church leaders. Rather than accepting Marcion's understanding of the Gospel, however, the Church expelled him for false teaching. Marcion then journeyed into Asia Minor, where he proved remarkably successful in converting others to his understanding of the Christian message. "Marcionite" churches were in existence for centuries after his death, around A.D. 160.

Marcion's understanding of the Gospel was rooted in his interpretation of the writings of the apostle Paul, whose differentiation between the Law (of the Old Testament) and the Gospel (of Christ) Marcion took to an extreme, claiming that the old and new were fundamentally different, so much so that they represented the religions of different Gods. Marcion, in other words, was a *ditheist*, who thought that the Old Testament God—who had created the world, called Israel to be his people, and gave them his Law—was a different god from the God of Jesus, who came into the world in the "appearance" of human flesh (because he was not actually part of the material world of the creator-god) to save people from the just but wrathful God of the Jews. Marcion's views were based on his canon of Scripture—the first canon known to be formally advanced by a Christian—which did not, obviously, contain anything from the Old Testament but comprised a form of the Gospel of Luke and 10 of Paul's letters (all those in the present New Testament except 1 and 2 Timothy and Titus).

Marcus Aurelius: Marcus Aurelius (A.D. 121–180) ruled as Roman emperor from A.D. 161–180. He is probably best known as a "philosopher"-emperor, because he was one of the leading spokespersons for the philosophy of Stoicism in the ancient world. His private journal, *The Meditations*, still survives; in it, he reflects on his life and urges himself to live rationally in light of his inner resources.

It was during the reign of Marcus Aurelius that Christians in Lyons and Vienne (in Gaul) were subject to the horrendous persecutions described in the Letter of Lyons and Vienne preserved for us in the writings of Eusebius.

Minucius Felix: Minucius Felix is an otherwise unknown Christian author from Latin-speaking North Africa who, sometime in the second half of the 2nd century, wrote an apology called the *Octavian*. The book is named after one of the characters in the book, "Octavius," who is said to enter into a long discussion with a pagan, Caecillian, over the competing virtues of the Christian versus the pagan religion. In the course of the discussion, Octavius not only lays out arguments for the superiority of the Christian philosophy, but he also describes the superior moral rectitude of the Christians. In so doing, he is compelled to address the charges leveled against the Christians that they are, in fact, prone to wild and licentious activities that make them socially disruptive and dangerous.

Nero: Nero (A.D. 37–68) was the Roman emperor in A.D. 54–68, during the time that the apostle Paul, for example, wrote his letters. For the history of early Christianity, he is probably best known as being the first emperor to persecute the Christians. According to the Roman historian Tacitus, Nero arranged for the city of Rome to be burned to allow implementation of some of his own architectural designs for its reconstruction. When the populace came to suspect Nero's involvement in the fire, he decided to lay the blame on the Christians, who were a widely despised group in any event; he had Christians rounded up, condemned for arson, and executed in gruesome and humiliating ways. Nero's treatment of Christians may have set the stage for subsequent imperial persecutions.

Papias: Papias was an early- to mid-2nd-century proto-orthodox bishop of Hierapolis who is best known to history as author of a now-lost work called An Exposition of the Sayings of the Lord. In this five-volume work, Papias describes the information he had received about Jesus' teachings from the companions of his disciples. We know of the book only as it was quoted on occasion by later authors. These quotations show that numerous legendary expansions of the Gospel traditions were in circulation for decades after the composition of the New Testament Gospels. They also show that

Papias was a *chiliast*, that is, that he subscribed to the view that there would be a literal 1,000-year reign of Christ on Earth in which paradisiacal conditions would prevail. Later theologians considered this view naive and dangerous and, thus, chose not to preserve Papias's writings.

Paul the Apostle: Paul was a Hellenistic Jew who was born and raised outside of Palestine. We do not know when he was born, but it was probably sometime during the first decade A.D. Through his own letters and the encomiastic account found in the book of Acts, we can learn something of his history. He was raised as a strict Pharisaic Jew and prided himself in his scrupulous religiosity. At some point in his early adulthood, he learned of the Christians and their proclamation of the crucified man Jesus as the messiah; incensed by this claim, Paul began a rigorous campaign of persecution against the Christians—only to be converted himself to faith in Jesus through some kind of visionary experience.

Paul then became an ardent proponent of the faith and its best-known missionary. He saw his call as a missionary to the Gentiles and worked in major urban areas in the regions of Asia Minor, Macedonia, and Achaia to establish churches through the conversion of former pagan. A distinctive aspect of his message was that all people, Jew and Gentile, are made right with God through Jesus' death and resurrection, and by no other means; the practical payoff was that Gentiles did not need to become Jewish in order to be among the people of the Jewish God—in particular, the men did not need to become circumcised.

We know about Paul principally through the letters he wrote to his churches when problems had arisen that he wanted to address. There are seven letters in the New Testament that indisputably come from his hand; six others claim him as an author, but there are reasons to doubt these claims. According to the book of Acts, Paul was eventually arrested for socially disruptive behavior and sent to Rome to face trial. An early tradition outside of the New Testament indicates that Paul was martyred there, in Rome, during the reign of the emperor Nero, in A.D. 64.

Philotheus Bryennios: Philotheus Bryennios (1833–1914) was a Greek scholar important in the annals of history for discovering the Didache in 1873, in the library of the Jerusalem Monastery of the

Holy Sepulchre in Constantinople. He was born in Constantinople but was educated in Germany. The manuscript he discovered contained not only the Didache (which before this was unknown) but also the Letter of Barnabas, 1 and 2 Clement, and the epistles of Ignatius. It appears to have been produced in A.D. 1056. Many scholars hail this discovery as one of the greatest of the entire 19th century.

Pliny the Younger: Pliny the Younger (A.D. 62–113) is so named to differentiate him from his uncle, Pliny the Elder, a famous natural scientist and author who perished in the eruption of Mount Vesuvius in A.D. 79. As a young Roman aristocrat, Pliny the Younger received a top-rate literary education and is known from his literary remains, chiefly letters that he sent to the then-emperor Trajan from his post in the Asia Minor province of Bythinia, where he was appointed in the early 2nd century to serve as governor.

Among the valuable information to be gleaned from these letters is an account of Pliny's proceedings against Christians, whom he treated as criminals deserving of death. When Christians were brought before him, he ordered them to perform a sacrifice to the image of the emperor; if they refused, he had them executed. Any Christians, however, who recanted their faith and made the sacrifice were released. This legal proceeding against the Christians was sanctioned by Trajan himself and may represent the typical judicial actions against Christians in the early 2nd century throughout the empire.

Polycarp of Smyrna: Polycarp was the bishop of Smyrna, in Asia Minor, for most of the first half of the 2nd century. Born around A.D.70, he was martyred as a Christian in 156; the account of his arrest, trial, and execution (by being burned at the stake) is preserved for us in a firsthand report written in a letter by fellow Christians in Smyrna. This is the first detailed account of a martyrdom to survive from ancient Christianity outside the New Testament.

Some 45 years before his death, Polycarp had received a letter from Ignatius of Antioch, which still survives; Ignatius indicates that he had stayed in Smyrna en route to his own martyrdom in Rome and had come to know and respect the bishop there. In addition, we have a letter (or more likely, two letters, later spliced together) written by Polycarp himself to the Christians of Philippi, addressing ethical and theological issues that had arisen in their church.

Although not an original thinker, Polycarp was, thus, one of the most well known and important proto-orthodox leaders of the early and mid-2nd century. Later legend indicates that he had once been a companion of the apostle John and later became the teacher of Irenaeus; the latter claim may be right, but there appears to be little credible evidence for the former.

Bibliography

Akroyd, Peter R., ed. *Cambridge History of the Bible*, vol. 1. Cambridge: Cambridge University Press, 1970. A comprehensive survey of how the Bible was collected into a canon and interpreted down through the centuries.

Aune, David. *The New Testament in Its Literary Environment.* Philadelphia: Westminster, 1987. A valuable discussion of the different literary genres represented in the New Testament and how they reflect the literary styles of the period.

Barnard, L. W. *Studies in the Apostolic Fathers and Their Background.* New York: Schocken, 1966. A collection of essays on a broad range of important aspects of the Apostolic Fathers.

Bauer, Walter. *Orthodoxy and Heresy in Earliest Christianity.* Philadelphia: Fortress, 1971. One of the most important books of the 20th century on the history of early Christianity. Bauer argues against the classical understanding of orthodoxy and heresy by maintaining that what was later called *heresy* was, in many regions of early Christendom, the oldest and most widely held form of Christian belief.

Bisbee, Gary. *Pre-Decian Acts of Martyrs and Commentarii.* Philadelphia: Fortress, 1988. A valuable account of the earliest Christian martyrologies (prior to the persecution of A.D. 250).

Bowe, Barbara. *A Church in Crisis: Ecclesiology and Paraenesis in Clement of Rome.* Philadelphia: Fortress, 1988. A study of the church in Rome at the end of the first Christian century, based on an analysis of 1 Clement.

Bradshaw, Paul. *The Search for the Origins of Christian Worship.* Oxford: Oxford University Press, 1992. One of the most thorough studies of the original forms of Christian liturgy available.

Burtchaell, James. *From Synagogue to Church: Public Services and Offices in the Earliest Christian Communities.* Cambridge: Cambridge University Press, 1992. A useful study of the development of Christian Church offices from their roots in the Jewish synagogue.

Campenhausen, Hans von. *Ecclesiastical Authority and Spiritual Power in the Church of the First Three Centuries.* Peabody, MA: Hendrickson, 1997 (reprint of 1969 ed.). A classical study by an important German scholar of the formation of Church structure over the formative periods of Christianity. For advanced students.

Collins, John. *Apocalypse: Morphology of a Genre*. Missoula, MT: Scholars Press 1979. A scholarly assessment of the leading characteristics of the apocalypse genre that considers all of the important surviving examples of the genre from Jewish and Christian antiquity.

Corwin, Virginia. *St. Ignatius and Christianity in Antioch*. New Haven: Yale University Press, 1960. A classical study of Ignatius and the church over which he presided as bishop in Antioch.

Dix, Gregory. *The Shape of the Liturgy*. London: Dacre, 1945. A classical study of how Christian liturgical rituals took the shape they did in the early centuries of the Church.

Donfried, Karl. *The Setting of Second Clement in Early Christianity*. Leiden: Brill, 1974. A controversial study of 2 Clement that argues that it was written by one of the "deposed" presbyters of Corinth restored to office at the urging of the letter of 1 Clement.

Draper, Jonathan, ed. *The Didache in Modern Research*. Leiden: Brill, 1996. An important collection of scholarly essays on a variety of issues involving the history and interpretation of the Didache.

Droge, Arthur. *Moses or Homer: Early Christian Interpretations of the History of Culture*. Tuebingen: Mohr/Siebeck, 1989. An intriguing study of the early Christian apologists and their assertion that the Christian faith could claim greater antiquity than pagan religions, in a world that respected antiquity.

Ehrman, Bart D., ed. *After the New Testament: A Reader in Early Christianity*. New York: Oxford University Press, 1999. A collection of some of the most important early Christian writings from the 2nd and 3rd centuries, in quality English translations, dealing with a range of issues covered in this course, including persecution and martyrdom, Jewish-Christian relations, apostolic pseudepigrapha, the formation of canon, and the development of Christian theology. All in all, probably the best companion volume for the course.

————. *Lost Christianities: The Battles for Scripture and the Faiths We Never Knew*. New York: Oxford University Press, 2003. A study of the wide-ranging diversity of Christianity in the 2nd and 3rd centuries, of the sacred texts (many of them forged) produced and revered by different Christian groups of the period, and of the struggles that led to the emergence of "orthodox" Christianity prior to the conversion of Constantine. For popular audiences.

————, ed. *The Apostolic Fathers*, 2 vols. The Loeb Classical Library. Cambridge, MA: Harvard University Press, 2003. A two-volume edition of all the writings of the Apostolic Fathers, with original Greek (and Latin) texts and English translations on facing pages, along with introductions to each work.

————, ed. *The New Testament and Other Early Christian Writings*, 2nd ed. New York: Oxford University Press, 2004. This is a collection of all the writings by the early Christians from within the first century after Jesus death (that is, written before A.D. 130), both canonical and non-canonical. It includes several of the texts discussed in this course. Ideal for beginning students.

————, and Andrew Jacobs, eds. *Christianity in Late Antiquity, 300–450 C.E.: A Reader*. New York: Oxford University Press, 2004. A collection of some of the most important Christian writings of the 4th and early 5th centuries, in quality English translations, dealing with a range of important social and historical issues from the period.

————. *The New Testament: A Historical Introduction to the Early Christian Writings*, 3rd ed. New York: Oxford University Press, 2004. This volume provides a historically oriented introduction to all of the issues dealt with in this course, by the instructor. It is designed both for use as a college-level textbook and as a resource for anyone interested in the New Testament.

Ferguson, Everett, ed. *Worship in Early Christianity*. New York: Garland, 1993. A collection of important articles on various aspects of worship in the early Church.

Frend, W. H. C. *Martyrdom and Persecution in the Early Church*. Oxford: Basil Blackwell, 1965. This classic is the best full-length study of Christian persecution and martyrdom during the first three centuries A.D., which tries to understand Christian views of martyrdom in light of the martyrdoms in the Jewish tradition.

————. *The Rise of Christianity*. Philadelphia: Fortress, 1984. A full introductory discussion of the major issues involved with the history of the first six centuries of Christianity, packed with important information and full of names and dates.

Froehlich, Karlfried. *Biblical Interpretation in the Early Church*. Philadelphia: Fortress, 1984. A useful discussion of the methods of interpretation prevalent in early Christianity, especially in view of their roots in other interpretive practices of the ancient world.

Gager, John. *The Origins of Anti-Semitism: Attitudes Toward Judaism in Pagan and Christian Antiquity.* New York: Oxford University Press, 1985. A seminal study of anti-Jewish attitudes and activities in the Roman world, especially within early Christianity.

Gamble, Harry. *The New Testament Canon: Its Making and Meaning.* Philadelphia: Fortress, 1985. A clearly written and informative overview of the formation of the canon that shows how, why, and when Christians chose the present 27 books to include in their sacred Scriptures of the New Testament.

Grant, Robert M. *Greek Apologists of the Second Century.* Philadelphia: Westminster, 1988. A learned discussion of the teachings of the 2nd-century Christian apologists, with a particular focus on the sources for their information.

———, and David Tracy. *A Short History of the Interpretation of the Bible*, 2nd ed. Philadelphia: Fortress, 1983. A survey of the methods used to interpret the Bible from the earliest of times onward.

Hanson, R. P. C. *Allegory and Event.* Richmond, VA: John Knox Press, 1959. A seminal study of the allegorical method of interpretation as used by the famous biblical interpreter of the early 3rd century, Origen of Alexandria.

Harrison, P. N. *Polycarp's Two Epistles to the Philippians.* Cambridge: Cambridge University Press, 1936. A classical study of the Letter of Polycarp, which argues that the current text represents two *different* letters written by Polycarp, three decades apart.

Hurtado, Larry. *One God, One Lord: Early Christian Devotion and Ancient Jewish Monotheism.* Philadelphia: Fortress, 1988. A brief study that tries to understand the worship of Jesus as divine within the context of Christian claims that there is only one God.

Hvalvik, Reidar. *The Struggle for Scripture and Covenant: The Purpose of the Epistle of Barnabas.* Tuebingen: Mohr-Siebeck, 1996. A useful study of the function of Scripture in the exposition of the Letter of Barnabas.

Jeffers, James. *Conflict at Rome: Social Order and Hierarchy in Early Christianity.* Minneapolis: Fortress, 1991. A social analysis of the church of Rome and its internal tensions, as evident in the writings of 1 Clement and The Shepherd, both of them produced by Roman Christians.

Jefford, Clayton, ed. *The Didache in Context: Essays on Its Text, History, and Transmission*. Leiden: Brill, 1995. A useful collection of essays on important aspects of the Didache, by some of the leading scholars in the field.

————. *Reading the Apostolic Fathers: An Introduction*. Peabody, MA: Hendrickson, 1996. For beginning students, the most useful introductory discussion of all the major aspects of each of the writings of the Apostolic Fathers.

Kelly, J. N. D. *Early Christian Doctrines*. San Francisco: Harper, 1978. A historical survey of the development of such fundamental Christian doctrines as those involving Christ and the Trinity.

Maier, Harry. *The Social Setting of the Ministry as Reflected in the Writings of Hermas, Clement, and Ignatius*. Waterloo, Ont.: Wilfrid Laurier University, 1991. A detailed study of The Shepherd, 1 Clement, and the Letters of Ignatius that intends to explain the development of ecclesiastical offices in the early Church.

Meecham, Henry. *The Epistle to Diognetus*. Manchester: Manchester University Press, 1949. An important Greek-English edition of the Letter to Diognetus, with a full commentary.

Metzger, Bruce M. *The Canon of the New Testament: Its Origin, Development, and Significance*. Oxford: Clarendon Press, 1987. The most thorough and informative account of the formation of the New Testament canon, by one of the world's eminent scholars of early Christianity.

Musurillo, H., ed. *The Acts of the Christian Martyrs*. Oxford: Clarendon Press, 1972. This is an intriguing collection of 28 accounts of Christian martyrdom in English translation, taken from eyewitness sources of the 2nd to 4th centuries.

Norris, Richard. *The Christological Controversy*. Philadelphia: Fortress, 1980. A useful presentation of some of the major texts from antiquity involving the controversies over the nature and person of Christ.

Ong, W. J. *Orality and Literacy*. London: Routledge, 1982. A seminal study of the differences between oral and literary cultures.

Paget, James Carleton. *The Epistle of Barnabas: Outlook and Background*. Tuebingen: Mohr-Siebeck, 1994. A broad but useful study of the historical context and themes of the Letter of Barnabas.

Pelikan, Jeroslav. *The Christian Tradition*, vol. 1. Chicago: University of Chicago Press, 1971. A useful exploration of the development of major theological topics in the early centuries of the Christian Church.

Perkins, Judith. *The Suffering Self*. New York: Routledge, 1995. An intriguing investigation of early Christian understandings of pain, suffering, and persecution in light of a broader cultural shift in the understanding of the self in the early centuries of Christianity, in which one's own bodily suffering became a celebrated mark of self-identity.

Rowland, Christopher. *The Open Heaven: A Study of Apocalyptic in Judaism and Early Christianity*. New York: Crossroad, 1982. One of the most important studies of the worldview of apocalypticism in both Jewish and Christian writings of antiquity.

Ruether, Rosemary. *Faith and Fratricide: The Theological Roots of Anti-Semitism*. New York: Seabury, 1974. A controversial discussion of the early Christian attitudes toward Jews and Judaism, which maintains that anti-Semitism is the necessary corollary of Christian belief in Jesus as the messiah.

Schoedel, William R. "Fragments of Papias," in *The Apostolic Fathers: A New Translation*, vol. 5, Robert M. Grant, ed. Camden, NJ: Thomas Nelson, 1967. An English translation, with notes, of the surviving fragments of Papias's book, *An Exposition of the Sayings of the Lord*.

―――. *Ignatius of Antioch: A Commentary on the Letters of Ignatius of Antioch*. Philadelphia: Fortress Press, 1985. A comprehensive and valuable commentary on the Letters of Ignatius, by one of the leading scholars in the study of the Apostolic Fathers.

―――. "Papias," in the *Anchor Bible Dictionary*, vol. 5, pp. 140–142, D. N. Freedman, ed. New York: Doubleday, 1992. A brief and incisive assessment of what we can know about Papias and his writings.

―――. "Papias," in the series *Aufstieg und Niedergang der Roemischen Welt* (the article is in English), II, 27, 1 (1993): 235–

270. A full survey of all the major scholarship on Papias and his work.

Simon, Marcel. *Verus Israel: A Study of the Relations between Christians and Jews in the Roman Empire (A.D. 135–425)*. H. McKeating, trans. Oxford: Oxford University Press, 1986. A standard study of Jewish-Christian relations in the early centuries of the Church.

Stewart-Sykes, Alistair. *From Prophecy to Preaching: A Search for the Origins of the Christian Homily*. Leiden: Brill, 2001. The best available study of preaching in earliest Christianity, with a focus on uncovering its historical roots.

Tugwell, Simon. *The Apostolic Fathers*. Harrisburg, PA: Morehouse, 1986. A good introduction to the writings of the Apostolic Fathers; useful for students at all levels.

Wilken, Robert. *The Christians as the Romans Saw Them*. New Haven, CT: Yale University Press, 1984. This is a popular and clearly written account of the mainly negative views of Christians held by several Roman authors. It is particularly suitable for beginning students.

Wilson, J. Christian. *Five Problems in the Interpretation of the Shepherd of Hermas*. Lewiston: Mellen Biblical Press, 1995. The author addresses several of the most puzzling aspects of The Shepherd and shows how scholars have come to deal with them in their writings.